WORD SMART

6th Edition

The Staff of The Princeton Review

princetonreview.com

Penguin
Random
House

The Princeton Review
555 West 18th Street
New York, NY 10011
Email: editorialsupport@review.com

Published in the United States by Penguin
Random House LLC, New York, and in Canada
by Random House of Canada, a division of
Penguin Random House Ltd., Toronto.

ISBN: 978-1-5247-1071-2
eBook ISBN: 978-1-5247-1087-3
ISSN: 1559-8659

The Princeton Review is not affiliated with
Princeton University.

Editor: Colleen Day
Production Editors: Emily Epstein White and Dallin Law
Production Artist: Gabriel Berlin

Printed in the United States of America.

6th Printing

6th Edition

Editorial

Rob Franek, Editor-in-Chief
Casey Cornelius, VP Content Development
Mary Beth Garrick, Director of Production
Selena Coppock, Managing Editor
Meave Shelton, Senior Editor
Colleen Day, Editor
Sarah Litt, Editor
Aaron Riccio, Editor
Orion McBean, Associate Editor

Penguin Random House Publishing Team

Tom Russell, VP, Publisher
Alison Stoltzfus, Publishing Director
Jake Eldred, Associate Managing Editor
Ellen Reed, Production Manager
Suzanne Lee, Designer

Acknowledgments

The Princeton Review would like to thank Gina Donegan for her fantastic contributions to this edition, as well as Gabriel Berlin, Emily Epstein White, and Dallin Law for their time and attention to each page.

Special thanks to Adam Robinson, who conceived of and perfected the Joe Bloggs approach to standardized tests and many of the other successful techniques used by The Princeton Review.

Contents

Register Your

1 Go to **PrincetonReview.com/cracking**

2 You'll see a welcome page where you can register your book using the following ISBN: 9781524710712

3 After placing this free order, you'll either be asked to log in or to answer a few simple questions in order to set up a new Princeton Review account.

4 Finally, click on the "Student Tools" tab located at the top of the screen. It may take an hour or two for your registration to go through, but after that, you're good to go.

If you have noticed potential content errors, please email EditorialSupport@review.com with the full title of the book, its ISBN (located above), and the page number of the error.

Experiencing technical issues? Please email TPRStudentTech@review.com with the following information:

- your full name
- email address used to register the book
- full book title and ISBN
- your computer OS (Mac or PC) and Internet browser (Firefox, Safari, Chrome, etc.)
- description of technical issue

Book Online!

Once you've registered, you can...

- Find printable lists of essential SAT and GRE vocabulary so you can study on the go

- Check out articles with valuable advice about college admissions

- Sort colleges by whatever you're looking for (such as Best Theater or Dorm), learn more about your top choices, and see how they all rank according to *The Best 382 Colleges*

- Check to see if there have been any corrections or updates to this edition

Offline Resources

- *More Word Smart*
- *Grammar Smart*
- *SAT Power Vocab*

The
Princeton
Review®

Introduction

Your Vocabulary Has Been Talking About You Behind Your Back

The words you use say a lot about you. Knowing which words to use and understanding how to use them are both key to communicating effectively and accurately. People often say in frustration, "I know what I mean, but I don't know how to say it." If the right words aren't there, the right ideas can't get through. Your vocabulary is the foundation of your ability to share your thoughts with other people. When you improve your vocabulary, you improve your ability to bring your intelligence and ideas to bear on the world around you.

"Big" Words Aren't Necessarily Better

When people say that someone has a "good vocabulary," they usually mean that he or she uses a lot of important-sounding words—words like *jactitation, demulcent,* and *saxicolous.* But a vocabulary consisting of words like these isn't necessarily a "good" vocabulary. Why?

Because almost no one knows what *jactitation, demulcent,* and *saxicolous* mean. If you used these words in conversation, chances are no one listening to you would know what you were talking about. Big, difficult words have important uses, but improving a vocabulary involves much more than merely decorating your speech or your writing with a few polysyllabic zingers.

The goal of communication is clarity. We write and speak in order to make ourselves understood. A good vocabulary is one that makes communication easy and efficient. One mark of an effective speaker or writer is his or her ability to express complex ideas with relatively simple words.

Most discourse among educated people is built on words that are fairly ordinary—words you've heard before, even if you aren't exactly certain what they mean. The best way to improve your vocabulary isn't to comb the dictionary for a handful of tongue twisters to throw at unsuspecting strangers. Instead, you need to hone your understanding of words that turn up again and again in intelligent communication. A person who has a clear understanding of every word in an issue of *The New York Times* or *The Wall Street Journal* would have a powerful vocabulary—a vocabulary sophisticated enough to impress almost any teacher, admissions officer, colleague, or employer.

Why You Need This Book

An effective vocabulary is one that enables you to convey ideas easily. Do you know what *inveterate* means? Do you know the difference between *flaunt* and *flout*? Do you know why an artist might be insulted if you called his or her work *artful*?

None of these words is particularly difficult. But each has its own meaning or meanings. If you misuse these words, you communicate that you are in over your head.

When people get into trouble with words, it usually isn't because they don't know the meaning of a seldom-used word like *termagant* but because they are confused about the meaning of a much more common word—a word they hear, read, and even use with regularity.

Take the word *peruse,* for example. Many people think that it means "skim" or "glance over." However, it also means very nearly the opposite. To *peruse* can also mean to read very carefully.

The number of words you know is less important than the care you take in learning the ones you really use. Speaking or writing well doesn't require an enormous vocabulary—but it does require a confident one. And the way to gain confidence in your vocabulary is to buckle down and learn the words you need to make yourself clearly understood.

The Princeton Review Approach

The philosophy behind The Princeton Review is simple: We teach what you need to know and try to make it interesting and fun at the same time. In preparing students for various standardized tests, we spend much of our time working on vocabulary. Despite what many people think, many "intelligence" or "aptitude" tests are largely tests of vocabulary. The students who earn high scores on such tests are the students who know the right words. The success of our method is in part a result of our success in teaching vocabulary.

The methods we have developed are easy to use and, we believe, extremely effective. There's nothing particularly startling about them because they rely mostly on common sense, but they do work. And although they were developed primarily for students, these methods can be used by anyone who wants to build a stronger, smarter vocabulary.

How This Book Is Organized

This book is divided into three main sections. In Chapter 1, we describe some basic principles of vocabulary building. We also explain techniques for learning new words. You should apply these techniques as you work through the rest of the book. The more carefully you work, the more rapidly you'll enhance your ability to use words effectively.

The heart of *Word Smart* is Chapters 2 and 3. Chapter 2 is the largest section of the book, containing all of the words we think the savvy student should know. Each word is accompanied by a definition and one or more examples intended to help you understand how to use the word properly. Many entries also include discussions of related words as well as additional meanings or associations. Scattered throughout the book are quick quizzes that will help you strengthen your vocabulary skills and assess your progress as you work. The answers to these quick quizzes are found in Chapter 13.

Chapter 3 consists of "The Final Exam" covering all the words in Chapter 2. You can use this test to help firm up your new vocabulary knowledge and to help ensure that you'll retain all the new words you've learned. You can also use the test as a diagnostic tool. By trying your hand at the questions *before* working your way through the book, you'll give yourself a good idea of which words cause you the most trouble. And if you're preparing for a major standardized test such as the SAT or GRE, you and your friends can use the Final Exam as a handy review device. All of the answers to the drills in this section can be found in Chapter 13.

The third and final section of this book, Chapters 4 through 12, contain specialized lists of words, including need-to-know words for the SAT and GRE. These lists, which contain the most frequently tested (or appearing) words on the SAT and GRE, are the ones we use to help students boost their verbal scores on these exams. Sometimes simply knowing that a particular word is included on one of these lists is enough to lead students to a correct answer on the test.

Other specialized lists include frequently misused words, useful foreign words and phrases, common abbreviations, and words associated with science, finance, and the arts. If you learn the words on these lists, you'll improve your reading comprehension as well as increase your understanding of various disciplines.

How to Use This Book

Don't try to read this book in a single sitting. You'll learn much more if you tackle it a little at a time. You may feel comfortable with a number of the words already. You don't need to spend much time on those, but be certain you really *do* know a word as well as you think you do before you skip ahead. Some of the most embarrassing vocabulary blunders occur when we boldly misuse words we feel certain we understand.

The words in *Word Smart* are arranged alphabetically. You'll find a Quick Quiz every 10 words or so. You may find it convenient to tackle words in the main list in 10-word chunks, pausing at each Quick Quiz to make certain you have retained what you just learned. Don't forget to check your answers.

If you're trying to build your vocabulary in preparation for a test, you should set a schedule for yourself and work methodically from beginning to end. If you're simply trying to improve your vocabulary, you may find it more interesting to dip into the text at random. You can also use the book as a companion to your dictionary to zero in on the meanings of new words you've encountered in reading or in conversation.

When you finish this book, you will have a solid vocabulary that can help you in every facet of your life—studying in a classroom, communicating at work, even kicking back with a book on your couch. But don't stop there. Continue to expand your vocabulary by mastering the new words you encounter.

Let's begin!

CHAPTER 1

Learning New Words

Building a Vocabulary Is Child's Play

Young children learn new words by imitating the speakers around them. When a three-year-old hears a new word that catches her interest, she may use it repeatedly for a day or two until she feels comfortable with it. She establishes its meaning from context, often by trial and error. She adds new words to her vocabulary because she needs them to make herself understood.

Children have an easier time learning new words than most adults do. As we grow beyond childhood, our brains seem to lose their magical ability to soak up language from the environment. But adults can still learn a great deal from the way children learn new words.

Young children don't learn the meanings of new words by looking them up. Sometimes they ask grown-ups directly, but more often they simply infer meanings from context. They figure out what new words mean by paying attention to how they are used.

You need to do the same. Be receptive to new words by actively seeking to understand them. When you encounter an unfamiliar word in the newspaper, don't skim over it. Stop and try to figure out what it means. The words that surround it should provide a few clues. Put your mind to work.

A Word Is Useful Only If You Use It

Children learn words by using them. Adults who want to build their vocabularies must do the same. You can't incorporate a new word into your vocabulary unless you give it a thorough workout and then keep it in shape through regular exercise. Use new words over and over—at the dinner table, at school, in conversation with friends—even at the risk of making mistakes.

If you are a student preparing to enter college or graduate school, learning new words can help you perform better on tests like the SAT and GRE, improving your chances of being admitted to more competitive schools. An added bonus is that your writing and speaking skills will improve along with your vocabulary, which can help you in your classes as well. Nonstudents may have other vocabulary needs, but the same general rules apply. As with many other things, you have to use vocabulary if you don't want to lose it. Remember that the size and quality of a person's vocabulary correlate powerfully with his or her success in school, at work, and beyond.

Read, Read, Read!

The best way to build a solid, sophisticated vocabulary is to read voraciously. Careful reading not only brings you into contact with new words but also forces you to use your brain to figure out what those new words mean. If you read widely enough, you will find that your vocabulary will build itself. New words are contagious if you give yourself enough exposure to them. Reading any good book is better for your vocabulary than watching television. Reading well-written magazines and newspapers can help, too.

Use a Dictionary

When you read, you will undoubtedly come across words you don't know, and some will be critical to the meaning of the passages in which they appear. If you're serious about understanding what you read, as well as improving your vocabulary, you'll have to use the dictionary.

The natural way to learn words is to see how other people use them—that is, to see or hear the word in context. While context may tell you how to use the word, relying on context is not without pitfalls.

First, when you hear a new word, you can't be certain the speaker's pronunciation is correct. You also can't be certain the word is being used correctly. Even skillful writers and speakers occasionally misuse language. A writer or speaker may even misuse a word intentionally, perhaps for dramatic or comic effect.

Even more important, many words have multiple meanings and connotations. Sometimes the difference between one meaning and another is slight; sometimes it is significant. Even if you deduce the meaning from the context, you have no way of knowing whether the meaning you've deduced will apply in other cases.

Finally, context can be misleading. Take the word *formidable*, for example. When you hear this word, you may think of it in the context of "a *formidable* opponent." This might lead you to believe that *formidable* means something like "skillful" or "aggressive." But those definitions miss the mark, as *formidable* actually means "frightening" or "menacing." See how context can be misleading?

The point here is to understand the limits of context and always consult a dictionary if you're not sure of the meaning of a word.

Which Dictionary Should You Use?

Like cars, not all dictionaries have the same features. Dictionaries can range from children's editions with lots of pictures to humongous, unabridged dictionaries with lots of entries in tiny type. (By the way, *abridged* means "shortened." An unabridged dictionary is one that includes almost every single word in the English language!) And then there's the 20-volume *Oxford English Dictionary*.

For most people, however, a good college-edition dictionary is sufficient. (A "college" dictionary is not for use in college only; the phrase "college dictionary" is simply a rough indication of the vocabulary level of the readers for whom the dictionary is appropriate.)

We encourage you to get in the habit of carrying a portable dictionary with you wherever you go, so that when you encounter a word you don't know, you can look it up on the spot. Of course, we don't expect you to lug around a huge hardcover dictionary; try a small paperback copy or even a dictionary app that can be downloaded to your smartphone or tablet. We recommend using a hard-copy dictionary, as looking up a word in a real book creates a tactile memory so that you will have a better chance of remembering the meaning of the word. But ultimately, you should you use the dictionary that works best for you; that's the best approach for getting words to stick.

What Are the Features of a Good Dictionary?

We used several dictionaries in verifying the definitions and usages that appear in *Word Smart*. Let's take a look at a sample dictionary entry:

> **a•bridge** (ə brij'), *v.t.*, **a•bridged, a•bridg•ing.**
> **1.** to shorten by condensation or omission while retaining the basic contents: *to abridge a long novel.*
> **2.** to reduce or lessen in duration, scope, etc.; diminish, curtail. **3.** to deprive; cut off [1350–1400; ME *abregge, abrigge* < MF *abreg(i)er* < ML *abbreviare* to shorten. See ABBREVIATE] —**a•bridg'a•ble**; *esp.* Brit., **a•bridg'á•ble,** *adj.—* **a•bridg'ér,** *n.* —**Syn.1.** condense, abstract. See **shorten. 2.** contract.

Now let's examine this entry part by part:

a•bridge

The main entry—the dot separates the words into syllables. Sometimes the main entry includes stress marks to tell you which syllables to stress in pronouncing the word.

(ə brij')

The pronunciation—every dictionary includes a pronunciation key up front to explain symbols like the upside-down *e* known as a *schwa* and pronounced "uh." If a word has more than one acceptable pronunciation, the entry will list them.

Always observe the pronunciation of a word when you look it up. If you know how to pronounce a word, you're more likely to use it. (If you don't know how to pronounce a word, you're more likely to embarrass yourself at cocktail parties.) And the more you use a word, the more likely you'll be able to remember it.

Part of speech—this abbreviation means that *abridge* is a verb, specifically a transitive verb.

A transitive verb is one that carries action from a subject to a direct object. For example, in the sentence *The dog ate the book,* the verb *ate* carries action from the dog to the book. Similarly, in *The editor abridged the book,* the verb *abridged* carries action from the editor to the book.

An example of an *in*transitive verb is *to sleep.* In *The dog sleeps,* the verb does not carry any action from the subject (dog) to any other thing.

a•bridged, a•bridg•ing

Forms—these entries let us know that we should note the spellings of different forms of the word *abridge.* Notice, for example, that we drop the *e* before adding *ing.*

1. to shorten by condensation or omission while retaining the basic contents: *to abridge a long novel.*

The most common definition of the word. Some dictionaries include helpful phrases or sentences to show you how to use the word in context.

This feature is quite useful. The example tells us that we would not use *abridge* this way: *The tailor abridged Susan's long skirt to make it a mini.*

2. to reduce or lessen in duration, scope, etc.; diminish, curtail. **3.** to deprive; cut off.

Other definitions, generally in order of importance— sometimes a definition will include close synonyms.

[1350–1400; ME *abregge, abrigge* < MF *abreg(i)er* < ML *abbreviare* to shorten. See ABBREVIATE]

The etymology—some dictionaries include the etymology before the definitions.

You don't have to be a linguist, but the word *abridge* developed from medieval Latin to Middle French to Middle English: *abbreviare* (meaning "to shorten"), in medieval Latin became *abreg(i)er* in

Middle French, which became *abregge* or *abrigge* in Middle English, which finally became *abridge*.

The etymology suggests that we look up *abbreviate*. If you have the time, you should do so. It will reinforce your understanding of *abridge*.

We will discuss etymology in more detail later because it is a powerful *mnemonic*. (Look it up!)

—**a•bridg'a•ble**; *esp. Brit.,* **a•bridge'á•ble**, *adj.*
—**a•bridg'ér**, *n.*

Other parts of speech, along with an alternative (British) spelling.

—**Syn. 1.** condense, abstract. See **shorten. 2.** contract.

An abridged (!) list of synonyms—the numbers refer to the preceding order of definitions. The entry suggests that we look up *shorten*. Not all dictionaries include this feature, though.

Don't Stop with the Definition

The editors of the dictionary advise us to look up *shorten* if we want a better understanding of *abridge*, so let's do just that:

short•en (shôr'tən), *v.t.,* **1.** to make short or shorter. **2.** to reduce, decrease, take in, etc.: *to shorten sail.* **3.** to make (pastry, bread, etc.) short, as with butter or other fat. —*v.i.* **4.** to become short or shorter. **5.** (of odds) to decrease. —**short'ener**, *n.* —**Syn.** SHORTEN, ABBREVIATE, ABRIDGE, CURTAIL mean to make shorter or briefer. SHORTEN is a general word meaning to make less in extent or duration: *to shorten a dress, a prisoner's sentence.* The other three words suggest methods of shortening. To ABBREVIATE is to make shorter by omission or contraction: *to abbreviate a word.* To ABRIDGE is to reduce in length or size by condensing, summarizing, and the like: *to abridge a document.* CURTAIL suggests deprivation and lack of completeness because of cutting off part: *to curtail an explanation.*

This entry distinguishes *shorten* from a number of synonyms, including *abridge*. The digression took another minute or so, but we've come away with a better understanding of the meanings and their *nuances*. (Look it up!) We will consider synonyms in detail when we discuss how to use a thesaurus.

Why Don't Entries in *Word Smart* Look Like Standard Dictionary Entries?

We've tried to make *Word Smart* easier to read and understand than a big dictionary.

Don't get us wrong. We use dictionaries, we rely on dictionaries, but sometimes we wish that lexicographers (those fun-loving people who write dictionaries) would communicate in basic English.

For each word in *Word Smart*, we give you a basic definition. Sometimes a close synonym is enough. Then we give you—and this is important—a sentence or two so that you can see how to use the word. Our entry for *abridge* reads as follows:

ABRIDGE (uh BRIJ) *v* to shorten; to condense

- The thoughtful editor *abridged* the massive book by removing the boring parts.

An *abridged* dictionary is one that has been shortened to keep it from crushing desks and people's laps.

An *abridgment* is a shortened or condensed work.

The problem with most dictionaries is that they don't tell you how to *use* the word. You can always spot someone who has learned new words almost exclusively through the dictionary rather than through general reading supplemented with a dictionary. When you ask such people the definition of a word, it's almost as if they fall into a trance—their eyes glaze over as they rattle off the definition almost word for word from a dictionary.

So while it's important to use a dictionary, it's also important to think critically about the words as well, because...

You will not truly learn a word unless you can define it in your own words.

To understand a word completely, to make a word yours, you should try to define it in your own words. Don't settle for the dictionary definition. For that matter, don't settle for our definition.

Make up your own definition. You'll understand the meaning better. What's more, you'll be more likely to remember it.

Thesauruses: Don't Misuse, Abuse, Exploit, Corrupt, Misapply, or Misemploy Them

A thesaurus is a dictionary-like reference book that lists synonyms for many words. A thesaurus can be another useful tool in your word-building campaign, but only if you use it properly. Many people don't.

Thesaurus abuse is common. Students often try to make their vocabularies seem bigger than they actually are by using a thesaurus to beef up the papers they write. (*Neophytes chronically endeavor to induce their parlance to portend more magisterially by employing a lexicon of synonyms to amplify the theses they inscribe.*) They write their papers in their own words, and then they plug in words from a thesaurus. That's what we did with the silly-sounding sentence in the parentheses above. You'd be surprised how many students actually compose their papers that way.

Still, a Thesaurus Can Be Useful

A thesaurus can be helpful—if you use it properly.

The best way to use a thesaurus is as a supplement to your dictionary, as a reference work that can help you find the word that expresses precisely what you are trying to say. A good thesaurus is intended to help a speaker or writer distinguish the shades of difference between words of similar meaning.

How to Use the Thesaurus: An Example

Let's say you're trying to describe Randolph, someone who never lends money to anyone. Randolph examines his monthly bank statement with a calculator to make sure that his interest has been properly computed to the penny. Randolph is someone who would have to think long and hard if a mugger presented him with the dilemma "Your money or your life."

The first word that comes to mind in describing Randolph may be *cheap*. Being the careful writer you are, you decide to see whether *cheap* is the most precise word you can come up with.

In your thesaurus, you find the following entry:

> **cheap** *adj.* **1.** *Chicken is not as cheap as it was:* inexpensive, low-priced, economical, reasonable. **2.** *Talk is cheap:* effortless, costless, easy. **3.** *The coat may be expensive, but it looks cheap:* shoddy, shabby, inferior, worthless, poor, second-rate, trashy, meager, paltry, gimcrack, flashy, gaudy, in bad taste, tawdry, tacky, common, inelegant. **4.** *Spreading gossip is a cheap thing to do:* contemptible, petty, despicable, sordid, ignoble, wretched, mean, base. *Slang:* two-bit, vulgar, immoral, indecent. **5.** *He's too cheap to pick up the check:* tight,

The entry *cheap* lists five primary meanings, each preceded by an illustrative sentence. You scan the sentences until you find the one you want: the last one. Now you examine the synonyms.

> *tight:* Okay, but perhaps it's too informal or colloquial—might be confused with other definitions of the word *tight*. Forget this one.

stingy: A possibility.

miserly: Let's say you're not exactly sure what this one means. You decide to look this one up in the regular dictionary.

penurious: Better look this one up, too.

tightfisted: A little better than *tight,* though perhaps still too slangy—you'll think about it.

close: Nope—too many other definitions.

Before leaving the thesaurus, however, you decide to check out the listing for *miserly* and come up with the following additional words:

parsimonious: Look it up.

avaricious: Look it up.

mean: Too many other definitions.

grasping: More a synonym of *greedy.* Randolph isn't precisely greedy. He doesn't want to accumulate a lot; he just wants to hold on to what he has. Forget this one.

scrimping: Doesn't sound right—forget this one.

pinching: Nope.

penny-pinching: Better than *pinching* alone, but colloquial—maybe.

frugal: Look it up.

illiberal: Too vague.

closehanded: Nah.

closefisted: Similar to *tightfisted* and *penny-pinching,* but not as good—drop.

selfish: Too general—Randolph is selfish only with money.

ungenerous: Nope—Randolph isn't particularly generous, but you want to say what he *is* rather than what he is *not.*

greedy: You ruled this out earlier.

near: Nope.

meager: Look it up.

grudging: Not precisely what you mean.

You decide you have enough synonyms to work with. Now you have to look up and verify definitions.

You are left with three synonyms you know (*stingy, tightfisted,* and *penny-pinching*) and seven you don't know. Just to be orderly, you look up the seven words alphabetically in your dictionary:

avaricious characterized by avarice (insatiable greed for riches; inordinate desire to gain and hoard wealth); covetous

Nope, you don't mean greedy. *Avaricious* is out.

frugal 1. economical in use or expenditure; prudently saving or sparing. **2.** entailing little expense; requiring few resources; meager, scanty.

The first definition means careful with money. *Economical* and *prudent* both have positive connotations, but Randolph's obsession with money is not something good. The second definition is not the one we want—out.

meager 1. deficient in quantity or quality; lacking fullness or richness; poor; scanty. **2.** having little flesh; lean; thin. **3.** maigre.

Nope, none of these seems to convey the meaning you want.

miserly of, like, or befitting a miser (one who lives in wretched circumstances in order to save and hoard money); penurious.

Well, this might be right. You have to think about Randolph a little more. What are his circumstances like? Is he willing to live in wretched circumstances?

parsimonious characterized by or showing parsimony; sparing or frugal, esp. to excess.

Now you have established that *parsimonious* means stingier than frugal. This seems to hit the mark.

penurious 1. extremely stingy. **2.** extremely poor; indigent. **3.** poorly or inadequately supplied.

The first definition works, but the second definition seems to imply a stinginess perhaps resulting from poverty. The third definition does not apply. Now you have to think again about Randolph. Is he poor as well as cheap? If so, this is the right word.

You're still left with *stingy, tightfisted, penny-pinching, miserly, parsimonious,* and *penurious.* Oh, and there's still the blunt, if unassuming, *cheap,* which you started with. Which word is the right word?

Stingy is the right word if you want to use a simple, no-nonsense word.

Tightfisted is the word if you want something a little more slangy and graphic.

Penny-pinching is right if you want the image to be a little more explicit than tightfisted.

Miserly could be the right word, depending on Randolph's living circumstances.

Parsimonious is the right word if you want a multisyllabic synonym for *cheap* or *stingy.* From the definitions, *parsimonious* seems more extreme than *stingy.*

Penurious is the right word if Randolph is poor as well as stingy.

To decide which word is the right word, you must give more thought to precisely what aspect of Randolph you're trying to capture and convey.

The right word is not merely the accurate word with the proper connotations.

We don't want to get into writing style, but other considerations to keep in mind when choosing the right word include the following:

Rhythm, or Cadence
Which word best fits in with the overall flow of the sentence and paragraph? Perhaps you want to achieve alliteration *(Randolph is a pretentious, penny-pinching poet)* or a certain rhyme *(Alimony drove Randolph to parsimony)*.

Part of Speech
Miserly seems okay as an adjective, but *miserliness* seems a little awkward as a noun.

Vocabulary Level
Who will read your description of Randolph? Your word choice may be limited by your potential reader or audience. Other things being equal, the simple word is the better word.

Variety
If you've used *cheap* several times already in the same piece of writing, you may want to use a different word.

Repetition
On the other hand, repeating the same word may have a powerful effect.

Dramatic Effect
A simple word in an academic setting, or an academic word in a simple setting, can have a dramatic effect. Comic effects can also be achieved by using a word in an inappropriate or incongruous context.

Editing Is More Than Choosing the Right Word

Word Smart is a book on words rather than on writing. Still, we want to note in passing that good editing is more than simply reviewing the words you use.

Editing means refining your ideas. Editing means deciding on the ordering and presentation of your ideas. Editing means deciding which ideas you're going to present at all.

Which Thesaurus Should I Use?

We recommend that the thesaurus you use be one that lists words alphabetically in the text itself. Ideally, the thesaurus should include sample sentences that distinguish at least some of the different shades of meanings.

Reading This Book

Reading widely—with the help of a dictionary and perhaps also a thesaurus—is a great way to build a vocabulary. But it's also a slow way. Which words you encounter in your reading depend on which words the writers happen to use.

That's where we come in. The main section of *Word Smart* is a concentrated source of the words you want to know—the words you need to help yourself build an educated vocabulary. We've also included fun facts, etymology, and usage, which are integral to the vocabulary learning methods you're about to encounter. If you want a better vocabulary, you have to put the time and effort in.

As you work through this book, you'll undoubtedly find that you need to tailor your approach to the way you think and learn best. You may discover that for a particular word one method works best and that for another word a different method works best. That's fine.

The best method for memorizing words is the method that works best for *you*.

We'll show you the methods we have found to be the most successful for our students. Use the one or ones that suit *you* best.

Basic Method #1: Tricks and Mnemonics

A mnemonic is a device or trick that helps you remember something specific. Grade schoolers are sometimes taught to remember the spelling of *arithmetic* by using the following mnemonic: *A Rat In The House Might Eat Tom's Ice Cream*. The first letter in each word in this silly sentence stands for the letters in *arithmetic*. Remember the sentence and you remember how to spell the word.

Mnemonics can appeal to our ears, too. How about the history mnemonic: *In fourteen hundred ninety-two, Columbus sailed the ocean blue...*? Or the spelling mnemonic: i *before* e *except after* c, *and in words that say* a, *as in* neighbor *and* weigh?

You Already Know How to Use Mnemonics

Whether you realize it or not, you use mnemonics all the time. When you make up a little game to remember your locker combination or a friend's birthday, you're using a mnemonic.

How Do Mnemonics Work?

All mnemonics work in the same way: they force you to associate what you're trying to remember with something that you already know, or with something that is easier to memorize. Patterns and rhymes are easy to memorize, which explains why so many mnemonics use them.

Incidentally, it may also explain why rhyming became a part of poetry. The earliest poets and balladeers didn't write down their compositions because many didn't know how to write. Instead, they kept the poems in their heads. Among other things, the rhymes at the ends of the lines made the poems easier to remember.

Basic Method #2: Seeing Is Remembering

Letting a new word suggest a vivid mental image to you is a powerful and effective way to remember that word. Mental images are really mnemonics, too. They help you remember. The emphasis here is on suggestive mental pictures rather than on tricky abbreviations or coincidences of spelling.

Let's look at an example. We'll start with a word we've already used in this chapter: *abridge*. As you know, to *abridge* is to shorten or condense.

What image pops into your mind when you think of the word *abridge*? That's easy: a bridge. Now you need to picture something happening on or to that bridge that will help you remember the meaning of the word *abridge*. Your goal is to create such a vivid and memorable image in your mind that the next time you encounter *abridge* in your reading, you'll instantly remember what it means.

To be useful, your image must have something to do with the meaning of the word rather than merely with the way it sounds or looks. If you merely think of a bridge when you see *abridge,* you won't help yourself remember what you want to remember.

What you need is an image that suggests shortening or condensing. A dinosaur taking a big bite out of the middle of a bridge? Carpenters sawing it? The image you choose is up to you.

And Now for Another Example...

Another useful word is *gregarious,* which means sociable, enjoying the company of others. What image springs to mind? Really think now.

Can't think of an image? Be creative. A party animal is *gregarious.* How about imagining a party animal named Greg Arious. Don't stop with his name. You need a picture. So give Greg a funny hat, a noisemaker, and some polka-dot dancing shoes. Or put a lampshade on his head. Think of something that will make you think of sociability the next time you see Greg's name in a book or a magazine you read. The more real you make Greg Arious seem in your imagination, the less trouble you'll have remembering the meaning of *gregarious.*

The Crazier the Mental Image, the Better

It's better to choose an interesting mental image that you'll remember. If you choose an image that is bland or boring, you may have trouble remembering the word. Interesting, even weird, mental images are more likely to stick in your memory.

Memory Aids Should Be Personal

Sometimes we'll give you a mnemonic for the listings in *Word Smart,* but we won't do this very often. Memory aids work best when you have to struggle a little to come up with them.

If you come up with your own memory aid, if it really means something to you, it will likely become a permanent part of your memory.

Basic Method #3: Etymological Clues

Although the English language contains hundreds of thousands of words, you will discover that many groups of words are related in meaning because they developed from a common root. When you recognize that a group of words shares a similar root, you will more easily remember the entire group.

For example, take the word *mnemonic*. You know now, if you hadn't already, that a *mnemonic* is a device that helps you remember something. We're going to show you two other words that are related to this word.

> **mne**monic: device to help you remember something
>
> **amne**sty: a general pardon for offenses against a government (an official "forgetting")
>
> **amne**sia: loss of memory

Pretty neat, eh? How about words from another common root:

> **chron**ological: in order according to time
>
> syn**chron**ize: to put on the same timetable
>
> ana**chron**ism: something out of place in time or history
>
> **chron**ic: continuing over a long time
>
> **chron**icle: chronological record of events
>
> **chron**ometer: device to measure time

Sometimes it is easier to learn a whole cluster of related words than to come up with mnemonics for them individually.

The Advantages of Etymology

Learning word roots is a key part of etymology, the study of the origin of words and how their meanings have changed over time. A word's etymology tells you something about the meaning of the word. Additionally, etymology can be shared among several words, which can help you remember the meanings of clusters of related words. Learning etymology can also get you interested in the origin of words and language in general; etymology tells you the story of a word over centuries. In Chapter 6 you will find a list of the most important roots with numerous examples following each.

The Pitfalls of Etymology

The etymology of a word will tell you something about the word, but it will rarely give you the full definition. Students often confuse a word's etymology with its meaning, which can lead to errors on tests.

Take the word *verdant*, for example. At first glance, you may think this word is etymologically related to words like *verify, verdict, verisimilitude,* and *veritable* and guess that the definition of *verdant* must have something to do with the concept of truth or reality.

This is clever guesswork, but *verdant* actually comes from a different family of words. It comes from the same old root as does the French word *vert,* which means green. If those same clever students had recognized that connection, they might have realized that *verdant* means green with vegetation, as in *a verdant forest.*

Similarly, a lot of words that begin with *ped-* have something to do with foot: *pedestrian, pedal, pedestal, pedometer, impede, expedite.* A *pediatrician,* however, is *not* a foot doctor. A *pediatrician* is a doctor for children. A *podiatrist* is a foot doctor. (The word *pediatrician* is, however, related to the word meaning a strict teacher of children: *pedagogue.*)

Etymology is a powerful tool to remember words that you already know, but it can't always be relied upon to determine the meanings of words you *don't* know.

Basic Method #4: Writing on Your Brain

Many people find that they can learn new information more readily if they write it down. The physical act of writing seems to plant the information more firmly. Perhaps the explanation is that by writing you are bringing another sense into play (you've seen the word, you've said and heard the word, and now you're *feeling* the word).

You may find it useful to spend some time writing down phrases or sentences incorporating each new word. This is a good way to practice and strengthen your spelling as well.

You'll probably have more luck if you don't merely write down the word and its definition over and over again. If you've hit upon a good mnemonic or mental image to help you remember it, or you liked the etymology, write it down. You can even draw a picture or a diagram.

Basic Method #5: Putting It All Together with Flashcards and a Notebook

A flashcard, usually made with an index card, contains a word on one side and its definition on the reverse side. You may have used flashcards when you were first learning to read or when you were first tackling a foreign language. Flashcards can turn learning into a game and is an effective way to study and commit words to memory.

Along with the word's definition, you should also include the pronunciation if you aren't sure you'll remember it. Then you can either practice independently or have a friend quiz you.

Here's a basic flashcard, front and back.

Front

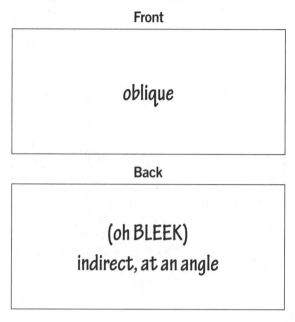

oblique

Back

(oh BLEEK)

indirect, at an angle

You'll learn even more if you use your imagination to make the backs of your flashcards a bit more elaborate. For example, you might decorate the back of this card with a diagram of *oblique* lines—that is, lines that are neither parallel nor perpendicular to each other.

Back

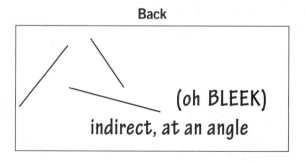

(oh BLEEK)

indirect, at an angle

Your diagram now gives you a mental image that can help you remember the word. You'll probably think of your own mental image, one that means something to you. You could even use the word itself to create a picture that conveys the meaning of the word and that will stick in your mind to help you remember it.

Here's one possibility. We've divided the word into two parts and written them on two different lines that are at an *oblique* angle to each other.

Back

(oh BLEEK) oblique

indirect, at an angle

Practicing with flashcards can be fun. Parents, siblings, and friends sometimes might lend a hand and discover that they learn new words, too. And every time you look at the back of the card, you'll be reminded of the mnemonic, trick, or mental image you've devised to keep the word firmly in your memory.

Tuck a few flashcards in your pocket when you head out the door in the morning, and work on them in spare moments, like when you're riding on a bus or listening to the radio. The more often you flash through your flashcards, the faster you'll build your vocabulary.

Reading your flashcards isn't enough, of course. You also need to make an effort to use the words on them. Using the words, much more than reading the cards, makes the definitions sink in and take hold.

We also encourage you to write down new words you learn in a note-book. If you devote an entire page to each new word, the notebook will give you room to practice "writing on your brain." It will also give you plenty of space to doodle or jot down images that will help you remember the word.

Even better, you can use your notebook as a place to record actual uses of new words that you discover in your own reading. If, while reading a magazine, you come across one of the words you're working on, you can copy the sentence into your notebook, giving you a brand-new example of the word in context.

Students who keep notebooks report a sense of accomplishment when they look back through their notebooks at the hundreds of new words they have learned. A notebook gives you tangible (a good word) evidence of the progress you're making.

A Memorization Game Plan

Here is our step-by-step approach to memorizing new words.

Step 1	Try to deduce the word's meaning from context.
Step 2	Look it up!
Step 3	Note the spelling.
Step 4	Say the word out loud.
Step 5	Read the main definition. Scan the secondary definitions.
Step 6	Compare the definition with the definitions and usages of the word's synonyms.
Step 7	Define the word using your own words.
Step 8	Use it in a sentence.
Step 9	Attach the word to a mnemonic, mental image, or other memory aid.
Step 10	Fill out a flashcard and make a new entry in your notebook.
Step 11	Use the new word every chance you get.

Let's take a look at each of these steps.

Step 1: Try to Deduce the Word's Meaning From Context

Context will often lead you astray, but doing a bit of detective work is a good way to sharpen your mind and hone your reading comprehension skills. And who knows? You might even guess the right meaning.

Step 2: Look It Up!

Most people try to skip this step. Don't you dare! You won't know whether you're correct about the meaning of a new word until you've made sure by looking it up.

No one can learn new words without a dictionary. If you don't have one, get one now, whether a physical copy from your local bookstore or library or a downloadable app on your smartphone or tablet.

Step 3: Note the Spelling

Look closely at the word's spelling. Then close your eyes and try to reconstruct the spelling. If you have trouble visualizing, test yourself by writing out the spelling on scrap paper and checking it against the dictionary.

You should also compare the spelling variations with other spelling variations you know. This is a nice trick that helps you recognize words that you think you don't know.

For example, *sober* is an adjective; the noun form is *sobriety*. Okay, with that as a clue, the noun *propriety* relates to what adjective? *Proper. Propriety* means what is socially proper or acceptable.

Here's another example: Do you know what *incisive* means? Give up? Well, you know what *decisive* means, don't you? *Decisive* relates to what word you know? *Decision,* of course. Now, what noun do you think *incisive* relates to? *Incision. Incisive* means sharp or cutting, as in an incisive remark or an incisive observation.

Step 4: Say the Word Out Loud

Say the word *out loud*. Hearing the word will bring another sense into play and help you remember the word. And as we noted earlier, you don't want to make a fool of yourself by mispronouncing words.

Our Pronunciation Key

We've never liked the pronunciation keys most dictionaries use. Our key is based on consistent phonetic sounds, so you don't have to memorize it. Still, it would be a good idea to take a few minutes now and familiarize yourself with the table below. Be sure to note how the *e* and *i* are used.

The letter(s)	is (are) pronounced like the letter(s)	in the word(s)
a	a	bat, can
ah	o	con, bond
aw	aw	paw, straw
ay	a	skate, rake
e	e	stem, hem
ee	ea	steam, clean
i	i	rim, chin, hint
ing	ing	sing, ring
oh	o	row, tow
oo	oo	room, boom
ow	ow	cow, brow
oy	oy	boy, toy
u, uh	u	run, bun
y (ye, eye)	i	climb, time
ch	ch	chair, chin
f	f, ph	film, phony
g	g	go, goon
j	j	join, jungle
k	c	cool, cat
s	s	solid, wisp
sh	sh	shoe, wish
z	z	zoo, razor
zh	s	measure
uh	a	apologize

All other consonants are pronounced as you would expect. Capitalized letters are accented.

Step 5: Read the Main Definition; Scan the Secondary Definitions

Most dictionaries list the definitions in order of importance. That does not mean, of course, that the first definition is the one you are looking for. Read all the definitions; each will add to your understanding of the word.

Step 6: Compare the Definition with the Definitions and Usages of the Word's Synonyms

As we showed you with the earlier examples, this step takes a little extra time. Believe us when we say that it is time well spent. Again, seeing how a word is similar to or different from synonyms or related words enhances your understanding of all of them.

Step 7: Define the Word Using Your Own Words

We said it before, and we'll say it again: you don't truly know what a word means unless you can define it yourself in your own way.

Step 8: Use It in a Sentence

Now that you know what the word means and what it doesn't mean, use it. Make up a sentence.

It helps to use the word in a sentence that includes a person or thing or event that you know and that creates a concrete feeling or image. For example, the sentence *They are gregarious* is not as good as *Greg, Gertrude, and Gretchen are gregarious.*

Step 9: Attach the Word to a Mnemonic, Mental Image, or Other Memory Aid

With all that you've done with the word in the previous steps, you may already have memorized it. The only way to be sure, however, is to fix the word with a mnemonic.

Step 10: Fill Out A Flashcard and Make a New Entry in Your Notebook

The paperwork is very important, particularly if you're trying to learn a lot of new words in a short period of time.

Step 11: Use the New Word Every Chance You Get

Dare to be repetitious. If you don't keep new knowledge in shape, you won't keep it at all.

Two Final Words of Advice: Be Suspicious

You already know some of the words in the book. You may know quite a few of them. Naturally, you don't need to drill yourself on words you already know and use. But be careful. Before skipping a word, make certain you really do know what it means. Some of the most embarrassing vocabulary mistakes occur when a person confidently uses familiar words incorrectly. Now on to the words. Remember that you'll retain more (and have more fun) if you tackle this book a little at a time.

CHAPTER 2

The Words

A

ABASH (uh BASH) *v* to make ashamed; to embarrass
- Meredith felt *abashed* by her inability to remember her lines in the school chorus of "Old McDonald Had a Farm."

To do something without shame or embarrassment is to do it *unabashedly*.
- Karl handed in a term paper that he had *unabashedly* copied from Wikipedia.

ABATE (uh BAYT) *v* to subside; to reduce
- George spilled a cup of hot coffee on his leg. It hurt quite a bit. Then, gradually, the agony *abated*.
- Bad weather *abates* when good weather begins to return. A rainstorm that does not let up continues *unabated*.

A tax *abatement* is a reduction in taxes. Businesses are sometimes given tax *abatements* in return for building factories in places where there is a particular need for jobs.

ABDICATE (AB duh kayt) *v* to step down from a position of power or responsibility
- When King Edward VIII of England decided he would rather be married to Wallis Warfield Simpson, an American divorcée, than be king of England, he turned in his crown and *abdicated*.

Even people who aren't monarchs can *abdicate* their duties and responsibilities.
- Abby *abdicated* her responsibilities as a vice president by dumping in the garbage the reports she was supposed to present to the board of directors and flying to the Bahamas.

ABERRATION (ab uh RAY shun) *n* something not typical; a deviation from the standard
- Søren's bad behavior was an *aberration*. So was Harry's good behavior. That is, Søren's was usually good, and Harry's was usually bad.
- The chef at this restaurant is dreadful; the decent meal we just had was an *aberration*.
- A snowstorm in June is an *aberration;* snow doesn't normally fall in June.

An *aberration* is an *aberrant* (uh BER unt) occurrence.
- Søren's behavior was *aberrant*. The summer snowstorm was *aberrant*.

ABHOR (ab HOR) *v* to hate very, very much; to detest

- Emanuel *abhorred* having to wake up before dawn.

To *abhor* something is to view it with horror. Hating a person is almost friendly in comparison with *abhorring* him or her.

To *abhor* raw chicken livers is to have an *abhorrence* of them or to find them *abhorrent.*

ABJECT (AB jekt) *adj* hopeless; extremely sad and servile; defeated

- While most people would quickly recover from a stumble on stage, Mia felt *abject* humiliation.

An *abject* person is one who is crushed and without hope. A slave would be *abject,* in all likelihood.

Perhaps 90 percent of the time, when you encounter this word it will be followed by the word *poverty. Abject poverty* is hopeless, desperate poverty. The phrase "abject poverty" is overused. Writers use it because they are too lazy to think of anything original.

ABNEGATE (AB nuh gayt) *v* to deny oneself things; to reject; to renounce

- Ascetics practice *self-abnegation* because they believe it will bring them closer to spiritual purity.

Self-abnegation is giving up oneself, usually for some higher cause.

ABORTIVE (uh BOR tiv) *adj* unsuccessful

- Marie and Elizabeth made an *abortive* effort to bake a birthday cake; that is, their effort did not result in a birthday cake.
- Fred's attempt to climb the mountain was *abortive;* he injured himself when he was halfway up.

To *abort* something is to end it before it is completed. An *aborted* pregnancy, called an *abortion,* is one that ends before the baby is born. An *abortion* in this sense doesn't have to be the result of a controversial medical procedure.

ABRIDGE (uh BRIJ) *v* to shorten; to condense

- The thoughtful editor *abridged* the massive book by removing the boring parts.

An *abridged* dictionary is one that has been shortened to keep it from crushing desks and people's laps.

An *abridgment* is a shortened or condensed work.

ABSOLUTE (AB suh loot) *adj* total; unlimited

An *absolute* ruler is one who is ruled by no one else. An *absolute* mess is a total mess. An *absolute* rule is one that has no exceptions and that you must follow, no two ways about it.

Absolute is also a noun. It means something that is total, unlimited, or perfect. Death, for living things, is an *absolute.* There just isn't any way around it.

ABSOLVE (ab ZOLV) *v* to forgive or free from blame; to free from sin; to free from an obligation

- The priest *absolved* the sinner who had come to church to confess.
- Tom's admission of guilt *absolved* Mary, who had originally been accused of the crime.

It is also possible to *absolve* someone of a responsibility.

- Jake *absolved* Ciara of her obligation to go to the prom with him; he told her it was all right if she went with the captain of the football team instead.

The act of *absolving* is called *absolution* (ab suh LOO shun).

Quick Quiz #1

Match each word in the first column with its definition in the second column. Check your answers in the back of the book.

1.	abash	a.	step down from power
2.	abate	b.	hopeless
3.	abdicate	c.	unsuccessful
4.	aberration	d.	forgive
5.	abhor	e.	total
6.	abject	f.	subside
7.	abnegate	g.	detest
8.	abortive	h.	shorten
9.	abridge	i.	deviation
10.	absolute	j.	embarrass
11.	absolve	k.	renounce

ABSTINENT (AB stuh nunt) *adj* abstaining; voluntarily not doing something, especially something pleasant that is bad for you or has a bad reputation
- Beulah used to be a smoker; now she's *abstinent.*
- Cynthia, who was dieting, tried to be *abstinent,* but when she saw the chocolate cake, she realized that she would probably have to eat the entire thing.

A person who *abstains* from something is an *abstainer* and engages in *abstinence.*

ABSTRACT (AB strakt) *adj* theoretical; impersonal
- He liked oysters in the *abstract,* but when he actually tried one he became nauseated.

To like something in the *abstract* is to like the idea of it.
- Bruno doesn't like *abstract* art; he thinks that a painting should resemble something real, not a lot of splattered paint.

ABSTRUSE (ab STROOS) *adj* hard to understand
- The professor's article, on the meaning of meaning, was *abstruse.* Michael couldn't even pronounce the words in it.

Nuclear physics is a subject that is too *abstruse* for most people.

ABYSMAL (uh BIZ mul) *adj* extremely hopeless or wretched; bottomless

An *abyss* (uh BIS) is a bottomless pit, or something so deep that it seems bottomless. *Abysmal* despair is despair so deep that no hope seems possible.
- The nation's debt crisis was *abysmal;* there seemed to be no possible solution.

Abysmal is often used somewhat sloppily to mean very bad. You might hear a losing baseball team's performance referred to as *abysmal.* This isn't strictly correct, but many people use the word this way.

ACCOLADE (AK uh layd) *n* an award; an honor

This word is generally used in the plural.
- The first break-dancing troupe to perform in Carnegie Hall, the Teflon Toughs, received *accolades* from the critics as well as from the fans.

ACCOST (uh KAWST) *v* to approach and speak to someone aggressively

- Amanda karate-chopped the stranger who *accosted* her in the street and was embarrassed to find he was an old, blind man.

ACERBIC (uh SUR bik) *adj* sour; severe; like acid in temper, mood, or tone

- Barry sat silently as his friends read the teacher's *acerbic* comments on his paper.

Acerb and *acerbic* are synonyms. *Acerbity* is the state of being *acerbic*.

ACQUIESCE (ak wee ES) *v* to comply passively; to accept; to assent; to agree

- The pirates asked Pete to walk the plank; he took one look at their swords and then *acquiesced.*

To *acquiesce* is to do something without objection—to do it *quietly.* As the similarity of their spellings indicates, the words *acquiesce* and *quiet* are closely related. They are both based on Latin words meaning to rest or to be quiet.

Acquiesce is sometimes used sloppily as a simple synonym for *agree* in situations in which it isn't really appropriate. For example, it isn't really possible to *acquiesce* noisily, enthusiastically, or eagerly. Don't forget the *quiet* in the middle.

To *acquiesce* is to exhibit *acquiescence.*

ACRID (AK rid) *adj* harshly pungent; bitter

- The cheese we had at the party had an *acrid* taste; it was harsh and unpleasant.
- Long after the fire had been put out, we could feel the *acrid* sting of smoke in our nostrils.

Acrid is used most often with tastes and smells, but it can be used more broadly to describe anything that is offensive in a similar way. A comment that stings like acid could be called *acrid*—so could a harsh personality.

ACRIMONIOUS (ak ruh MOH nee us) *adj* full of spite; bitter; nasty

- George and Elizabeth's discussion turned *acrimonious* when Elizabeth introduced the subject of George's perennial, incorrigible stupidity.

- Relations between the competing candidates were so *acrimonious* that each refused to acknowledge the presence of the other.

ACUMEN (AK yoo mun) *n* **keenness of judgment; mental sharpness**

- A woman who knows how to turn one dollar into a million overnight might be said to have a lot of business *acumen*.
- Ernie's lack of *acumen* led him to invest all his money in a company that had already gone out of business.

Note carefully the pronunciation of this word.

Quick Quiz #2

Match each word in the first column with its definition in the second column. Check your answers in the back of the book.

1.	abstinent	a.	hard to understand
2.	abstract	b.	voluntarily avoiding
3.	abstruse	c.	wretched
4.	abysmal	d.	bitter
5.	accolade	e.	comply
6.	accost	f.	harsh
7.	acerbic	g.	mental sharpness
8.	acquiesce	h.	theoretical
9.	acrid	i.	award
10.	acrimonious	j.	approach someone aggressively
11.	acumen	k.	sour

ACUTE (uh KYOOT) *adj* **sharp; shrewd**

If your eyesight is *acute,* you can see things that other people can't. You have visual *acuity* (uh KYOO uh tee). An *acute* mind is a quick, intelligent one. You have mental *acuity*. An *acute* pain is a sharp pain.

Acute means sharp only in a figurative sense. A knife, which is sharp enough to *cut,* is never said to be *acute*.

Acute is a word doctors throw around quite a bit. An *acute* disease is one that reaches its greatest intensity very quickly and then goes away. What could a disease be if it isn't *acute*? See *chronic*.

ADAMANT (AD uh munt) *adj* stubborn; unyielding; completely inflexible
- Candice was *adamant:* she would never go out with Paul again.

A very hard substance, like a diamond, is also *adamant. Adamantine* (ad uh MAN teen) and *adamant* are synonyms. *Adamancy* is being *adamant.*

ADDRESS (uh DRES) *v* to speak to; to direct one's attention to

To *address* a convention is to give a speech to the convention. To *address* a problem is to face it and set about solving it.
- Ernie *addressed* the problem of *addressing* the convention by sitting down and writing his speech.

ADHERENT (ad HEER unt) *n* follower; supporter; believer
- The king's *adherents* threw a big birthday party for him, just to show how much they liked him.

To *adhere* to something is to stick to it. *Adherents* are people who *adhere* to, or stick to, something or someone. Following someone or something, especially rules or laws, is *adherence.*

A religion could be said to have *adherents,* assuming there are people who believe in it. Governments, causes, ideas, people, philosophies, and many other things can have *adherents,* too.

> **Note carefully the pronunciation of this word.**

ADMONISH (ad MAHN ish) *v* to scold gently; to warn
- The boys' father *admonished* them not to eat the pie he had just baked. When they did so anyway, he *admonished* them.

In the first sentence, *admonish* means warn, and in the second, it means scold gently. Consider yourself *admonished* not to misuse this word.

The noun is *admonition* (ad muh NISH un), and the adjective is *admonitory* (ad MAHN i tor ee).

ADROIT (uh DROYT) *adj* skillful; dexterous; clever; shrewd; socially at ease
- Julio was an *adroit* salesperson: his highly skilled pitch, backed up by extensive product knowledge, nearly always resulted in a sale.

Adroit comes from the French word for right (as in the direction) and refers to an old superstition that right-handedness is superior. It's a synonym of *dexterous* (which comes from the Latin for right) and an antonym of *gauche* and *maladroit.*
- My brilliant accountant *adroitly* whipped my taxes into shape, then made a *gauche* remark about my ignorance of financial matters.

ADULATION (aj uh LAY shun) *n* **wild or excessive admiration; flattery**
- The boss thrived on the *adulation* of his scheming secretary.
- The rock star grew to abhor the *adulation* of his fans.

The verb is *adulate* (AJ uh layt).

ADULTERATE (uh DUL tuh rayt) *v* **to contaminate; to make impure**
- We discovered that the town's drinking water had radioactive waste in it; we discovered, in other words, that it had been *adulterated.*

Vegetarians do not like their foods *adulterated* with animal fats.

Unadulterated means pure. *Unadulterated* joy is joy untainted by sadness.

ADVERSE (ad VURS) *adj* **unfavorable; antagonistic**
- We had to play our soccer match under *adverse* conditions: It was snowing, and only three members of our team had bothered to show up.

Airplanes often don't fly in *adverse* weather. An airplane that took off in bad weather and reached its destination safely would be said to have overcome *adversity*. *Adversity* means misfortune or unfavorable circumstances. To do something "in the face of *adversity*" is to undertake a task despite obstacles. Some people are at their best in *adversity* because they rise to the occasion.

A word often confused with *adverse* is *averse* (uh VURS). The two are related but they don't mean quite the same thing. A person who is *averse* to doing something is a person who doesn't want to do it. To be *averse* to something is to be opposed to doing it—to have an *aversion* to doing it.

AESTHETIC (es THET ik) *adj* having to do with artistic beauty; artistic

- Our art professor had a highly developed *aesthetic* sense; he found things to admire in paintings that, to us, looked like garbage.

Someone who greatly admires beautiful things can be called an *aesthete* (ES theet). *Aesthetics* is the study of beauty or principles of beauty.

AFFABLE (AF uh bul) *adj* easy to talk to; friendly

- Susan was an *affable* girl; she could strike up a pleasant conversation with almost anyone.
- The Jeffersons' dog was big but *affable;* it liked to lick little children on the face.

The noun is *affability*.

AFFECTATION (af ek TAY shun) *n* unnatural or artificial behavior, usually intended to impress

- Becky's English accent is an *affectation*. She spent only a week in England, and that was several years ago.
- Elizabeth had somehow acquired the absurd *affectation* of pretending that she didn't know how to turn on a television set.

A person with an *affectation* is said to be *affected*.

To *affect* a characteristic or habit is to adopt it consciously, usually in the hope of impressing other people.

- Edward *affected* to be more of an artist than he really was. Everyone hated him for it.

AFFINITY (uh FIN uh tee) *n* sympathy; attraction; kinship; similarity

- Ducks have an *affinity* for water; that is, they like to be in it.
- Children have an *affinity* for trouble; that is, they often find themselves in it.
- Magnets and iron have an *affinity* for each other; that is, each is attracted to the other.

Affinity also means similarity or resemblance. There is an *affinity* between snow and sleet.

AFFLUENT (AF loo unt) *adj* rich; prosperous

A person can be *affluent;* all it takes is money. A country can be *affluent,* too, if it's full of *affluent* people.

Affluence means the same thing as wealth or prosperity.

> **Note carefully the pronunciation of this word.**

AGENDA (uh JEN duh) *n* program; the things to be done
- What's on the *agenda* for the board meeting? A little gossip, then lunch.

A politician is often said to have an *agenda.* The politician's *agenda* consists of the things he or she wishes to accomplish.

An *agenda,* such as that for a meeting, is often written down, but it doesn't have to be. A person who has sneaky ambitions or plans is often said to have a secret or hidden *agenda.*

Quick Quiz #4

Match each word in the first column with its definition in the second column. Check your answers in the back of the book.

1.	adulterate	a.	opposed to
2.	adverse	b.	friendly
3.	averse	c.	rich
4.	aesthetic	d.	unnatural behavior
5.	affable	e.	artistic
6.	affectation	f.	contaminate
7.	affinity	g.	sympathy
8.	affluent	h.	unfavorable
9.	agenda	i.	program

AGGREGATE (AG ruh gut) *n* sum total; a collection of separate things mixed together
- Chili is an *aggregate* of meat and beans.

Aggregate (AG ruh gayt) can also be a verb or an adjective. You would make chili by *aggregating* meat and beans. Chili is an *aggregate* (AG ruh gut) food.

Similar and related words include *congregate, segregate,* and *integrate*. To *aggregate* is to bring together; to *congregate* is to get together; to *segregate* is to keep apart (or separate); to *integrate* is to unite.

AGNOSTIC (ag NAHS tik) *n* one who believes that the existence of a god can be neither proven nor disproven

An *atheist* is someone who does not believe in a god. An *agnostic*, on the other hand, isn't sure. He or she doesn't believe, but doesn't *not* believe, either.

The noun is *agnosticism* (ag NAHS tih siz um).
- An *atheist* himself, Jon concluded from Jorge's spiritual skepticism that they shared similar beliefs. In fact, Jorge's reluctance to affirm or discredit a god's existence reflects his *agnosticism*.

AGRARIAN (uh GRAR ee un) *adj* relating to land; relating to the management or farming of land

Agrarian usually has to do with farming. Think of agriculture.
- Politics in this country often pit the rural, *agrarian* interests against the urban interests.

ALACRITY (uh LAK ri tee) *n* cheerful eagerness or readiness to respond
- David could hardly wait for his parents to leave; he carried their luggage out to the car with great *alacrity*.

> **Note carefully the pronunciation of this word.**

ALLEGE (uh LEJ) *v* to assert without proof
- If I say, "Cedrick *alleges* that I stole his hat," I am saying two things:

    1. Cedrick says I stole his hat.

    2. I say I didn't do it.

To *allege* something is to assert it without proving it. Such an assertion is called an *allegation* (al uh GAY shun).

The adjective is *alleged* (uh LEJD). If the police accuse someone of having committed a crime, newspapers will usually refer to that person as an *alleged* criminal.
- The police have *alleged* that Mary committed the crime, but a jury hasn't made a decision yet.

ALLEVIATE (uh LEE vee ayt) *v* to relieve, usually temporarily or incompletely; to make bearable; to lessen

- Visiting the charming pet cemetery *alleviated* the woman's grief over the death of her canary.
- Aspirin *alleviates* headache pain. When your headache comes back, take some more aspirin.

ALLOCATE (AL uh kayt) *v* to distribute; to assign; to allot

- The event had been a big failure, and David, Aaliyah, and Jan spent several hours attempting to *allocate* the blame. In the end, they decided it had all been Jan's fault.
- The office manager had *allocated* just seven paper clips for our entire department.

ALLOY (AL oy) *n* a combination of two or more things, usually metals

- Brass is an *alloy* of copper and zinc, meaning you make brass by combining copper and zinc.

Alloy (uh LOY) is often used as a verb. To *alloy* two things is to mix them together. There is usually an implication that the mixture is less than the sum of the parts. That is, there is often something undesirable or debased about an *alloy* (as opposed to a pure substance).

Unalloyed means undiluted or pure. *Unalloyed* dislike is dislike undiminished by any positive feelings; *unalloyed* love is love undiminished by any negative feelings.

Match each word in the first column with its definition in the second column. Check your answers in the back of the book.

1.	aggregate	a.	get together
2.	congregate	b.	unite
3.	segregate	c.	someone unconvinced about the existence of a god
4.	integrate		
5.	agnostic		
6.	agrarian	d.	relieve
7.	alacrity	e.	keep apart
8.	allege	f.	combination of metals
9.	alleviate	g.	sum total
10.	allocate	h.	distribute
11.	alloy	i.	assert
		j.	cheerful eagernes
		k.	relating to the land

ALLUSION (uh LOO zhun) *n* **an indirect reference (often to a literary work); a hint**

To *allude* to something is to refer to it indirectly.

- When Ralph said, "I sometimes wonder whether to be or not to be," he was *alluding* to a famous line in *Hamlet*. If Ralph had said, "As Hamlet said, 'To be or not to be, that is the question,'" his statement would have been a direct reference, not an *allusion*.

An *allusion* is an *allusion* only if the source isn't identified directly. Anything else is a reference or a quotation.

- If Andrea says, "I enjoyed your birthday party," she isn't *alluding* to the birthday party; she's mentioning it. But if she says, "I like your choice of party music," she is *alluding* to the party.

ALOOF (uh LOOF) *adj* **uninvolved; standing off; keeping one's distance**

- Al, on the roof, felt very aloof.

To stand *aloof* from a touch-football game is to stand on the sidelines and not take part.

Cats are often said to be *aloof* because they usually mind their own business and don't crave the affection of people.

ALTRUISM (AL troo iz um) *n* selflessness; generosity; devotion to the interests of others

- The private foundation depended on the *altruism* of the extremely rich old man. When he decided to start spending his money on yachts and sports cars, the foundation went out of business.

To be *altruistic* is to help others without expectation of personal gain. Giving money to charity is an act of *altruism.* The *altruist* does it just to be nice, although he or she will probably also remember to take a tax deduction.

An *altruistic* act is also an act of *philanthropy,* which means almost the same thing.

AMBIENCE (AM bee uns) *n* atmosphere; mood; feeling

- By decorating their house with plastic beach balls and Popsicle sticks, the Cramers created a playful *ambience* that delighted young children.

A restaurant's *ambience* is the look, mood, and feel of the place. People sometimes say that a restaurant has "an atmosphere of *ambience.*" To do so is redundant—*atmosphere* and *ambience* mean the same thing.

Ambience is a French word that can also be pronounced "ahm BYAHNS." The adjective *ambient* (AM bee unt) means surrounding or circulating.

AMBIGUOUS (am BIG yoo us) *adj* unclear in meaning; confusing; capable of being interpreted in different ways

- We listened to the weather report, but the forecast was *ambiguous;* we couldn't tell whether the day was going to be rainy or sunny.
- The poem we read in English class was *ambiguous;* no one had any idea what the poet was trying to say.

The noun is *ambiguity* (am bih GYOO uh tee).

AMBIVALENT (am BIV uh lunt) *adj* undecided; having opposed feelings simultaneously

- Susan felt *ambivalent* about Alec as a boyfriend. Her frequent desire to break up with him reflected this *ambivalence.*

AMELIORATE (uh MEEL yuh rayt) *v* to make better or more tolerable

- The mood of the prisoners was *ameliorated* when the warden gave them extra free time outside.
- My great-uncle's gift of several million dollars considerably *ameliorated* my financial condition.

AMENABLE (uh MEE nuh bul) *adj* obedient; willing to give in to the wishes of another; agreeable

- I suggested that Brad pay for my lunch as well as for his own; to my surprise, he was *amenable.*
- The plumber was *amenable* to my paying my bill with jelly beans, which was lucky because I had more jelly beans than money.

Note carefully the pronunciation of this word.

AMENITY (uh MEN i tee) *n* pleasantness; attractive or comfortable feature

- The *amenities* at the local club include a swimming pool, a golf course, and a tennis court.

If an older guest at your house asks you where the *amenities* are, he or she is probably asking for directions to the bathroom.

Those little bars of soap and bottles of shampoo found in hotel rooms are known in the hotel business as *amenities.* They are meant to increase your comfort. People like them because people like almost anything that is free (although, of course, the cost of providing such *amenities* is simply added to the price of hotel rooms).

AMIABLE (AY mee uh bul) *adj* friendly; agreeable

- Our *amiable* guide made us feel right at home in what would otherwise have been a cold and forbidding museum.
- The drama critic was so *amiable* in person that even the subjects of negative reviews found it impossible not to like her.

Amicable is a similar and related word. Two not very *amiable* people might nonetheless make an *amicable* agreement. *Amicable* means politely friendly or not hostile. Two countries might trade *amicably* with each other even while technically remaining enemies.

- Julio and Clarissa had a surprisingly *amicable* divorce and remained good friends even after paying their lawyers' fees.

AMNESTY (AM nuh stee) *n* an official pardon for a group of people who have violated a law or policy

Amnesty comes from the same root as *amnesia,* the condition that causes characters in movies to forget everything except how to speak English and drive their cars.

An *amnesty* is an official forgetting. When a state government declares a tax *amnesty,* it is saying that if people pay the taxes they owe, the government will officially "forget" that they broke the law by not paying them in the first place.

The word *amnesty* always refers to a pardon given to a group or class of people. A pardon granted to a single person is simply a pardon.

AMORAL (ay MOR ul) *adj* lacking a sense of right and wrong; neither good nor bad, neither moral nor immoral; without moral feelings

- Very young children are *amoral;* when they cry, they aren't being bad or good—they're merely doing what they have to do.

A *moral* person does right; an *immoral* person does wrong; an *amoral* person simply does.

AMOROUS (AM ur us) *adj* feeling loving, especially in a sexual sense; in love; relating to love

- The *amorous* couple made quite a scene at the movie. The movie they were watching, *Love Story,* was pretty *amorous* itself. It was about an *amorous* couple, one of whom died.

AMORPHOUS (uh MOR fus) *adj* shapeless; without a regular or stable shape; bloblike

- Ed's teacher said that his term paper was *amorphous;* it was as shapeless and disorganized as a cloud.

- The sleepy little town was engulfed by an *amorphous* blob of glowing protoplasm—a higher intelligence from outer space.

To say that something has an "*amorphous* shape" is a contradiction. How can a shape be shapeless?

ANACHRONISM (uh NAK ruh niz um) *n* something out of place in time or history; an incongruity

- In this day of impersonal hospitals, a doctor who remembers your name seems like an *anachronism*.

ANALOGY (uh NAL uh jee) *n* a comparison of one thing to another; similarity

- To say having an allergy feels like being bitten by an alligator would be to make or draw an *analogy* between an allergy and an alligator bite.

Analogy usually refers to similarities between things that are not otherwise very similar. If you don't think an allergy is at all like an alligator bite, you might say, "That *analogy* doesn't hold up." To say that there is no *analogy* between an allergy and an alligator bite is to say that they are not *analogous* (uh NAL uh gus).

Something similar in a particular respect to something else is its *analog* (AN uh lawg), sometimes spelled *analogue*.

Quick Quiz #7

Match each word in the first column with its definition in the second column. Check your answers in the back of the book.

1.	ameliorate	a.	pleasantness
2.	amenable	b.	comparison
3.	amenity	c.	obedient
4.	amiable	d.	without moral feeling
5.	amicable	e.	feeling loving
6.	amnesty	f.	make better
7.	amoral	g.	shapeless
8.	amorous	h.	politely friendly
9.	amorphous	i.	official pardon
10.	anachronism	j.	friendly
11.	analogy	k.	incongruity

ANARCHY (AN ur kee) *n* absence of government or control; lawlessness; disorder

- The country fell into a state of *anarchy* after the rebels kidnapped the president and locked the legislature inside the Capitol.

The word doesn't have to be used in its strict political meaning. You could say that there was *anarchy* in the kindergarten when the teacher stepped out of the door for a moment. You could say it, and you would probably be right.

The words *anarchy* and *monarchy* are closely related. *Anarchy* means no leader; *monarchy*, a government headed by a king or queen, means one leader.

ANECDOTE (AN ik doht) *n* a short account of a humorous or revealing incident

- The old lady kept the motorcycle gang thoroughly amused with *anecdote* after *anecdote* about her cute little dog.
- Alvare told an *anecdote* about the time Jessica got her big toe stuck in a bowling ball.
- The vice president set the crowd at ease with an *anecdote* about his childhood desire to become a vice president.

To say that the evidence of life on other planets is merely *anecdotal* is to say that we haven't captured any aliens, but simply heard a lot of stories from people who claimed to have been kidnapped by flying saucers.

ANGUISH (ANG gwish) *n* agonizing physical or mental pain

- Theresa had been a nurse in the emergency room for twenty years, but she had never gotten used to the *anguish* of accident victims.

ANIMOSITY (an uh MAHS uh tee) *n* resentment; hostility; ill will

- The rivals for the state championship felt great *animosity* toward each other. Whenever they ran into each other, they snarled.

A person whose look could kill is a person whose *animosity* is evident.

ANOMALY (uh NAHM uh lee) *n* an aberration; an irregularity; a deviation

- A snowy winter day is not an *anomaly*, but a snowy July day is.
- A house without a roof is an *anomaly*—a cold, wet *anomaly*.

A roofless house could be said to be *anomalous*. Something that is *anomalous* is something that is not normal or regular.

ANTECEDENT (an tuh SEED unt) *n* someone or something that went before; something that provides a model for something that came after it

- Your parents and grandparents could be said to be your *antecedents;* they came before you.
- The horse-drawn wagon is an *antecedent* of the modern automobile.

Antecedent can also be used as an adjective. The oil lamp was *antecedent* to the light bulb.

In grammar, the *antecedent* of a pronoun is the person, place, or thing to which it refers. In the previous sentence, the *antecedent* of *it* is *antecedent.* In the sentence "Bill and Harry were walking together, and then he hit him," it is impossible to determine what the *antecedents* of the pronouns (*he* and *him*) are.

Antecedent is related to a word that is similar in meaning: *precedent.*

ANTIPATHY (an TIP uh thee) *n* firm dislike

- I feel *antipathy* toward bananas wrapped in ham. I do not want them for dinner. I also feel a certain amount of *antipathy* toward the cook who keeps trying to force me to eat them. My feelings on these matters are quite *antipathetic* (an tip uh THET ik).

I could also say that ham-wrapped bananas and the cooks who serve them are among my *antipathies.* My *antipathies* are the things I don't like.

> Note carefully the pronunciation of this word.

ANTITHESIS (an TITH uh sis) *n* the direct opposite

- Erin is the *antithesis* of Aaron: Erin is bright and beautiful; Aaron is dull and plain.

> Note carefully the pronunciation of this word.

APARTHEID (uh PAHRT hyte) *n* the former policy of racial segregation and oppression in the Republic of South Africa

The word *apartheid* is related to the word *apart.* Under *apartheid* in South Africa, blacks were kept apart from whites and denied all rights.

The word *apartheid* is sometimes applied to less radical forms of racial injustice and to other kinds of separation. Critics have sometimes accused American public schools of practicing educational *apartheid* by providing substandard schooling for nonwhites.

Quick Quiz #8

Match each word in the first column with its definition in the second column. Check your answers in the back of the book.

1.	anarchy	a.	resentment
2.	monarchy	b.	racial oppression
3.	anecdote	c.	firm dislike
4.	anguish	d.	irregularity
5.	animosity	e.	what went before
6.	anomaly	f.	agonizing pain
7.	antecedent	g.	amusing account
8.	antipathy	h.	government by king or queen
9.	antithesis	i.	lawlessness
10.	apartheid	j.	direct opposite

APATHY (AP uh thee) *n* lack of interest; lack of feeling

- The members of the student council accused the senior class of *apathy* because none of the seniors had bothered to sign up for the big fundraiser.
- Jill didn't care one bit about current events; she was entirely *apathetic*.

APHORISM (AF uh riz um) *n* a brief, often witty saying; a proverb

- Benjamin Franklin was fond of *aphorisms*. He was frequently *aphoristic*.
- Chef Hussain is particularly fond of Woolf's *aphorism*, "One cannot think well, love well, or sleep well, if one has not dined well."

APOCALYPSE (uh PAHK uh lips) *n* a prophetic revelation, especially one concerning the end of the world

In strict usage, *apocalypse* refers to specific Christian writings, but most people use it more generally in connection with predictions of things like nuclear war, the destruction of the ozone layer, and the spread of fast-food restaurants to every corner of the universe. To make such predictions, or to be deeply pessimistic, is to be *apocalyptic* (uh pahk uh LIP tik).

APOCRYPHAL (uh POK ruh ful) *adj* of dubious authenticity; fictitious; spurious
- Brandi's blog discredited the *apocryphal* report of Martians in Congress.

An *apocryphal* story is one whose truth is not proven or whose falsehood is strongly suspected. Like *apocalypse,* this word has a religious origin. The *Apocrypha* are a number of "extra" books of the Old Testament that Protestants and Jews don't include in their Bibles because they don't think they're authentic.

APOTHEOSIS (uh pahth ee OH sis) *n* elevation to divine status; the perfect example of something
- Some people think that the Corvette is the *apotheosis* of American car making. They think it's the ideal.
- Geoffrey is unbearable to be with. He thinks he's the *apotheosis* of masculinity.

APPEASE (uh PEEZ) *v* to soothe; to pacify by giving in to
- Jaleel *appeased* his angry mother by promising to make his bed every morning without fail until the end of time.
- The trembling farmer handed over all his grain, but still the emperor was not *appeased.*

The noun is *appeasement.*

APPRECIATE (uh PREE shee ayt) *v* to increase in value
- The Browns bought their house twenty years ago for a hundred thousand dollars, but it has *appreciated* considerably since then; today it's worth almost two million dollars.
- Harry bought Joe's collection of old chewing tobacco tins as an investment. His hope was that the tins would *appreciate* over the next few years, enabling him to turn a profit by selling them to someone else.

The opposite of *appreciate* is *depreciate.* When a car loses value over time, we say it has *depreciated.*

APPREHENSIVE (ap ruh HEN siv) *adj* worried; anxious
- The *apprehensive* child clung to his father's leg as the two of them walked into the main circus tent to watch the lion tamer.
- Rhea was *apprehensive* about the exam because she had forgotten to go to class for several months. As it turned out, her *apprehensions* were justified. She couldn't answer a single question on the test.

A *misapprehension* is a misunderstanding.

- Rhea had no *misapprehensions* about her lack of preparation; she knew perfectly well she would fail abysmally.

Quick Quiz #9

Match each word in the first column with its definition in the second column. Check your answers in the back of the book.

1.	apathy	a.	of dubious authenticity
2.	aphorism	b.	misunderstanding
3.	apocalypse	c.	increase in value
4.	apocryphal	d.	lack of interest
5.	apotheosis	e.	soothe
6.	appease	f.	prophetic revelation
7.	appreciate	g.	decrease in value
8.	depreciate	h.	the perfect example
9.	apprehensive	i.	witty saying
10.	misapprehension	j.	worried

APPROBATION (ap ruh BAY shun) *n* approval; praise

- The crowd expressed its *approbation* of the team's performance by gleefully covering the field with toilet paper.
- The ambassador's actions met with the *approbation* of his commander in chief.

Approbation is a fancy word for *approval,* to which it is closely related. *Disapprobation* is disapproval.

APPROPRIATE (uh PROH pree ayt) *v* to take without permission; to set aside for a particular use

- Nick *appropriated* my lunch; he grabbed it out of my hands and ate it. So I *appropriated* Ed's.
- The deer and raccoons *appropriated* the vegetables in our garden last summer. This year we'll build a better fence.

Don't confuse the pronunciation of the verb *to appropriate* with the pronunciation of the adjective *appropriate* (uh PROH pree it). When Congress decides to buy some new submarines, it *appropriates* money for them. That is, it sets some money aside. The money thus set aside is called an *appropriation*.

When an elected official takes money that was supposed to be spent on submarines and spends it on a Rolls-Royce and a few mink coats, he or she is said to have *misappropriated* the money.

When the government decides to build a highway through your backyard, it *expropriates* your property for this purpose. That is, it uses its official authority to take possession of your property.

Cultural *appropriation* is when one group adopts elements of another group's culture, usually in an offensive manner.

APTITUDE (AP tuh tood) *n* capacity for learning; natural ability

- Some rare students have a marked *aptitude* for taking the SAT. They earn high scores without any preparation.
- I tried to repair my car, but as I sat on the floor of my garage, surrounded by mysterious parts, I realized that I had no *aptitude* for automobile repair.

The opposite of *aptitude* is *ineptitude*.

ARBITER (AHR buh tur) *n* one who decides; a judge

- An *arbiter* of fashion determines what other people will wear by wearing it herself.

An *arbiter arbitrates,* or weighs opposing viewpoints and makes decisions. The words *arbiter* and *arbitrator* mean the same thing. An *arbiter* presides over an *arbitration,* which is a formal meeting to settle a dispute.

ARBITRARY (AHR buh trer ee) *adj* random; capricious

- The grades Mr. Simone gave his English students appeared to be *arbitrary;* they didn't seem related to the work the students had done in class.
- The old judge was *arbitrary* in sentencing criminals; there was no sensible pattern to the sentences she handed down.

ARCANE (ahr KAYN) *adj* mysterious; known only to a select few

- The rites of the secret cult were *arcane;* no one outside the cult knew what they were.
- The *arcane* formula for the cocktail was scrawled on a faded scrap of paper.
- We could make out only a little of the *arcane* inscription on the old trunk.

ARCHAIC (ahr KAY ik) *adj* extremely old; ancient; outdated

- The tribe's traditions are *archaic.* They have been in force for thousands of years.

Archaic civilizations are ones that disappeared a long time ago.

An *archaic* meaning of a word is one that isn't used anymore.

ARCHETYPE (AHR kuh type) *n* an original model or pattern

An *archetype* is similar to a *prototype*. A *prototype* is a first, tentative model that is made but that will be improved in later versions. Henry Ford built a *prototype* of his Model T in his basement. His mother kicked him out, so he had no choice but to start a motor car company.

An *archetype* is usually something that precedes something else.

- Plato is the *archetype* of all philosophers.

An *archetype* is *archetypal* or *archetypical*.

Note carefully the pronunciation of this word.

ARDENT (AHR dunt) *adj* passionate; enthusiastic

- Larry's *ardent* wooing finally got on Cynthia's nerves, and she told him to get lost.
- Blanche happily made cakes from morning to night. She was an *ardent* baker.

To be *ardent* is to have *ardor*.

- The young lovers were oblivious to everything except their *ardor* for each other.

ARDUOUS (AHR joo us) *adj* hard; difficult

- Climbing the mountain was *arduous*. We were so exhausted when we got to the top that we forgot to enjoy the view.

- The *arduous* car trip was made even more difficult by the fact that all four tires went flat, one after another.

ARISTOCRATIC (uh ris tuh KRAT ik) *adj* of noble birth; snobbish
- Prince Charles is *aristocratic*. He is a member of the British *aristocracy*.
- Polo, which Prince Charles enjoys, is often said to be an *aristocratic* sport because it is typically played by privileged people.

It is possible to be an *aristocrat* (uh RIS tuh krat) without being rich, although *aristocrats* tend to be quite wealthy. There is nothing you can do to become an *aristocrat*, short of being born into a family of them.

People who act as though they think they are better than everyone else are often said to be *aristocratic*. A person with an "*aristocratic* bearing" is a person who keeps his or her nose in the air and looks down on everyone else.

ARTFUL (AHRT ful) *adj* crafty; wily; sly
- After dinner, the *artful* counselor told the campers that there was a madman loose in the woods, thus causing them to lie quietly in the tent.

The *Artful* Dodger is a sly con man in Charles Dickens's *Oliver Twist*.

Someone who is *artless*, on the other hand, is simple and honest. Young children are charmingly *artless*.

ARTIFICE (AHRT uh fus) *n* a clever trick; cunning
- The Trojan Horse was an *artifice* designed to get the soldiers inside the walls.
- Mrs. Baker had to resort to *artifice* to get her children to take their medicine: she told them that it tasted like chocolate syrup.

Artifice and *artificial* are related words.

ASCENDANCY (uh SEN dun see) *n* supremacy; domination
- Handheld gadgets have been in *ascendancy* for the past few years.
- The *ascendancy* of the new regime had been a great boon for the economy of the tiny tropical kingdom.

When something is in *ascendancy*, it is *ascendant*.

ASCETIC (uh SET ik) *adj* hermitlike; practicing self-denial
- The college student's apartment, which contained no furniture except a single tattered mattress, was uncomfortably *ascetic*.
- In his effort to save money, Roy led an *ascetic* existence: he never went out, never ate anything but soup, and never had any fun.

Ascetic can also be a noun. A person who leads an *ascetic* existence is an *ascetic*. An *ascetic* is someone who practices *asceticism*.

A similar-sounding word with a very different meaning is *aesthetic* (es THET ik). Don't be confused.

ASSIDUOUS (uh SIJ oo us) *adj* hardworking; busy; quite diligent

- The workmen were *assiduous* in their effort to get nothing done; instead of working, they drank coffee all day long.
- Wendell was the only *assiduous* student in the entire math class; all the other students tried to copy their homework from him.

Quick Quiz #11

Match each word in the first column with its definition in the second column. Check your answers in the back of the book.

1.	archetype	a.	passionate
2.	ardent	b.	of noble birth
3.	arduous	c.	supremacy
4.	aristocratic	d.	hardworking
5.	artful	e.	difficult
6.	artifice	f.	trickery
7.	ascendancy	g.	hermitlike
8.	ascetic	h.	crafty
9.	assiduous	i.	original model

ASSIMILATE (uh SIM uh layt) *v* to take in; to absorb; to learn thoroughly

To *assimilate* an idea is to take it in as thoroughly as if you had eaten it. (Your body *assimilates* nutrients from the food you eat.) To *assimilate* knowledge is to absorb it, to let it soak in. People can be *assimilated*, too.

- Margaret didn't have any friends when she first went to the new school, but she was gradually *assimilated*—she became part of the new community. When she was chosen for the cheerleading squad, her *assimilation* was complete.

ASSUAGE (uh SWAYJ) *v* to soothe; to pacify; to ease the pain of; to relieve

- Beth was extremely angry, but I *assuaged* her by promising to leave the house and never return.

- The thunderstorm made the baby cry, but I *assuaged* her fears by singing her a lullaby.

> **Note carefully the pronunciation of this word.**

ASTUTE (uh STOOT) *adj* shrewd; keen in judgment
- Morris was an *astute* judge of character; he was very good at seeing what people were really like despite what they pretended to be.
- Yael notices everything important and many things that other people don't see; he is an *astute* observer.

ATHEIST (AY thee ist) *n* one who does not believe in the existence of any god or divine being
- Hadley had always imagined a big religious wedding, but Emma, a lifelong *atheist*, preferred a Vegas elopement.

The noun form is *atheism*. *Atheism* is often confused with *agnosticism*, but the two are not the same.

ATTRITION (uh TRISH un) *n* gradual wearing away, weakening, or loss; a natural or expected decrease in numbers or size
- Mr. Gregory did not have the heart to fire his workers even though his company was losing millions each year. He altruistically preferred to lose workers through *attrition* when they moved away, retired, or decided to change jobs.

AUDACITY (aw DAS uh tee) *n* boldness; reckless daring; impertinence
- Edgar's soaring leap off the top of the building was an act of great *audacity.*
- Ivan had the *audacity* to tell that nice old lady to shut up.

A person with *audacity* is said to be *audacious*.
- Bert made the *audacious* decision to climb Mt. Everest in bowling shoes.

AUGMENT (awg MENT) *v* to make bigger; to add to; to increase
- The army *augmented* its attack by sending in a few thousand more soldiers.

To *augment* a record collection is to add more records to it.

Adding another example to this definition would *augment* it.

The act of *augmenting* is called *augmentation*.

AUSPICIOUS (aw SPISH us) *adj* favorable; promising; pointing to a good result

- A clear sky in the morning is an *auspicious* sign on the day of a picnic.
- The first quarter of the football game was not *auspicious;* the home team was outscored by thirty points.

AUSTERE (aw STEER) *adj* unadorned; stern; forbidding; without excess

- The Smiths' house was *austere:* there was no furniture in it, and there was nothing hanging on the walls.
- Quentin, with his *austere* personality, didn't make many friends. Most people were too intimidated by him to introduce themselves or say hello.

The noun *austerity* (aw STER uh tee) is generally used to mean roughly the same thing as poverty. To live in *austerity* is to live without comforts.

- After the devastation of the war, the citizens in Austria lived in *austerity.*

AUTOCRATIC (aw tuh KRAT ik) *adj* ruling with absolute authority; extremely bossy

- The ruthless dictator's *autocratic* reign ended when the rebels blew up his palace with plastic explosives.
- This two-year-old can be very *autocratic*—he wants what he wants when he wants it.
- No one at our office liked the *autocratic* manager. He always insisted on having his own way, and he never let anyone make a decision without consulting him.

An *autocrat* is an absolute ruler. *Autocracy* (aw TAHK ruh see), a system of government headed by an *autocrat,* is not democratic—the people don't get a say.

> **Note carefully the pronunciation of these words.**

AUTONOMOUS (aw TAHN uh mus) *adj* acting independently

- The West Coast office of the law firm was quite *autonomous;* it never asked the East Coast office for permission before it did anything.

An *autonomous* nation is one that is independent—it governs itself. It is said to have *autonomy*.

To act *autonomously* is to act on your own authority. If something happens *autonomously*, it happens all by itself.

AVARICE (AV ur is) *n* greed; excessive love of riches

- The rich man's *avarice* was annoying to everyone who wanted to lay hands on his money.

Avarice is the opposite of generosity or philanthropy.

To be *avaricious* is to love wealth above all else and not to share it with other people.

AVOW (uh VOW) *v* to claim; to declare boldly; to admit

- At the age of twenty-five, Louis finally *avowed* that he couldn't stand his mother's apple pie.

To *avow* something is to declare or admit something that most people are reluctant to declare or admit.

- Mr. Smith *avowed* on television that he had never paid any income tax. Shortly after this *avowal,* he received a lengthy letter from the Internal Revenue Service.

An *avowed* criminal is one who admits he is a criminal. To *disavow* is to deny or repudiate someone else's claim.

- The mayor *disavowed* the allegation that she had embezzled campaign contributions.

AVUNCULAR (uh VUNG kyuh lur) *adj* like an uncle, especially a nice uncle

What's an uncle like? Kind, helpful, generous, understanding, and so on, in an uncle-y sort of way. This is a fun word to use, although it's usually hard to find occasions to use it.

- Professor Zia often gave us *avuncular* advice; he took a real interest in our education and helped us with other problems that weren't related to multidimensional calculus.

Note carefully the pronunciation of this word.

AWRY (uh RYE) *adj* off course; twisted to one side

- The hunter's bullet went *awry*. Instead of hitting the bear, it hit his truck.
- When we couldn't find a restaurant, our dinner plans went *awry*.
- The old woman's hat was *awry;* it had dipped in front of her left eye.

AXIOM (AK see um) *n* a self-evident rule or truth; a widely accepted saying

"Everything that is living dies" is an *axiom.*

An *axiom* in geometry is a rule that doesn't have to be proved because its truth is accepted as obvious, self-evident, or unprovable.

Quick Quiz #13

Match each word in the first column with its definition in the second column. Check your answers in the back of the book.

1.	autonomous	a.	greed
2.	avarice	b.	like an uncle
3.	avow	c.	self-evident truth
4.	avuncular	d.	acting independently
5.	awry	e.	claim
6.	axiom	f.	off course

B

BANAL (buh NAL) *adj* unoriginal; ordinary
- The dinner conversation was so *banal* that Amanda fell asleep in her dessert dish.

A *banal* statement is a boring, trite, and uncreative statement. It is a *banality*.
- What made Yu fall asleep was the *banality* of the dinner conversation.

This word can also be pronounced "BANE ul."

BANE (bayn) *n* poison; torment; cause of harm

Bane means poison (wolfbane is a kind of poisonous plant), but the word is usually used figuratively. To say that someone is the *bane* of your existence is to say that that person poisons your enjoyment of life.

Baneful means harmful.

BASTION (BAS chun) *n* stronghold; fortress; fortified place
- Mrs. Garnett's classroom is a *bastion* of banality; that is, it's a place where originality seldom, if ever, makes its way inside.
- The robbers terrorized the village for several weeks and then escaped to their *bastion* high in the treacherous mountains.

BEGET (bih GET) *v* to give birth to; to create; to lead to; to cause
- Those who lie should be creative and have good memories, because one lie often *begets* another lie, which *begets* another.

BELABOR (bi LAY bur) *v* to go over repeatedly or to an absurd extent
- For more than an hour, the boring speaker *belabored* her point about the challenge of foreign competition.
- Mr. Irving spent the entire period *belaboring* the obvious; he made the same dumb observation over and over again.

BELEAGUER (bih LEE gur) *v* to surround; to besiege; to harass
- No one could leave the *beleaguered* city; the attacking army had closed off all the exits.
- Oscar felt *beleaguered* at work. He was months behind in his assignments, and he had little hope of catching up.
- The *beleaguered* executive seldom emerged from the his office as he struggled to deal with the growing scandal.

BELIE (bih LYE) *v* to give a false impression of; to contradict

- Melvin's smile *belied* the grief he was feeling; despite his happy expression he was terribly sad inside.
- The messy appearance of the banquet table *belied* the huge effort that had gone into setting it up.

A word that is sometimes confused with *belie* is *betray*. To rework the first example above: Melvin was smiling, but a small tear in one eye *betrayed* the grief he was feeling.

BELITTLE (bih LIT ul) *v* to make to seem little; to put someone down

- We worked hard to put out the fire, but the fire chief *belittled* our efforts by saying she wished she had brought some marshmallows.
- The chairman's *belittling* comments made everyone feel small.

Quick Quiz #14

Match each word in the first column with its definition in the second column. Check your answers in the back of the book.

1.	banal	a.	make to seem little
2.	bane	b.	unoriginal
3.	bastion	c.	go over repeatedly
4.	beget	d.	stronghold
5.	belabor	e.	poison
6.	beleaguer	f.	give a false impression
7.	belie	g.	surround
8.	belittle	h.	give birth to

BELLIGERENT (buh LIJ ur unt) *adj* combative; quarrelsome; waging war

- Al was so *belligerent* that the party had the feel of a boxing match.

A bully is *belligerent*. To be *belligerent* is to push other people around, to be noisy and argumentative, to threaten other people, and generally to make a nuisance of oneself.

Opposing armies in a war are referred to as *belligerents.* Sometimes one *belligerent* in a conflict is more *belligerent* than the other.

BEMUSED (bih MYOOZD) *adj* confused; bewildered

- The two stood *bemused* in the middle of the parking lot at Disneyland, trying to remember where they had parked their car.

- Ralph was *bemused* when all lights and appliances in his house began switching on and off for no apparent reason.

To *muse* is to think about or ponder things. To be *bemused,* then, is to have been thinking about things to the point of confusion.

People often use the word *bemused* when they really mean amused, but *bemusement* is no laughing matter. *Bemused* means confused.

BENEFACTOR (BEN uh fak tur) *n* one who provides help, especially in the form of a gift or donation

To give benefits is to be a *benefactor.* To receive benefits is to be a *beneficiary.* People very, very often confuse these two words. It would be to their benefit to keep them straight.

If your next-door neighbor rewrites his life insurance policy so that you will receive all his millions when he dies, then you become the *beneficiary* of the policy. If your neighbor dies, he is your *benefactor.*

A *malefactor* (MAL uh fak tur) is a person who does bad things.
- Batman and Robin made life hell for *malefactors* in Gotham City.

Remember Maleficent, Sleeping Beauty's evil nemesis? Her name is a variation of this idea.

BENEVOLENT (beh NEV uh lunt) *adj* generous; kind; doing good deeds

Giving money to the poor is a *benevolent* act. To be *benevolent* is to bestow benefits. The United Way, like any charity, is a *benevolent* organization.

Malevolent (muh LEV uh lunt) means evil, or wishing to do harm.

BENIGN (bih NYNE) *adj* gentle; not harmful; kind; mild
- Karla has a *benign* personality; she is not at all unpleasant to be with.
- The threat of revolution turned out to be *benign;* nothing much came of it.
- Charlie was worried that he had cancer, but the lump on his leg turned out to be *benign.*

The difference between a *benign* person and a *benevolent* (see separate entry) one is that the *benevolent* one is actively kind and generous while the *benign* one is more passive. *Benevolence* is usually active generosity or kindness, while *benignancy* tends to mean simply not causing harm.

The opposite of a *benign* tumor is a *malignant* one. This is a tumor that can kill you. A *malignant* personality is one you wish a surgeon would remove. *Malignant* means nasty, evil, or full of ill will. The word *malignant* also conveys a sense that evil is spreading, as with a cancer. An adjective that means the same thing is *malign.*

As a verb, *malign* has a different meaning. To *malign* someone is to say unfairly bad things about that person, to injure that person by telling evil lies about him or her. *Slander* and *malign* are synonyms.

Quick Quiz #15

Match each word in the first column with its definition in the second column. Check your answers in the back of the book.

1.	belligerent	a.	intending harm
2.	bemused	b.	donor
3.	benefactor	c.	not harmful
4.	beneficiary	d.	deadly
5.	benevolent	e.	confused
6.	benign	f.	generous
7.	malignant	g.	combative
8.	malign	h.	injure with lies
9.	malevolent	i.	one who receives benefits
10.	malefactor	j.	evildoer

BEQUEST (bih KWEST) *n* something left to someone in a will

If your next-door neighbor leaves you all his millions in a will, the money is a *bequest* from him to you. It is not polite to request a *bequest*. Just keep smiling and hope for the best.

To leave something to someone in a will is to *bequeath* it. A *bequest* is something that has been *bequeathed.*

BEREAVED (buh REEVD) *adj* deprived or left desolate, especially through death

- The new widow was still *bereaved* when we saw her. Every time anyone mentioned her dead husband's name, she burst into tears.
- The children were *bereaved* by the death of their pet. Then they got a new pet.

Bereft (buh REFT) means the same thing as *bereaved.*

BESET (bih SET) *v* to harass; to surround

- The bereaved widow was *beset* by grief.

- Problems *beset* the expedition almost from the beginning, and the mountain climbers soon returned to their base camp.
- The little town was *beset* by robberies, but the police could do nothing.

BLASPHEMY (BLAS fuh mee) *n* irreverence; an insult to something held sacred; profanity

In the strictest sense, to commit *blasphemy* is to say nasty, insulting things about God. The word is used more broadly, though, to cover a wide range of nasty, insulting comments.

To *blaspheme* (blas FEEM) is to use swear words or say deeply irreverent things. A person who says such things is *blasphemous*.

BLATANT (BLAYT unt) *adj* unpleasantly or offensively noisy; glaring

- David was *blatantly* critical of our efforts; that is, he was noisy and obnoxious in making his criticisms.

Blatant is often confused with flagrant, because both words mean glaring. *Blatant* indicates that something was not concealed very well, whereas *flagrant* indicates that something was intentional. A *blatant* act is usually also a *flagrant* one, but a *flagrant* act isn't necessarily *blatant*. You might want to refer to the listing for *flagrant*.

Quick Quiz #16

Match each word in the first column with its definition in the second column. Check your answers in the back of the book.

1.	bequest	a.	left desolate
2.	bequeath	b.	something left in a will
3.	bereaved	c.	harass
4.	beset	d.	offensively noisy
5.	blasphemy	e.	leaving in a will
6.	blatant	f.	irreverence

BLIGHT (blyte) *n* a disease in plants; anything that injures or destroys

- An early frost proved a *blight* to the citrus crops last year, so we had no orange juice for breakfast.

BLITHE (blythe) *adj* carefree; cheerful

- The *blithe* birds in the garden were making so much noise that Jamilla began to think about the shotgun in the attic.

- The children were playing *blithely* next to the hazardous-waste dump. While they played, they were *blithely* unaware that they were doing something dangerous.

To be *blithely* ignorant is to be happily unaware.

BOURGEOIS (boor ZHWAH) *adj* middle class, usually in a pejorative sense; boringly conventional

The original *bourgeoisie* (boor zhwaw ZEE) were simply people who lived in cities, an innovation at the time. They weren't farmers and they weren't nobles. They were members of a new class—the middle class. Now the word is used mostly in making fun of or sneering at people who think about nothing but their possessions and conforming with other people like them.

A hip, young city dweller might reject life in the suburbs as being too *bourgeois*. A person whose dream is to have a swimming pool in his or her backyard might be called *bourgeois* by someone who thinks there are more important things in life. Golf is often referred to as a *bourgeois* sport.

Note carefully the pronunciation of these words.

BOVINE (BOH vyne) *adj* cow related; cowlike
- Cows are *bovine,* obviously. Eating grass is a *bovine* concern.

There are a number of similar words based on other animals:

> *canine* (KAY nyne): dogs
> *equine* (EE kwyne): horses
> *feline* (FEE lyne): cats
> *piscine* (PYE seen): fish
> *porcine* (POR syne): pigs
> *ursine* (UR syne): bears

BREVITY (BREV i tee) *n* briefness
- The audience was deeply grateful for the *brevity* of the after-dinner speaker's remarks.
- The reader of this book may be grateful for the *brevity* of this example.

Brevity is related to the word *abbreviate*.

BROACH (brohch) *v* to open up a subject for discussion, often a delicate subject
- Henrietta was proud of her new dress, so no one knew how to *broach* the subject with her of how silly grandmothers look in leather.

BUCOLIC (byoo KAHL ik) *adj* charmingly rural; rustic; country-like
- The changing of the autumn leaves, old stone walls, distant views, and horses grazing in green meadows are examples of *bucolic* splendor.
- The *bucolic* scene didn't do much for the city child, who preferred screaming fire engines and honking horns to the sounds of a babbling brook.

BUREAUCRACY (byoo RAHK ruh see) *n* a system of government administration consisting of numerous bureaus or offices, especially one run according to inflexible and inefficient rules; any large administrative system characterized by inefficiency, lots of rules, and red tape
- The Department of Motor Vehicles is a *bureaucracy*. The forms you have to fill out all request unnecessary information. After you finally get everything all filled out and handed in, you don't hear another word from the department for many months.

The people who work in a *bureaucracy* are called *bureaucrats*. These people and the inefficient procedures they follow might be called *bureaucratic*. Administrative systems outside the government can be *bureaucratic*, too. A high school principal who requires teachers and students to fill out forms for everything might be called *bureaucratic*.

BURGEON (BUR jun) *v* to expand; to flourish
- The *burgeoning* weeds in our yard soon overwhelmed the grass.

Note carefully the pronunciation of this word.

BURLESQUE (bur LESK) *n* a ludicrous, mocking, lewd imitation
- Vaudeville actors frequently performed *burlesque* works on the stage.

Burlesque, parody, lampoon, and *caricature* share similar meanings.

C

CACOPHONY (kuh KAHF uh nee) *n* harsh-sounding mixture of words, voices, or sounds

- The parade's two marching bands played simultaneously; the resulting *cacophony* drove many spectators to tears.

A *cacophony* isn't just a lot of noise—it's a lot of noise that doesn't sound good together. A steam whistle blowing isn't a *cacophony*. But a high school orchestra that had never rehearsed together might very well produce a *cacophony*. The roar of engines, horns, and sirens arising from a busy city street would be a *cacophony*. A lot of people all shouting at once would produce a *cacophony*.

Euphony is the opposite of *cacophony*. *Euphony* is pleasing sound.

CADENCE (KAYD uns) *n* rhythm; the rise and fall of sounds

- We wished the tone of Irwin's words would have a more pleasing *cadence,* but he spoke in a dull monotone.

CAJOLE (kuh JOHL) *v* to persuade someone to do something he or she doesn't want to do

- I didn't want to give the speech, but Enrique *cajoled* me into doing it by telling me what a good speaker I am. As it turned out, he simply hadn't been able to find anyone else.

CALLOW (KAL oh) *adj* immature

- The patient was alarmed by the *callowness* of the medical staff. The doctors looked too young to have graduated from high school, much less from medical school.

To be *callow* is to be youthfully naive, inexperienced, and unsophisticated.

CANDOR (KAN dur) *n* truthfulness; sincere honesty

- My best friend exhibited *candor* when she told me that for many years now she has believed me to be a jerk.
- Teddy appreciated Ross's *candor;* Teddy was glad to know that Ross thought Teddy's sideburns looked stupid.

To show *candor* is to be *candid*. What is *candid* about *candid* photos? The photos are *candid* because they are truthful in showing what people do. *Candid* does *not* mean concealed or hidden, even though the camera on the old television show "Candid Camera" was concealed. To be *candid* is to speak frankly.

CAPITALISM (KAP uh tuh liz um) *n* an economic system in which businesses are owned by private citizens (not by the government) and in which the resulting products and services are sold with relatively little government control

The American economy is *capitalist*. If you wanted to start a company to sell signed photographs of yourself, you could. You, and not the government, would decide how much you would charge for the pictures. Your success or failure would depend on how many people decided to buy your pictures.

CAPITULATE (kuh PICH uh layt) *v* to surrender; to give up or give in

- On the twentieth day of the strike, the workers *capitulated* and went back to work without a new contract.

- So few students paid attention to Mr. Hernandez that he had to *recapitulate* his major points at the end of the class.

To *recapitulate* is not to *capitulate* again. To *recapitulate* is to summarize.

CAPRICIOUS (kuh PRISH us) *adj* unpredictable; likely to change at any moment

- Arjun was *capricious.* One minute he said his favorite car was a Volkswagen; the next minute he said it was a Toyota.
- The weather is often said to be *capricious.* One minute it's snowing; the next minute it's 120 degrees in the shade.

A *caprice* (kuh PREES) is a whim.

- Kendra attempted a quadruple somersault off the ten-meter diving board as a *caprice.* It was a painful *caprice.*

Note carefully the pronunciation of this word.

CARICATURE (KAR uh kuh chur) *n* a portrait or description that is purposely distorted or exaggerated, often to prove some point about its subject

- Khoa sat for a *caricature* at the end of the marathon, but wasn't pleased with the result: the portrait exaggerated his already dominant acne.

Editorial cartoonists often draw *caricatures.* Big noses, enormous glasses, floppy ears, and other distortions are common in such drawings. A politician who has been convicted of bribery might be depicted in a prison uniform or with a ball and chain around his or her ankle. If the politician has big ears to begin with, the ears might be drawn vastly bigger.

A *caricature* uses exaggeration to bring out the hidden character of its subject.

The word can also be used as a verb. To *caricature* someone is to create such a distorted portrait.

CASTIGATE (KAS tuh gayt) *v* to criticize severely; to chastise

- Jose's mother-in-law *castigated* him for forgetting to pick her up at the airport.

CATALYST (KAT uh list) *n* in chemistry, something that changes the rate of a chemical reaction without itself being changed; anyone or anything that makes something happen without being directly involved in it

- When the mad scientist dropped a few grains of the *catalyst* into his test tube, the bubbling liquid began to boil furiously.

This word is often used outside the laboratory as well. The launching of *Sputnik* by the Russians provided the *catalyst* for the creation of the modern American space program.

- The tragic hijacking provided the *catalyst* for Congress's new anti-terrorist legislation.

Quick Quiz #18

Match each word in the first column with its definition in the second column. Check your answers in the back of the book.

1.	cacophony	a.	truthfulness
2.	cadence	b.	harsh mixture of sounds
3.	cajole	c.	surrender
4.	callow	d.	distorted portrait
5.	candor	e.	unpredictable
6.	capitalism	f.	immature
7.	capitulate	g.	free enterprise
8.	recapitulate	h.	something that makes
9.	capricious		things happen
10.	caricature	i.	summarize
11.	castigate	j.	persuade deceptively
12.	catalyst	k.	criticize severely
		l.	rhythm

CATEGORICAL (kat uh GOR uh kul) *adj* unconditional; absolute

A *categorical* denial is one without exceptions—it covers every *category*.

- Crooked politicians often make *categorical* denials of various charges against them. Then they go to jail.
- I *categorically* refuse to do anything whatsoever at any time, in any place, with anyone.

CATHARSIS (kuh THAR sis) *n* purification that brings emotional relief or renewal

To someone with psychological problems, talking to a psychiatrist can lead to a *catharsis*. A *catharsis* is a sometimes traumatic event after which one feels better.

A *catharsis* is *cathartic*. Some people find emotional movies *cathartic*—watching one often allows them to release buried feelings. *Cathartic* can also be a noun.

CATHOLIC (KATH lik) *adj* universal; embracing everything
- Da Vinci was a *catholic* genius who excelled at everything he did.

Parochial means narrow-minded, so *parochial* and *catholic* are almost opposites.

Catholic with a small *c* means universal. *Catholic* with a large *C* means *Roman Catholic* or pertaining to an ancient, undivided Christian church.

CAUSTIC (KAW stik) *adj* like acid; corrosive

Paint remover is a *caustic* substance; if you spill it on your skin, your skin will burn.
- The *caustic* detergent ate right through Henry's laundry.

Caustic can be used figuratively as well. A *caustic* comment is one that is so nasty or insulting that it seems to sting or burn the person to whom it is directed.
- The teacher's *caustic* criticism of Sally's term paper left her crestfallen.

CELIBACY (SEL uh buh see) *n* abstinence from sex

People who practice *celibacy* don't practice sex. To practice *celibacy* is to be *celibate*. Some people choose to be *celibate* for personal reasons.

CENSURE (SEN shur) *v* to condemn severely for doing something bad
- The Senate sometimes *censures* senators for breaking laws or engaging in behavior unbecoming to an elected official.

Censure can also be a noun.
- The clumsy physician feared the *censure* of her fellow doctors, so she stopped treating anything more complicated than the common cold.

A Senate that made a habit of *censuring* senators might be said to

A Senate that made a habit of *censuring* senators might be said to be *censorious*. To be *censorious* is to be highly critical—to do a lot of *censuring*.

CEREBRAL (suh REE brul) *adj* brainy; intellectually refined

Your *cerebrum* is the biggest part of your brain. To be *cerebral* is to do and care about things that really smart people do and care about.

A *cerebral* discussion is one that is filled with big words and concerns abstruse matters that ordinary people can't understand.

- Sebastian was too *cerebral* to be a baseball announcer; he kept talking about the existentialism of the outfield.

This word can also be pronounced "SER uh brul."

CHAGRIN (shuh GRIN) *n* humiliation; embarrassed disappointment

- Much to my *chagrin*, I began to giggle during the eulogy at the funeral.
- Doug was filled with *chagrin* when he lost the race because he had put his shoes on the wrong feet.

The word *chagrin* is sometimes used incorrectly to mean surprise. There is, however, a definite note of shame in *chagrin*.

To be *chagrined* is to feel humiliated or mortified.

CHARISMA (kuh RIZ muh) *n* a magical-seeming ability to attract followers or inspire loyalty

- The glamorous presidential candidate had a lot of *charisma;* voters didn't seem to support her so much as be entranced by her.
- The evangelist's undeniable *charisma* enabled him to bring in millions and millions of dollars in donations to his television show.

To have *charisma* is to be *charismatic*.

Quick Quiz #19

Match each word in the first column with its definition in the second column. Check your answers in the back of the book.

1.	categorical	a.	unconditional
2.	catharsis	b.	relieving purification
3.	catholic	c.	abstinence from sex
4.	caustic	d.	brainy
5.	celibacy	e.	humiliation
6.	censure	f.	magical attractiveness
7.	cerebral	g.	corrosive
8.	chagrin	h.	condemn severely
9.	charisma	i.	universal

CHARLATAN (SHAR luh tun) *n* fraud; quack; con man

- Buck was selling what he claimed was a cure for cancer, but he was just a *charlatan* (the pills were jelly beans).
- The flea market usually attracts a lot of *charlatans* who sell phony products that don't do what they claim they will.

CHASM (KAZ um) *n* a deep, gaping hole; a gorge

- Mark was so stupid that his girlfriend wondered whether there wasn't a *chasm* where his brain should be.
- The bad guys were gaining, so the hero grabbed the heroine and swung across the *chasm* on a slender vine.

Note carefully the pronunciation of this word.

CHASTISE (chas TYZE) *v* to inflict punishment on; to discipline

- Mother *chastised* us for firing our bottle rockets too close to the house.
- *Chastising* the dog for sleeping on the beds never seemed to do any good; the minute we turned our backs, she'd curl up next to the pillows.

CHICANERY (shi KAY nuh ree) *n* trickery; deceitfulness; artifice, especially legal or political

- Political news would be dull were it not for the *chicanery* of our elected officials.

CHIMERA (kye MEER uh) *n* an illusion; a foolish fancy

- Jie's dream of becoming a movie star was just a *chimera*.
- Could you take a picture of a *chimera* with a camera? No, of course not. It wouldn't show up on the film.

Be careful not to mispronounce this word. Its apparent similarity to *chimney* is just a *chimera*.

> **Note carefully the pronunciation of this word.**

CHOLERIC (KAHL ur ik) *adj* hot-tempered; quick to anger

- The *choleric* watchdog would sink his teeth into anyone who came within biting distance of his doghouse.
- When the grumpy old man was in one of his *choleric* moods, the children refused to go near him.
- The *choleric* administrator kept all the secretaries in a state of terror.

CHRONIC (KRAHN ik) *adj* constant; lasting a long time; inveterate

- DJ's *chronic* back pains often kept her from soccer practice.

Someone who always comes in last could be called a *chronic* loser.

Chronic is usually associated with something negative or undesirable: *chronic* illness, *chronic* failure, *chronic* depression. You would be much less likely to encounter a reference to *chronic* success or *chronic* happiness, unless the writer or speaker was being ironic.

A *chronic* disease is one that lingers for a long time, doesn't go away, or keeps coming back. The opposite of a *chronic* disease is an *acute* disease. An *acute* disease is one that comes and goes very quickly. It may be severe, but it doesn't last forever.

CHRONICLE (KRAHN uh kul) *n* a record of events in order of time; a history

- Sally's diary provided her mother with a detailed *chronicle* of her daughter's extracurricular activities.

Chronicle can also be used as a verb.

- The reporter *chronicled* all the events of the revolution.

Chronology and *chronicle* are nearly synonyms: Both provide a *chronological* list of events.

Chronological means in order of time.

Quick Quiz #20

Match each word in the first column with its definition in the second column. Check your answers in the back of the book.

1.	charlatan	a.	in order of occurrence
2.	chasm	b.	constant
3.	chastise	c.	hot-tempered
4.	chicanery	d.	punish
5.	chimera	e.	account of past times
6.	choleric	f.	list in time order
7.	chronic	g.	illusion
8.	chronological	h.	fraud
9.	chronology	i.	gaping hole
10.	chronicle	j.	trickery

CIRCUITOUS (sur KYOO uh tus) *adj* **roundabout; not following a direct path**

- The *circuitous* bus route between the two cities went here, there, and everywhere, and it took an extremely long time to get anywhere.
- The salesman's route was *circuitous*—it wound aimlessly through many small towns.

A *circuitous* argument is one that rambles around for quite a while before making its point.

A *circuitous* argument is very similar to a *circular* argument, which is one that ends up where it begins or attempts to prove something without offering any new information. To say, "Straight means not curved, and curved means not straight," is to give a circular, or tautological, definition of the word *straight*.

CIRCUMLOCUTION (sur kum loh KYOO shun) *n* **an indirect expression; use of wordy or evasive language**

- The lawyer's *circumlocution* left everyone in the courtroom wondering what had been said.
- The indicted executive evaded the reporters' questions by resorting to *circumlocution*.

To use a lot of big, vague words and to speak in a disorganized way is to be *circumlocutory*.

CIRCUMSCRIBE (SUR kum skrybe) *v* to draw a line around; to set the limits; to define; to restrict

- The Constitution clearly *circumscribes* the restrictions that can be placed on our personal freedoms.
- A barbed-wire fence and armed guards *circumscribed* the movement of the prisoners.

CIRCUMSPECT (SUR kum spekt) *adj* cautious

- As a public speaker, Nick was extremely *circumspect;* he always took great care not to say the wrong thing or give offense.
- The *circumspect* general did everything she could not to put her soldiers at unnecessary risk.

The word *circumspect* comes from Greek roots meaning around and look (as do the words *circle* and *inspect*). To be *circumspect* is to look around carefully before doing something.

CIRCUMVENT (sur kum VENT) *v* to frustrate as though by surrounding

- Our hopes for an early end of the meeting were *circumvented* by the chairperson's refusal to deal with the items on the agenda.
- The angry school board *circumvented* the students' effort to install televisions in every classroom.

CIVIL (SIV ul) *adj* polite; civilized; courteous

- Our dinner guests conducted themselves *civilly* when we told them we weren't going to serve them dinner after all. They didn't bang their cups on the table or throw their plates to the floor.

The word *civil* also has other meanings. *Civil* rights are rights established by law. *Civil* service is government service. Consult your dictionary for the numerous shades of meaning.

CLEMENCY (KLEM un see) *n* mercy; forgiveness; mildness

- The governor committed an act of *clemency* when he released all the convicts from the state penitentiary.

Mild weather is called *clement* weather; bad weather is called *inclement.*

- You should wear a coat and carry an umbrella in *inclement* weather.

CLICHÉ (klee SHAY) *n* an overused saying or idea

- The expression "you can't judge a book by its cover" is a *cliché;* it's been used so many times that it's become stale.

Clichés are usually true. That's why they've been repeated often enough to become overused. But they are boring. A writer who uses a lot of *clichés*—referring to a foreign country as "a land of contrasts," describing spring as "a time of renewal," saying that a snowfall is "a blanket of white"—is not interesting to read because there is nothing new about these observations.

Note carefully the pronunciation of this French word.

CLIQUE (kleek; klik) *n* an exclusive group bound together by some shared quality or interest
- The high school newspaper staff was a real *clique;* they all hung out together and wouldn't talk to anyone else. It was hard to have fun at that school if you weren't a member of the right *clique.* The cheerleaders were *cliquish* as well.

Note carefully the pronunciation of this word.

Quick Quiz #21

Match each word in the first column with its definition in the second column. Check your answers in the back of the book.

1.	circuitous	a.	cautious
2.	circumlocution	b.	draw a line around
3.	circumscribe	c.	mercy
4.	circumspect	d.	polite
5.	circumvent	e.	roundabout
6.	civil	f.	frustrate
7.	clique	g.	overused saying
8.	clemency	h.	indirect expression
9.	inclement	i.	exclusive group
10.	cliché	j.	bad, as in weather

COALESCE (koh uh LES) *v* to come together as one; to fuse; to unite
- When the dough *coalesced* into a big blob, we began to wonder whether the cookies would be edible.
- The people in our neighborhood *coalesced* into a powerful force for change in the community.
- The Southern *coalition* in Congress is the group of representatives from Southern states who often vote the same way.

A *coalition* is a group of people that has come together for some purpose, often a political one.

Coal miners and cola bottlers might *coalesce* into a *coalition* for the purpose of persuading coal mine owners to provide cola machines in coal mines.

COERCE (koh URS) *v* to force someone to do or not to do something

- Darth Vader tried to flatter, bribe, and even *coerce*, but he was never able to make Han Solo reveal the hidden rebel base.

The noun is *coercion* (koh UR shun).

COGENT (KOH junt) *adj* powerfully convincing

- Shaft was *cogent* in explaining why he needed the confidential files, so we gave them to him.
- The lawyer's argument on her client's behalf was not *cogent,* so the jury convicted her client. The jury was persuaded by the *cogency* of the prosecuting attorney's argument.

Cogent reasons are extremely persuasive ones.

COGNITIVE (KAHG nu tiv) *adj* dealing with how we know the world around us through our senses; mental

Scientists study the *cognitive* apparatus of human beings to pattern how computers should gather information about the world.

Cognition is knowing.

COGNIZANT (KAHG nu zunt) *adj* aware; conscious

To be *cognizant* of your responsibilities is to know what your responsibilities are.

- Al was *cognizant* of the dangers of sword swallowing, but he tried it anyway and hurt himself quite badly.

COHERENT (koh HEER unt) *adj* holding together; making sense

- After puzzling over Grace's disorganized Holy Roman Empire essay for almost an hour, Ms. Fabricius needed only twenty minutes to read Arjun's *coherent* paper on the Defenestration of Prague.

A *coherent* wad of cotton balls is one that holds together.

A *coherent* explanation is an explanation that makes sense; the explanation holds together.

To hold together is to *cohere.*

COLLOQUIAL (kul OH kwee ul) *adj* conversational; informal in language

A writer with a *colloquial* style is a writer who uses ordinary words and whose writing seems as informal as common speech.

"The way I figure it" is a *colloquial* expression, or a *colloquialism;* people often say it, but it isn't used in formal prose.

A *colloquy* (KAHL uh kwee) is a conversation or conference.

COLLUSION (kuh LOO zhun) *n* conspiracy; secret cooperation

- The increase in oil prices was the result of *collusion* by the oil-producing nations.
- There was *collusion* among the owners of the baseball teams; they agreed secretly not to sign any expensive free agents.

If the baseball owners were in *collusion,* then you could say that they had *colluded.* To *collude* is to conspire.

COMMENSURATE (kuh MEN sur it) *adj* equal; proportionate

- Ryan's salary is *commensurate* with his ability; like his ability, his salary is small.
- The number of touchdowns scored by the team and the number of its victories were *commensurate* (both zero).

COMPELLING (kum PEL ing) *adj* forceful; causing to yield

- A *compelling* argument for buying a security system is one that makes you go out and buy a security system.
- The recruiter's speech was so *compelling* that nearly everyone in the auditorium enlisted in the Army when it was over.

To *compel* someone to do something is to force him or her to do it.

- Our consciences *compelled* us to turn over the money we had found to the authorities.

The noun is *compulsion,* which also means an irresistible impulse to do something irrational.

COMPENDIUM (kum PEN dee um) *n* a summary; an abridgment

- A yearbook often contains a *compendium* of the offenses, achievements, and future plans of the members of the senior class.

Quick Quiz #22

Match each word in the first column with its definition in the second column. Check your answers in the back of the book.

1.	coalesce	a.	perceptive
2.	coalition	b.	unite
3.	coerce	c.	conversational
4.	cogent	d.	force someone to do
5.	cognitive		something
6.	cognizant	e.	proportionate
7.	coherent	f.	making sense
8.	colloquial	g.	group with a purpose
9.	collusion	h.	powerfully convincing
10.	commensurate	i.	summary
11.	compelling	j.	forceful
12.	compendium	k.	conspiracy
		l.	dealing with how we know our environment

COMPLACENT (kum PLAY sunt) *adj* self-satisfied; overly pleased with oneself; contented to a fault

- The *complacent* camper paid no attention to the poison ivy around his campsite, and ended up going to the hospital.
- The football team won so many games that it became *complacent*, and the worst team in the league won the game.

To fall into *complacency* is to become comfortably uncaring about the world around you.

- The president of the student council was appalled by the *complacency* of her classmates; not one of the seniors seemed to care about the theme.

Don't confuse *complacent* with *complaisant* (kum PLAY zunt), which means eager to please.

COMPLEMENT (KAHM pluh munt) *v* to complete or fill up; to be the perfect counterpart

This word is often confused with *compliment*, which means to praise. It's easy to tell them apart. *Complement* is spelled like *complete*.

- The flower arrangement *complemented* the table decorations.

Complement can also be a noun.

- Fish-flavored ice cream was a perfect *complement* to the seafood dinner.

COMPLICITY (kum PLIS uh tee) *n* participation in wrongdoing; the act of being an accomplice

- There was *complicity* between the bank robber and the dishonest teller. The teller neglected to turn on the alarm, and the robber rewarded him by sharing the loot.
- *Complicity* among the students made it impossible to find out which of them had pulled the fire alarm.

COMPREHENSIVE (kahm pruh HEN siv) *adj* covering or including everything

- The insurance policy was *comprehensive;* it covered all possible losses.
- Maria's knowledge of English is *comprehensive;* she even understands what *comprehensive* means.

A *comprehensive* examination is one that covers everything in the course or in a particular field of knowledge.

COMPRISE (kum PRYZE) *v* to consist of

- A football team *comprises* eleven players on offense and eleven players on defense.
- A company *comprises* employees.

Careful! This word is often misused. Players do *not* "comprise" a football team, and employees do *not* "comprise" a company. Nor can a football team be said to be "*comprised* of" players, or a company to be "*comprised* of" employees. These are common mistakes. Instead, you can say that players *constitute* or *compose* a team and that employees *constitute* or *compose* a company.

You can also say that a team *consists* of players or a company *consists* of employees.

CONCILIATORY (kun SIL ee uh tor ee) *adj* making peace; attempting to resolve a dispute through goodwill

To be *conciliatory* is to kiss and make up.

- Come on—be *conciliatory!*
- The formerly warring countries were *conciliatory* at the treaty conference.
- After dinner at the all-you-can-eat pancake house, the divorced couple began to feel *conciliatory,* so they flew to Las Vegas and were remarried.

When peace has been made, we say that the warring parties have come to a *reconciliation* (rek un sil ee AY shun). To *reconcile* (REK un syle) is to bring two things into agreement.

- The accountant managed to *reconcile* the company books with the cash on hand only with great creativity.

CONCISE (kun SYSE) *adj* brief and to the point; succinct

- The scientist's explanation was *concise;* it was brief and it helped us understand the difficult concept.

To be *concise* is to say much with few words. A *concise* speaker is one who speaks *concisely* or with *concision.*

Quick Quiz #23

Match each word in the first column with its definition in the second column. Check your answers in the back of the book.

1.	complacent	a.	covering everything
2.	complement	b.	complete
3.	complicity	c.	consist of
4.	comprehensive	d.	make up (2)
5.	comprise	e.	brief and to the point
6.	compose	f.	making peace
7.	constitute	g.	participation in wrongdoing
8.	conciliatory	h.	self-satisfied
9.	concise		

CONCORD (KAHN kord) *n* harmony; agreement

Nations that live in *concord* are nations that live together in peace.

- The war between the neighboring tribes ended thirty years of *concord.*
- The faculty meeting was marked by *concord;* no one yelled at anyone else.

Discord is the opposite of *concord.* A faculty meeting where everyone yelled at one another would be a faculty meeting marked by *discord.* It would be a *discordant* meeting.

An *accord* is a formal agreement, usually reached after a dispute.

CONCURRENT (kun KUR unt) *adj* happening at the same time; parallel

- The criminal was sentenced to two *concurrent* fifteen-year sentences; the sentences will run at the same time, and he will be out of jail in fifteen years.
- High prices, falling demand, and poor weather were three *concurrent* trends that made life especially difficult for corn farmers last month.

To *concur* means to agree.

- The assistant wanted to keep his job, so he always *concurred* with his boss.

CONDESCEND (KAHN duh send) *v* to stoop to someone else's level, usually in an offensive way; to patronize

- I was surprised that the president of the company had *condescended* to talk with me, a mere temporary employee.

Many grown-ups make the mistake of *condescending* to young children, who usually prefer to be treated as equals, or at least as rational beings.

CONDONE (kun DOHN) *v* to overlook; to permit to happen

To *condone* what someone does is to look the other way while it happens or to permit it to happen by not doing anything about it.

- The principal *condoned* the hoods' smoking in the bathroom; he simply ignored it.

CONDUCIVE (kun DOO siv) *adj* promoting

- The chairs in the library are *conducive* to sleep. If you sit in them to study, you will fall asleep.
- The foul weather was not *conducive* to our having a picnic.

CONFLUENCE (KAHN floo uns) *n* a flowing together, especially of rivers; the place where they begin to flow together

- The *confluence* of the Missouri and Mississippi rivers is at St. Louis; that's the place where they join together.
- There is a remarkable *confluence* in our thoughts: we think the same way about almost everything.
- A *confluence* of many factors (no ice, bad food, terrible music) made it inevitable that the party would be a flop.

CONGENIAL (kun JEEN yul) *adj* agreeably suitable; pleasant

- The little cabin in the woods was *congenial* to the writer; she was able to get a lot of writing done there.

- The new restaurant has a *congenial* atmosphere. We enjoy just sitting there playing with the ice in our water glasses.

When people get along together at a restaurant and don't throw food at one another, they are being *congenial.*

Genial and *congenial* share similar meanings. *Genial* means pleasing, kind, sympathetic, or helpful. You can be pleased by a *genial* manner or by a *genial* climate.

CONGENITAL (kun JEN uh tul) *adj* describing a trait or condition acquired between conception and birth; innate

A *congenital* birth defect is one that is present at birth but was not caused by one's genes.

The word is also used more loosely to describe any (usually bad) trait or behavior that is so firmly fixed it seems to be a part of a person's nature.

A *congenital* liar is a natural liar, a person who can't help but lie.

Quick Quiz #24

Match each word in the first column with its definition in the second column. Check your answers in the back of the book.

1.	concord	a.	agreeably suitable
2.	discord	b.	innate
3.	concurrent	c.	harmony
4.	condescend	d.	flowing together
5.	condone	e.	promoting
6.	conducive	f.	stoop or patronize
7.	confluence	g.	overlook
8.	congenial	h.	happening at the same time
9.	congenital	i.	disharmony

CONGREGATE (KAHN grih gayt) *v* to come together
- Protestors were granted permission to *congregate* peacefully on the plaza.

The noun form is *congregation* and can refer to the membership of a house of worship.
- About half the *congregation* attended the sunrise service.

Aggregate also has to do with coming together. Can you think of additional words with the same root?

CONJECTURE (kun JEK chur) *v* to guess; to deduce or infer on slight evidence
- If forced to *conjecture,* I would say the volcano will erupt in twenty-four hours.

Conjecture can also be a noun.
- The divorce lawyer for Mr. Davis argued that the putative cause of the lipstick on his collar was mere *conjecture.*

A *conjecture* is *conjectural.*

CONJURE (KAHN jur) *v* to summon or bring into being as if by magic
- The chef *conjured* (or *conjured* up) a fabulous gourmet meal using nothing more than the meager ingredients in Lucy's kitchen.
- The wizard *conjured* (or *conjured* up) an evil spirit by mumbling some magic words and throwing a little powdered eye of newt into the fire.

CONNOISSEUR (kahn uh SUR) *n* an expert, particularly in matters of art or taste
- The artist's work was popular, but *connoisseurs* rejected it as amateurish.
- Frank was a *connoisseur* of bad movies. He had seen them all and knew which ones were genuinely dreadful and which ones were merely poorly made.
- The meal was exquisite enough to impress a *connoisseur.*
- I like sculpture, but I'm no *connoisseur;* I probably can't describe to you why one statue is better than another.

CONSECRATE (KAHN suh krayt) *v* to make or declare sacred
- The Veterans Day speaker said that the battlefield had been *consecrated* by the blood of the soldiers who had died there.
- The priest *consecrated* the building by sprinkling holy water on it.
- The college chaplain delivered a sermon at the *consecration* (kahn suh KRAY shun) ceremony for the new chapel.

The opposite of *consecrate* is *desecrate* (DES uh krayt), which means to treat irreverently.
- The vandals *desecrated* the cemetery by knocking down all the tombstones.

Desecrate can also be applied to areas outside religion.
- Their act of vandalism was a *desecration.*
- Doodling in a book *desecrates* the book, even if the book isn't a Bible.
- The graffiti on the front door of the school is a *desecration.*

CONSENSUS (kun SEN sus) *n* unanimity or general agreement

When there is a *consensus,* everybody feels the same way.

Contrary to how the word is often used, *consensus* implies more than just a rough agreement or a majority opinion. Election results don't reflect a *consensus* unless everyone or nearly everyone votes for the same candidate.

CONSONANT (KAHN suh nunt) *adj* harmonious; in agreement

- Our desires were *consonant* with theirs; we all wanted the same thing.
- The decision to construct a new gymnasium was *consonant* with the superintendent's belief in physical education.

The opposite of *consonant* is *dissonant* (DIS uh nunt), which means inharmonious. *Dissonant* voices are voices that don't sound good together.

Quick Quiz #25

Match each word in the first column with its definition in the second column. Check your answers in the back of the book.

1.	congregate	a.	incompatible
2.	conjecture	b.	harmonious
3.	conjure	c.	make sacred
4.	connoisseur	d.	unanimity
5.	consecrate	e.	summon as if by magic
6.	desecrate	f.	treat irreverently
7.	consensus	g.	artistic expert
8.	consonant	h.	guess
9.	dissonant	i.	get together

CONSTRUE (kun STROO) *v* to interpret

- Preston *construed* his contract as giving him the right to do anything he wanted.
- The law had always been *construed* as permitting the behavior for which Katya had been arrested.
- The meaning of the poem, as I *construed* it, had to do with the love of a woman for her dog.

To *misconstrue* is to misinterpret.

- Tommy *misconstrued* Pamela's smile, but he certainly did not *misconstrue* the slap she gave him.

CONSUMMATE (KAHN sum it) *adj* perfect; complete; supremely skillful

- A *consummate* pianist is an extremely good one. Nothing is lacking in the way he or she plays.

Consummate (KAHN suh mayt) is also a verb. Notice the different pronunciation. To *consummate* something is to finish it or make it complete. Signing a contract would *consummate* an agreement.

Note carefully the pronunciation of both forms of this word.

CONTENTIOUS (kun TEN shus) *adj* argumentative; quarrelsome

- Liz figured that her *contentious* style would make her a perfect litigator; after law school, however, the would-be trial attorney discovered that passing the bar requires more than a will to argue.

A person looking for a fight is *contentious.*

Two people having a fight are *contentious.*

To be *contentious* in a discussion is to make a lot of noisy objections.

A *contender* is a fighter. To *contend* is to fight or argue for something. Someone who breaks the law may have to *contend* with the law.

CONTIGUOUS (kun TIG yoo us) *adj* side by side; adjoining

Two countries that share a border are *contiguous;* so are two events that happened one right after the other.

If two countries are *contiguous,* the territory they cover is continuous. That is, it spreads or continues across both countries without any interruption.

CONTINGENT (kun TIN junt) *adj* dependent; possible

- Our agreement to buy their house is *contingent* upon the sellers' finding another house to move into. That is, they won't sell their house to us unless they can find another house to buy.
- My happiness is *contingent* on yours; if you're unhappy, I'm unhappy.
- The Bowdens were prepared for any *contingency.* Their front hall closet contained a first-aid kit, a fire extinguisher, a life raft, a parachute, and a pack of sled dogs.

A *contingency* is something that may happen but is at least as likely not to happen.

- Several *contingencies* stand between us and the successful completion of our business proposal; several things could happen to screw it up.

CONTRITE (kun TRYTE) *adj* admitting guilt; especially feeling remorseful

To be *contrite* is to admit whatever terrible thing you did.
- Mira was *contrite* about her mistake, so we forgave her.

Criminals who won't confess their crimes are not *contrite*.

Saying that you're sorry is an act of *contrition* (kun TRISH un).

CONTRIVED (kun TRYVED) *adj* artificial; labored
- Sam's acting was *contrived:* no one in the audience believed his character or enjoyed his performance.
- The artist was widely admired for her originality, but her paintings seemed *contrived* to me.
- No one laughed at Mark's *contrived* attempt at humor.

A *contrivance* (kuhn TRY vuhns) is a mechanical device, usually something rigged up.

CONVENTIONAL (kun VEN shun nul) *adj* common; customary; unexceptional
- The architect's *conventional* designs didn't win him awards for originality.

Tipping the server in a restaurant is a *conventional* courtesy.

Conventional wisdom is what everyone thinks.
- The bland politician maintained her popularity by never straying far from the *conventional* wisdom about any topic.

CONVIVIAL (kun VIV ee ul) *adj* fond of partying; festive

A *convivial* gathering is one in which the people present enjoy eating, drinking, and being together.

To be *convivial* is to be an eager but generally well-behaved party animal.

A *convivial* person is the opposite of an antisocial person.

Note carefully the pronunciation of this word.

COPIOUS (KOH pee us) *adj* abundant; plentiful
- The champagne at the wedding reception was *copious* but not very good.
- Matt had a *copious* supply of nails in his workshop. Everywhere you stepped, it seemed, there was a pile of nails.
- Phil ate *copiously* at the banquet and went home feeling quite sick.

Match each word in the first column with its definition in the second column. Check your answers in the back of the book.

1.	construe	a.	admitting guilt
2.	consummate	b.	interpret
3.	contentious	c.	perfect
4.	contiguous	d.	labored
5.	contingent	e.	dependent
6.	contrite	f.	abundant
7.	contrived	g.	adjoining
8.	conventional	h.	argumentative
9.	convivial	i.	festive
10.	copious	j.	common

COROLLARY (KOR uh ler ee) *n* something that follows; a natural consequence

In mathematics, a *corollary* is a law that can be deduced without further proof from a law that has already been proven.

- Bloodshed and death are *corollaries* of any declaration of war.
- Higher prices were a *corollary* of the two companies' agreement not to compete.

CORROBORATE (kuh ROB uh rayt) *v* to confirm; to back up with evidence

- I knew my statement was correct when my colleague *corroborated* it.
- Henny Penny's contention that the sky was falling could not be *corroborated*. That is, no one was able to find any fallen sky.
- The police could find no evidence of theft and thus could not *corroborate* Greg's claim that he had been robbed.

Note carefully the pronunciation of this word.

COSMOPOLITAN (kahz muh PAHL uh tun) *adj* at home in many places or situations; internationally sophisticated

- Marcello's interests were *cosmopolitan*—he liked Greek wine, German beer, Dutch cheese, Japanese cars, and French fries.

- A truly *cosmopolitan* traveler never feels like a foreigner anywhere on Earth.
- New York is a *cosmopolitan* city; you can hear nearly every language spoken there.

COUNTENANCE (KOWN tuh nuns) *n* face; facial expression, especially an encouraging one

- Her father's confident *countenance* gave Liz the courage to persevere.
- Ed's harsh words belied his *countenance,* which was kind and encouraging.

Countenance can also be a verb. To *countenance* something is to condone it or tolerate it.

- Dad *countenanced* our backyard rock fights even though he didn't really approve of them.

COUP (koo) *n* a brilliant victory or accomplishment; the violent overthrow of a government by a small internal group

- Winning a gold medal at the Olympics was a real *coup* for the fifty-year-old woman.
- The student council's great *coup* was persuading Drake to play at our prom.
- In the attempted *coup* in the Philippines, some army officers tried to take over the government.

The full name for this type of *coup* is *coup d'état* (koo day TAH). A *coup de grace* (koo duh GRAHS) is a final blow or concluding event.

> **Note carefully the pronunciation of these words.**

COVENANT (KUV uh nunt) *n* a solemn agreement; a contract; a pledge

- The warring tribes made a *covenant* not to fight each other anymore.
- We signed a *covenant* never to drive Masha's father's car without permission again.

COVERT (koh VURT) *adj* secret; hidden

To be *covert* is to be covered.

Covert activities are secret activities.

A *covert* military operation is one the public knows nothing about.

The opposite of *covert* is *overt. Overt* (oh VURT) means open or unconcealed.

COVET (KUV it) *v* to wish for enviously

- To *covet* thy neighbor's wife is to want thy neighbor's wife for thyself.
- Any position at MTV is a highly *coveted* job.

To be *covetous* is to be envious.

Quick Quiz #27

Match each word in the first column with its definition in the second column. Check your answers in the back of the book.

1.	corollary	a.	worldly and sophisticated
2.	corroborate	b.	face
3.	cosmopolitan	c.	wish for enviously
4.	countenance	d.	confirm
5.	coup	e.	solemn agreement
6.	covenant	f.	brilliant victory
7.	covert	g.	natural consequence
8.	covet	h.	secret

CREDULOUS (KREJ uh lus) *adj* eager to believe; gullible

- The *credulous* housewife believed that she had won a million dollars through an email scam.
- Judy was so *credulous* that she simply nodded happily when Kirven told her he could teach her how to fly. Judy's *credulity* (kri DYOOL uh tee) was limitless.

Credulous should not be confused with *credible* (CRED uh buhl). To be *credible* is to be believable. Almost anything, however *incredible,* is *credible* to a *credulous* person.

- Larry's implausible story of heroism was not *credible.* Still, *credulous* old Louis believed it.

A story that cannot be believed is *incredible.* If you don't believe that story someone just told you, you are *incredulous.* If something is *credible,* it may gain *credence* (KREED uns), which means belief or intellectual acceptance.

- No one could prove Frank's theory, but his standing at the university helped it gain *credence.*

Another similar word is *creditable* (CRED i tuh bul), which means worthy of credit or praise.

- Our record in raising money was very *creditable;* we raised several thousand dollars every year.

CRITERION (krye TEER ee un) *n* standard; basis for judgment
- When Norm judges a meal, he has only one *criterion:* is it edible?
- In choosing among the linemen, the most important *criterion* was quickness.

The plural of *criterion* is *criteria.* You can't have *one criteria;* you can only have one *criterion.* If you have two or more, you have *criteria.* There is no such thing as *criterions* and no such thing as *a criteria.*

CRYPTIC (KRIP tik) *adj* mysterious; mystifying
- Elaine's remarks were *cryptic;* Jerry was baffled by what she said.

A *cryptic* statement is one in which something important remains hidden.
- The ghost made *cryptic* comments about the *crypt* from which she had just emerged; that is, no one could figure out what the ghost meant.

CULINARY (KYOO luh ner ee) *adj* relating to cooking or the kitchen

A cooking school is sometimes called a *culinary* institute.
- Allison pursued her *culinary* interests by attending the *culinary* institute. Her first meal, which was burned beyond recognition, was a *culinary* disaster.

> **Note carefully the pronunciation of this word.**

CULMINATE (KUL muh nayt) *v* to climax; to reach full effect
- Connie's years of practice *culminated* in a great victory at the international juggling championship.
- The masquerade ball was the *culmination* of our fund-raising efforts.

Quick Quiz #28

Match each word in the first column with its definition in the second column. Check your answers in the back of the book.

1.	credulous	a.	related to cooking
2.	credible	b.	believable
3.	incredible	c.	believability
4.	incredulous	d.	worthy of praise
5.	credence	e.	eager to believe
6.	creditable	f.	unbelieving
7.	criterion	g.	unbelievable
8.	cryptic	h.	climax
9.	culinary	i.	standard
10.	culminate	j.	mysterious

CULPABLE (KUL puh bul) *adj* deserving blame; guilty

- The accountant's failure to spot the errors made her *culpable* in the tax-fraud case.
- We all felt *culpable* when the homeless old man died in the doorway of our apartment building.

A person who is *culpable* (a *culprit* [CUHL prit]) is one who can be blamed for doing something.

To decide that a person is not *culpable* after all is to *exculpate* (EK skul payt) that person.

- Lou's confession didn't *exculpate* Bob, because one of the things that Lou confessed was that Bob had helped him do it.

The opposite of *exculpate* is *inculpate* (IN kul payt). To *inculpate* is to accuse someone of something.

CURSORY (KUR suh ree) *adj* hasty; superficial

- To give a book a *cursory* reading is to skim it quickly without comprehending much.
- The *cursor* on Dave's computer made a *cursory* sweep across the data as he scrolled down the page.

To make a *cursory* attempt at learning French is to memorize a couple of easy words and then give up.

CURTAIL (kur TAYL) *v* to shorten; to cut short

- Curt had so much homework to do that night that he *curtailed* the amount of television he wanted to watch.

To *curtail* a tale is to cut it short.

CYNIC (SIN ik) *n* one who deeply distrusts human nature; one who believes humans are motivated only by selfishness

- When the pop star gave a million dollars to the museum, *cynics* said he was merely trying to buy himself a reputation as a cultured person.

To be *cynical* is to be extremely suspicious of the motivations of other people.

Cynicism is general grumpiness and pessimism about human nature.

Quick Quiz #29

Match each word in the first column with its definition in the second column. Check your answers in the back of the book.

1.	culpable	a.	free from guilt
2.	exculpate	b.	shorten
3.	cursory	c.	one who distrusts
4.	curtail		humanity
5.	cynic	d.	hasty
		e.	guilty

D

DAUNT (dawnt) *v* to make fearful; to intimidate
- The steepness of the mountain *daunted* the team of amateur climbers, because they hadn't realized what they were in for.
- The size of the players on the visiting team was *daunting;* the players on the home team began to perspire nervously.

To be *dauntless* or *undaunted* is to be fearless or unintimidated.
- The rescue crew was *undaunted* by the flames and ran into the burning house to look for survivors. The entire crew was *dauntless* in its effort to save the people inside.

DEARTH (durth) *n* lack; scarcity
- There is no *dearth* of comedy at a convention of clowns.
- When there is a *dearth* of food, many people may starve.
- There was a *dearth* of gaiety at the boring Christmas party.

DEBACLE (di BAHK ul) *n* violent breakdown; sudden overthrow; overwhelming defeat
- A political debate would become a *debacle* if the candidates began screaming and throwing dinner rolls at each other.

This word can also be pronounced "day BAHK ul."

DEBAUCHERY (di BAW chuh ree) *n* wild living; excessive intemperance
- *Debauchery* can be expensive; fortunately for Jeff, his wallet matched his appetite for extravagant pleasures. He died a poor, albeit happy, man.

To *debauch* is to seduce or corrupt. Someone who is *debauched* has been seduced or corrupted.

DEBILITATE (di BIL uh tayt) *v* to weaken; to cripple
- The football player's career was ended by a *debilitating* injury to his knee.

To become *debilitated* is to suffer a *debility,* which is the opposite of an ability.
- A surgeon who becomes *debilitated* is one who has lost the ability to operate on the *debilities* of other people.

DECADENT (DEK uh dunt) *adj* decaying or decayed, especially in terms of morals

A person who engages in *decadent* behavior is a person whose morals have decayed or fallen into ruin.

- Carousing in local bars instead of going to class is *decadent*.

Decadent behavior is often an affectation of bored young people.

The noun is *decadence*.

DECIMATE (DES uh mayt) *v* to kill or destroy a large part of

To *decimate* an army is to come close to wiping it out.
- When locusts attack a crop, they sometimes *decimate* it, leaving very little that's fit for human consumption.
- You might say in jest that your family had *decimated* its turkey dinner on Thanksgiving, leaving nothing but a few crumbs and a pile of bones.

The noun is *decimation*.

DECOROUS (DEK ur us) *adj* proper; in good taste; orderly

Decorous behavior is good, polite, orderly behavior.

To be *decorous* is to be sober and tasteful.
- The New Year's Eve crowd was relatively *decorous* until midnight, when they went wild.

To behave *decorously* is to behave with *decorum* (di KOR um).

DEDUCE (di DOOS) *v* to conclude from the evidence; to infer

To *deduce* something is to conclude it without being told it directly.
- From the footprints on the ground, Clarice *deduced* that the criminal had feet.
- Daffy *deduced* from the shape of its bill that the duck was really a chicken. That the duck was really a chicken was Daffy's *deduction*.

DEFAME (di FAYM) *v* to libel or slander; to ruin the good name of

To *defame* someone is to make accusations that harm the person's reputation.
- The local businessman accused the newspaper of *defaming* him by publishing an article that said his company was poorly managed.

To *defame* is to take away fame, to take away a good name.

To suffer such a loss of reputation is to suffer *defamation*.
- The businessman who believed he had been *defamed* by the newspaper sued the paper's publisher for *defamation*.

DEFERENCE (DEF ur uns) *n* submission to another's will; respect; courtesy

To show *deference* to another is to place that person's wishes ahead of your own.

- Dean showed *deference* to his grandfather: he let the old man have first dibs on the birthday cake.
- Danielle stopped texting at the dinner table in *deference* to the wishes of her mother.

To show *deference* to another is to *defer* (dih FUR) *to* that person.

- Joe was supposed to go first, but he *deferred* to Steve, who had been waiting longer.

To show *deference* is also to be *deferential* (def uh REN shul).

- Joe was being *deferential* when he allowed Steve to go first.

DEFINITIVE (di FIN uh tiv) *adj* conclusive; providing the last word

- Walter wrote the *definitive* biography of Keats; nothing more could have been added by another book.
- The army completely wiped out the invaders; its victory was *definitive*.
- No one could find anything to object to in Cindy's *definitive* explanation of how the meteorite had gotten into the bathtub.

DEGENERATE (di JEN uh rayt) *v* to break down; to deteriorate

- The discussion quickly *degenerated* into an argument.
- Over the years, the nice old neighborhood had *degenerated* into a terrible slum.
- The fans' behavior *degenerated* as the game went on.

A person whose behavior has *degenerated* can be referred to as a *degenerate* (di JEN ur it).

- The mood of the party was spoiled when a drunken *degenerate* wandered in from off the street.

Degenerate (di JEN ur it) can also be an adjective, meaning *degenerated*.

- The slum neighborhood was *degenerate*.
- The fans' *degenerate* behavior prompted the police to make several arrests.

Note carefully the pronunciation of the various parts of speech.

DELETERIOUS (del uh TIR ee us) *adj* harmful

- Smoking cigarettes is *deleterious* to your health.
- Is watching a lot of TV really *deleterious?* Of course not.

DELINEATE (di LIN ee ayt) *v* to describe accurately; to draw in outline

- After Jack had *delineated* his plan, we had no doubt about what he intended to do.
- Sharon's peculiar feelings about her pet gorilla were *delineated* in the newspaper article about her.
- The portrait artist *delineated* Sarah's features then filled in the shading.

The noun is *delineation*.

DELUDE (dye LOOD) *v* to deceive

- The con man *deluded* us into thinking that he would make us rich. Instead, he tricked us into giving him several hundred dollars.
- The *deluded* mental patient believed that he was a chicken sandwich.
- Lori is so persuasive that she was able to *delude* Leslie into thinking she was a countess.

To be *deluded* is to suffer from a *delusion*.

- That she was a great poet was the *delusion* of the English teacher, who could scarcely write two complete sentences in a row.
- Todd, the well-known jerk, suffered from the *delusion* that he was a genuinely nice man.

DELUGE (DEL yooj) *n* a flood; an inundation

A *deluge* is a flood, but the word is often used figuratively.

- The $1 million reward for the lost poodle brought in a *deluge* of hot leads. The distraught owner was *deluged* by phone calls all week.

Note carefully the pronunciation of this word.

DEMAGOGUE (DEM uh gawg) *n* a leader who uses prejudice to get more power

A *demagogue* is a leader, but not in a good sense of the word. *Demagogues* manipulate the public to support their aims, but they are little different from dictators. A *demagogue* is often a despot.

This word can also be spelled *demagog*. The methods a *demagogue* uses are *demagoguery* (DEM uh gahg uh ree) or *demagogy* (DEM uh gahg ee).

DENIZEN (DEN i zun) *n* inhabitant

To be a *denizen* of a country is to live there. A citizen of a country is usually also a *denizen*.

To be a *denizen* of a restaurant is to go there often—so often that people begin to wonder whether you live there.

Fish are sometimes referred to as "*denizens* of the deep." Don't refer to them this way yourself; the expression is a cliché.

DEPRAVITY (di PRAV uh tee) *n* extreme wickedness or corruption

- Mrs. Prudinkle wondered whether the *depravity* of her class of eight-year-olds was the result of their watching Saturday morning television.

To exhibit *depravity* is to be *depraved* (di PRAYVD).

DEPRECATE (DEP ruh kayt) *v* to express disapproval of

- To *deprecate* a colleague's work is to risk making yourself unwelcome in your colleague's office.

"This stinks!" is a *deprecating* remark.

- The critic's *deprecating* comments about my new novel put me in a bad mood for an entire month.

To be *self-deprecating* is to belittle one's own efforts, often in the hope that someone else will say, "No, you're wonderful!"

A very similar word is *depreciate* (dih PREE shee ayt). To *depreciate* a colleague's work would be to represent it as being of little value.

For another meaning of *depreciate,* see *appreciate.*

DERIDE (di RYDE) *v* to ridicule; to laugh at contemptuously
- Gerald *derided* Diana's driving ability after their hair-raising trip down the twisting mountain road.
- Sportswriters *derided* Columbia's football team, which hadn't won a game in three years.
- The boss *derided* her secretary mercilessly, so he quit his job. He was someone who could not accept *derision* (di RIZH un).

Quick Quiz #31

Match each word in the first column with its definition in the second column. Check your answers in the back of the book.

1.	deference	a.	deteriorate
2.	definitive	b.	ridicule
3.	degenerate	c.	describe accurately
4.	deleterious	d.	respect
5.	delineate	e.	conclusive
6.	delude	f.	express disapproval of
7.	deluge	g.	harmful
8.	demagogue	h.	inhabitant
9.	denizen	i.	deceive
10.	depravity	j.	flood
11.	deprecate	k.	extreme wickedness
12.	deride	l.	rabble-rousing leader

DEROGATORY (dih RAHG uh tor ee) *adj* disapproving; degrading

Derogatory remarks are negative remarks expressing disapproval. They are nastier than merely critical remarks.
- Stephen could never seem to think of anything nice to say about anyone; virtually all of his comments were *derogatory.*

DESICCATE (DES uh kayt) *v* to dry out
- The hot wind *desiccated* the few grapes remaining on the vine; after a day or two, they looked like raisins.
- After a week without water, the *desiccated* plant fell over and died.

Plums become prunes through a process of *desiccation.*

DESPONDENT (dih SPAHN dunt) *adj* extremely depressed; full of despair
- The cook became *despondent* when the wedding cake fell on the floor fifteen minutes before the reception.
- After the death of his wife, the man was *despondent* for many months.
- The team fell into *despondency* after losing the state championship game by a single point.

DESPOT (DES puht) *n* an absolute ruler; an autocrat
- Stephen was a *despot;* workers who disagreed with him were fired.
- The island kingdom was ruled by a ruthless *despot* who executed suspected rebels at noon each day in the village square.

To act like a *despot* is to be *despotic* (di SPAH tik).
- There was cheering in the street when the country's *despotic* government was overthrown.

DESTITUTE (DES tuh toot) *adj* extremely poor; utterly lacking

Destitute people are people who don't have, or severely lack, money and possessions.

To be left *destitute* is to be left without money or property. The word can also be used figuratively. A teacher might accuse her students of being *destitute* of brains or intellectually *destitute.*

DESULTORY (DES ul tor ee) *adj* without a plan or purpose; disconnected; random
- Aadi made a few *desultory* attempts to start a garden, but nothing came of them.
- In his *desultory* address, Rizal skipped from one topic to another and never came to the point.
- The discussion at our meeting was *desultory;* no one's comments seemed to bear any relation to anyone else's.

Note carefully the pronunciation of this word.

DEXTROUS (DEX trus) *adj* skillful; adroit

Dextrous often, but not always, connotes physical ability. Like *adroit*, it comes from the Latin word for right (as in the direction), because right-handed people were once considered physically and mentally superior.
- Though not imposing in stature, Rashid was the most *dextrous* basketball player on the court; he often beat taller competitors with his nimble management of the ball.

- Alexandra was determined not to sell the restaurant on eBay; even the most *dextrous* negotiator could not sway her.

You may also see this word spelled *dexterous*. *Dexterity* is the noun form. For an antonym, see *gauche*.

DIALECTICAL (dye uh LEK ti kul) *adj* relating to discussions; relating to the rules and methods of reasoning; approaching truth in the middle of opposing extremes

The game of Twenty Questions is *dialectical*, in that the participants attempt to narrow down a chosen object by asking a series of ever more specific questions.

The noun is *dialectic*.

DICTUM (DIK tum) *n* an authoritative saying; an adage; a maxim; a proverb

"No pain, no gain" is a hackneyed *dictum* of sadistic coaches everywhere.

DIDACTIC (dye DAK tik) *adj* intended to teach; morally instructive; pedantic

- Natalia's seemingly amusing talk had a *didactic* purpose; she was trying to show her listeners the difference between right and wrong.
- The priest's conversation was always *didactic*. He never said anything that wasn't intended to teach a lesson.
- The new novel is painfully *didactic;* the author's aim is always to instruct and never to entertain.

DIFFIDENT (DIF i dunt) *adj* timid; lacking in self-confidence

Diffident and *confident* are opposites.
- The *diffident* student never made a single comment in class.
- Sebastian's stammer made him *diffident* in conversation and shy in groups of strangers.
- Carla's *diffidence* led many participants to believe she hadn't been present at the meeting, even though she had.

DIGRESS (dye GRES) *v* to stray from the main subject

Speaking metaphorically, to *digress* is to leave the main highway in order to travel aimlessly on back roads. When a speaker *digresses, he or she* departs from the main topic and tells a story only distantly related to it.

Such a story is called a *digression*. Sometimes a writer's or speaker's *digressions* are more interesting than his or her main points.
- After a lengthy *digression,* the lecturer returned to his speech and brought it to a conclusion.

DILETTANTE (DIL uh tahnt) *n* someone with superficial knowledge of the arts; an amateur; a dabbler

To be a *dilettante* is to dabble in something rather than doing it in a serious way.

- Reginald said he was an artist, but was merely a *dilettante;* he didn't know a pencil from a paintbrush.
- Antonella dismissed the members of the ladies' sculpture club as nothing more than a bunch of *dilettantes.*

Quick Quiz #32

Match each word in the first column with its definition in the second column. Check your answers in the back of the book.

1.	derogatory	a.	without purpose
2.	desiccate	b.	extremely depressed
3.	despondent	c.	amateur
4.	despot	d.	stray from the main subject
5.	destitute	e.	extremely poor
6.	desultory	f.	timid
7.	dextrous	g.	dry out
8.	dialectical	h.	disapproving
9.	dictum	i.	absolute ruler
10.	didactic	j.	intended to teach
11.	diffident	k.	relating to discussions
12.	digress	l.	authoritative saying
13.	dilettante	m.	skillful

DISCERN (dih SURN) *v* to have insight; to see things clearly; to discriminate; to differentiate

To *discern* something is to perceive it clearly. A writer whose work demonstrates *discernment* is a writer who is a keen observer.

- The ill-mannered people at Tisha's party proved that she had little *discernment* when it came to choosing friends.

DISCREET (dih SKREET) *adj* prudent; judiciously reserved

To make *discreet* inquiries is to ask around without letting the whole world know you're doing it.

- The psychiatrist was very *discreet;* no matter how much we pestered him, he wouldn't gossip about the problems of his famous patients.

He had *discretion* (di SKRESH un).

To be *indiscreet* is to be imprudent and especially to say or do things you shouldn't.

- It was *indiscreet* of Laura to tell Salima how much she hated Bailey's new hairstyle, because Salima always tells Bailey everything.
- When Laura told Salima, she committed an *indiscretion.*

DISCRETE (dih SKREET) *adj* unconnected; separate; distinct

Do not confuse *discrete* with *discreet.*

- The twins were identical, but their personalities were *discrete.*
- The drop in the stock market was not the result of any single force but of many *discrete* trends.

When things are all jumbled up together, they are said to be *indiscrete,* which means not separated or sorted.

DISCRIMINATE (dih SKRIM uh nayt) *v* to notice or point out the difference between two or more things; to discern; to differentiate

A person with a refined aesthetic sense is able to *discriminate* subtle differences where a less observant person would see nothing. Such a person is *discriminating.* This kind of *discrimination* is a good thing. To *discriminate* unfairly, though, is to dwell on differences that shouldn't make a difference. It is unfair and illegal to *discriminate* based on ethnicity when selling a house. Such a practice is not *discriminating* (which is good), but *discriminatory* (which is wrong).

Indiscriminate means not *discriminating;* in other words, random or haphazard.

DISDAIN (dis DAYN) *n* arrogant scorn; contempt

- Bertram viewed the hot dog with *disdain,* believing that to eat such a disgusting food was beneath him.
- The millionaire looked upon the poor workers with evident *disdain.*

Disdain can also be a verb. The millionaire in the previous example could be said to have *disdained* those workers.

To be filled with *disdain* is to be *disdainful.*

DISINTERESTED (dis IN truh stid) *adj* not taking sides; unbiased

Disinterested should *not* be used to mean *uninterested.* If you don't care about knowing something, you are *uninterested,* not *disinterested.*

- A referee should be *disinterested*. He or she should not be rooting for one of the competing teams.

A *disinterested* observer is one who has no personal stake in or attachment to what is being observed.

- Meredith claimed that the accident had been Louie's fault, but several *disinterested* witnesses said that Meredith had actually bashed into his car after jumping the median and driving in the wrong lane for several miles.

DISPARAGE (dih SPAR ij) *v* to belittle; to say uncomplimentary things about, usually in a somewhat indirect way

- The mayor *disparaged* our efforts to beautify the town square when she said that the flower bed we had planted looked somewhat worse than the bed of weeds it had replaced.
- My guidance counselor *disparaged* my high school record by telling me that not everybody belongs in college.

Quick Quiz #33

Match each word in the first column with its definition in the second column. Check your answers in the back of the book.

1.	discern	a.	have insight
2.	discreet	b.	belittle
3.	discrete	c.	not separated
4.	indiscrete	d.	not taking sides
5.	discriminate	e.	arrogant scorn
6.	disdain	f.	prudent
7.	disinterested	g.	unconnected
8.	disparage	h.	differentiate

DISPARATE (DIS pur it) *adj* different; incompatible; unequal

- Our interests were *disparate:* Cathy liked to play with dolls, and I liked to throw her dolls out the window.
- The *disparate* interest groups were united only by their intense dislike of the candidate.
- The novel was difficult to read because the plot consisted of dozens of *disparate* threads that never came together.

The noun form of *disparate* is *disparity* (dih SPAR i tee). *Disparity* means inequality. The opposite of *disparity* is *parity*.

DISSEMINATE (dih SEM uh nayt) *v* to spread the seeds of something; to scatter; to make widely known

News is *disseminated* through many media: internet, radio, television, newspapers, magazines, and gossips.

DISSIPATE (DIS uh payt) *v* to thin out, drift away, or dissolve; to cause to thin out, drift away, or dissolve; to waste or squander

- The smoke *dissipated* as soon as we opened the windows.
- Ilya's anger *dissipated* as the day wore on, and he gradually forgot what had upset him.
- The police *dissipated* the riotous crowd by spraying the demonstrators with fire hoses and firing rubber bullets over their heads.
- Alex won the weekly lottery but *dissipated* the entire winnings in one abandoned, fun-filled weekend.

We can also say that a person is *dissipated,* by which we mean that he or she indulges in wild living. Alex is *dissipated.*

DISSOLUTION (dis uh LOO shun) *n* the breaking up or dissolving of something into parts; disintegration

- Nothing could prevent the *dissolution* of the famous actor's fan club after he retired to seek a political career.

A person who is *dissolute* has lived life in the fast lane too long. *Dissolute* and *dissipated* are synonyms in this sense.

DISTEND (di STEND) *v* to swell; to extend a great deal

- The tire *distended* alarmingly as the forgetful gas station attendant kept pumping more and more air into it.
- A *distended* belly is one symptom of malnutrition.

A swelling is a *distension.*

DISTINGUISH (di STING gwish) *v* to tell apart; to cause to stand out

- The rodent expert's eyesight was so acute that she was able to *distinguish* between a shrew and a vole at more than a thousand paces.
- I studied and studied but I was never able to *distinguish* between *discrete* and *discreet.*
- His face had no *distinguishing* characteristics; there was nothing about his features that stuck in your memory.
- Lou's uneventful career as a dogcatcher was not *distinguished* by adventure or excitement.

DOCILE (DAHS ul) *adj* easily taught; obedient; easy to handle

- The *docile* students quietly memorized all the lessons their teacher told them.
- The baby raccoons appeared *docile* at first, but they were almost impossible to control.
- Mia's *docility* (dah SIL i tee) fooled the professor into believing that she was incapable of thinking for herself.

Note carefully the pronunciation of the various parts of speech.

DOCTRINAIRE (dahk truh NAYR) *adj* inflexibly committed to a doctrine or theory without regard to its practicality; dogmatic

A *doctrinaire* supporter of manned space flights to Pluto would be someone who supported such space flights even though it might be shown that such lengthy journeys could never be undertaken.

A *doctrinaire* opponent of fluoridation of water would be someone whose opposition could not be shaken by proof that fluoride is good for teeth and not bad for anything else.

A person with *doctrinaire* views can be called a *doctrinaire*.

DOGMATIC (dawg MAT ik) *adj* arrogantly assertive of unproven ideas; stubbornly claiming that something (often a system of beliefs) is beyond dispute

A *dogma* is a belief. A *dogmatic* person, however, is stubbornly convinced of his or her beliefs.

- Marty is *dogmatic* on the subject of the creation of the world; he sneers at anyone whose views are not identical to his.
- The philosophy professor became increasingly *dogmatic* as she grew older and became more firmly convinced of her strange theories.

The opinions or ideas *dogmatically* asserted by a *dogmatic* person are known collectively as *dogma*.

DOMESTIC (duh MES tik) *adj* having to do with the household or family; not foreign

A home that enjoys *domestic* tranquility is a happy home.

A maid is sometimes referred to as a *domestic* engineer or simply as a *domestic*.

To be *domestic* is to enjoy being at home or to be skillful at doing things around the house.

Domestic wine is wine from this country, as opposed to wine imported from, say, France.

The *domestic* steel industry is the steel industry in this country.

A country that enjoys *domestic* tranquility is a happy country on the homefront.

Quick Quiz #34

Match each word in the first column with its definition in the second column. Check your answers in the back of the book.

1.	disparate	a.	committed to a theory
2.	disseminate	b.	thin out
3.	dissipate	c.	of the household
4.	dissolution	d.	firmly held system of ideas
5.	distend	e.	easily taught
6.	distinguish	f.	arrogantly assertive
7.	docile	g.	swell
8.	doctrinaire	h.	tell apart
9.	dogmatic	i.	incompatible
10.	dogma	j.	spread seeds
11.	domestic	k.	disintegration

DORMANT (DOR munt) *adj* **inactive; as though asleep; asleep**

Dormant, like *dormitory,* comes from a root meaning sleep.
- Mt. Vesuvius erupted violently and then fell *dormant* for several hundred years.

Many plants remain *dormant* through the winter; that is, they stop growing until spring.
- Frank's interest in playing the piano was *dormant* and, quite possibly, dead.
- The snow fell silently over the *dormant* village, which became snarled in traffic jams the following morning.

The noun is *dormancy.*

DUBIOUS (DOO bee us) *adj* **full of doubt; uncertain**
- I was fairly certain that I would be able to fly if I could merely flap my arms hard enough, but Mary was *dubious;* she said I'd better flap my legs as well.

- We were *dubious* about the team's chance of success, and, as it turned out, our *dubiety* (doo BYE uh tee) was justified: the team lost.

Dubious and *doubtful* don't mean exactly the same thing. A *dubious* person is a person who has doubts. A *doubtful* outcome is an outcome that isn't certain to occur.

- Sam's chances of getting the job were *doubtful* because the employer was *dubious* of his claim that he had been president of the United States while in high school.

Something beyond doubt is *indubitable.* A dogmatic person believes his or her opinions are *indubitable.*

DUPLICITY (doo PLIS uh tee) *n* the act of being two-faced; double-dealing; deception

- Dave, in his *duplicity,* told us he wasn't going to rob the bank and then went right out and robbed it.
- Liars engage in *duplicity* all the time; they say one thing and do another.
- The *duplicitous* salesman sold the red sports car to someone else even though she had promised to sell it to us.

Quick Quiz #35

Match each word in the first column with its definition in the second column. Check your answers in the back of the book.

1.	dormant	a.	uncertainty
2.	dubiety	b.	double-dealing
3.	duplicity	c.	inactive

E

EBULLIENT (ih BUL yunt) *adj* boiling; bubbling with excitement; exuberant

A boiling liquid can be called *ebullient.* More often, though, this word describes excited or enthusiastic people.

The roaring crowd in a full stadium before the World Series might be said to be *ebullient.*

A person overflowing with enthusiasm might be said to be *ebullient.*

- Cammie was *ebullient* when her fairy godmother said she could use one of her three wishes to wish for three more wishes.

Someone or something that is *ebullient* is characterized by *ebullience.*

Note carefully the pronunciation of this word.

ECCENTRIC (ek SEN trik) *adj* not conventional; a little kooky; irregular

- The *eccentric* inventor spent all her waking hours fiddling with what she said was a time machine, but it was actually just an old telephone booth.
- Fred's political views are *eccentric:* he believes that we should have kings instead of presidents and that the government should raise money by holding bake sales.
- The rocket followed an *eccentric* course; first it veered in one direction, then it veered in another, and then it crashed.

An *eccentric* person is a person who has *eccentricities* (ek sen TRIS uh teez).

ECLECTIC (ih KLEK tik) *adj* choosing the best from many sources; drawn from many sources

- Adolfo's taste in art was *eclectic.* He liked the Old Masters, the Impressionists, and Walt Disney.
- The *eclectic* menu included dishes from many different countries.
- Giulia's *eclectic* reading made her well-rounded.

EDIFY (ED uh fye) *v* to enlighten; to instruct, especially in moral or religious matters

- We found the pastor's sermon on the importance of not eating beans to be most *edifying.*
- The teacher's goal was to *edify* her students, not to force a handful of facts down their throats.
- We would have felt lost at the art show had not the excellent and informative programs been provided for our *edification.*

EFFACE (ih FAYS) *v* to erase; to rub away the features of

- The inscription on the tombstone had been *effaced* by centuries of weather.
- The vandals *effaced* the delicate carving by rubbing it with sandpaper.

- We tried to *efface* the dirty words that had been written on the front of our house, but nothing would remove them.

To be *self-effacing* is to be modest.

- John is *self-effacing:* when he won an Olympic gold medal, all he said was, "Aw, shucks. I'm just a regular fella."

EFFUSION (ih FYOO zhun) *n* a pouring forth

- When the child was rescued from the well, there was an intense *effusion* of emotion from the crowd that had gathered around the hole.
- The madman's writings consisted of a steady *effusion* of nonsense.

To be *effusive* is to be highly emotional.

- Anna's *effusive* thanks for our silly little present made us feel somewhat embarrassed, so we decided to move to a different lunch table.

EGALITARIAN (ih gal uh TAYR ee un) *adj* believing in the social and economic equality of all people

- People often lose interest in *egalitarian* measures when such measures interfere with their own interests.

Egalitarian can also be used as a noun to characterize a person.

An *egalitarian* advocates *egalitarianism.*

EGOCENTRIC (ee goh SEN trik) *adj* selfish; believing that one is the center of everything

- Nellie was so *egocentric* that she could never give anyone else credit for doing anything.
- *Egocentric* Lou never read the newspaper unless there was something in it about him.
- It never occurred to the *egocentric* musician that her audiences might like to hear someone else's songs every once in a while.

An *egoist* is an *egocentric* person. He or she believes the entire universe exists for his benefit.

An *egotist* is another type of *egocentric.* An *egotist* is an *egoist* who tells everyone how wonderful he is.

EGREGIOUS (ih GREE jus) *adj* extremely bad; flagrant

Save this word for things that are worse than bad.

- The mother's *egregious* neglect was responsible for her child's accidental cross-country ride on the freight train.
- Erik's manners were *egregious;* he ate his mashed potatoes with his fingers and slurped the peas right off his plate.

Quick Quiz #36

Match each word in the first column with its definition in the second column. Check your answers in the back of the book.

1.	ebullient	a.	pouring forth
2.	eccentric	b.	self-obsessed person
3.	eclectic	c.	extremely bad
4.	edify	d.	not conventional
5.	efface	e.	drawn from many sources
6.	effusion	f.	bubbling with excitement
7.	egalitarian	g.	erase
8.	egocentric	h.	selfish
9.	egotist	i.	enlighten
10.	egregious	j.	believing in social equality

ELICIT (ih LIS it) *v* to bring out; to call forth

- The interviewer skillfully *elicited* our true feelings by asking us questions that got to the heart of the matter.
- The defendant tried to *elicit* the sympathy of the jury by appearing at the trial in a wheelchair, but the jury convicted her anyway.

Don't confuse this word with *illicit*.

ELLIPTICAL (ih LIP ti kul) *adj* oval; missing a word or words; obscure

This word has several meanings. Consult a dictionary if you are uncertain.

- The orbit of the earth is not perfectly round; it is *elliptical*.

An egg may have an *elliptical* shape.

An *elliptical* statement is one that is hard or impossible to understand, either because something is missing from it or because the speaker or writer is trying to be hard to understand.

- The announcement from the State Department was purposely *elliptical*—the government didn't really want reporters to know what was going on.

ELUSIVE (ih LOO siv) *adj* hard to pin down; evasive

To be *elusive* is to *elude,* which means to avoid, evade, or escape.

- The answer to the problem was *elusive;* every time the mathematician thought she was close, she discovered another error. (Or, one could say that the answer to the problem *eluded* the mathematician.)
- The *elusive* criminal was next to impossible for the police to catch. (The criminal *eluded* the police.)
- The team played hard, but victory was *elusive* and they suffered another defeat. (Victory *eluded* the hard-playing team.)

EMIGRATE (EM uh grayt) *v* to leave a country permanently; to expatriate

- Pierre *emigrated* from France because he had grown tired of speaking French. Pierre became an *émigré* (EM uh gray).
- The Soviet dissidents were persecuted by the secret police, so they sought permission to *emigrate.*

At the heart of this word is the word *migrate,* which means to move from one place or country to another. *Emigrate* adds to *migrate* the sense of moving *out of* some place in particular.

On the other end of every *emigration* is an *immigration* (think of this as "in-migration"). See *immigration.*

- When Solange *emigrated* from France, she *immigrated* to the United States.

EMINENT (EM uh nunt) *adj* well-known and respected; standing out from all others in quality or accomplishment; outstanding

- The visiting poet was so *eminent* that our English teacher asked the poet for his autograph. Our English teacher thought the poet was *preeminent* in his field.
- The entire audience fell silent when the *eminent* musician walked onto the stage and picked up her banjo and bongo drums.

Don't confuse this word with *imminent.*

EMPIRICAL (em PIR uh kul) *adj* relying on experience or observation; not merely theoretical

- The apple-dropping experiment gave the scientists *empirical* evidence that gravity exists.
- Nicky's idea about the moon being made of pizza dough was not *empirical.*
- We proved the pie's deliciousness *empirically,* by eating it.

Quick Quiz #37

Match each word in the first column with its definition in the second column. Check your answers in the back of the book.

1.	elicit	a.	well-known
2.	elliptical	b.	bring out
3.	elusive	c.	hard to pin down
4.	emigrate	d.	relying on experience
5.	immigration	e.	move from a country
6.	eminent	f.	moving into a country
7.	empirical	g.	obscure

EMULATE (EM yuh layt) *v* to strive to equal or excel, usually through imitation

- To *emulate* someone is to try to be just as good as, or better than, him or her.
- The American company *emulated* its successful Japanese competitor but never quite managed to do as well.
- Little Joey imitated his athletic older brother in the hope of one day *emulating* his success.
- I got ahead by *emulating* those who had succeeded before me.

ENCROACH (en KROHCH) *v* to make gradual or stealthy inroads into; to trespass

- As the city grew, it *encroached* on the countryside surrounding it.
- With an *encroaching* sense of dread, I slowly pushed open the blood-spattered door.
- My neighbor *encroached* on my yard by building her stockade fence a few feet on my side of the property line.

ENDEMIC (en DEM ik) *adj* native; restricted to a particular region or era; indigenous

- You won't find that kind of tree in California; it's *endemic* to our part of the country.
- That peculiar strain of influenza was *endemic* to a small community in South Carolina; there were no cases anywhere else.
- The writer Tom Wolfe coined the term "Me Decade" to describe the egocentricity *endemic* in the 1970s.

ENERVATE (EN ur vayt) *v* to reduce the strength or energy of, especially to do so gradually

- Sander felt *enervated* by his long ordeal and couldn't make himself get out of bed.
- Clinging to a flagpole for a month without food or water *enervated* me, and one day I fell asleep and ended up on the ground.
- Life itself seemed to *enervate* the old woman. She grew weaker and paler with every breath she drew.

ENFRANCHISE (en FRAN chyze) *v* to grant the privileges of citizenship, especially the right to vote

- In the United States, citizens become *enfranchised* on their eighteenth birthdays. American women were not *enfranchised* until the adoption of the Nineteenth Amendment in 1920, which gave them the right to vote.

To *disfranchise* (or *disenfranchise*) someone is to take away the privileges of citizenship or to take away the right to vote.

- One of the goals of the reform candidate was to *disfranchise* the bodies at the cemetery, which had somehow managed to vote for the crooked mayor.

ENGENDER (en JEN dur) *v* to bring into existence; to create; to cause

- My winning lottery ticket *engendered* a great deal of envy among my co-workers; they all wished that they had won.
- Smiles *engender* smiles.
- The bitter lieutenant *engendered* discontent among his troops.

ENIGMA (uh NIG muh) *n* a mystery

- Ben is an *enigma;* he never does any homework but he always gets good grades.
- The wizard spoke in riddles and *enigmas,* and no one could understand what he was saying.

An *enigma* is *enigmatic* (en ig MAT ik).

- Ben's good grades were *enigmatic.* So was the wizard's speech.

ENORMITY (i NOR muh tee) *n* extreme evil; a hideous offense; immensity

- Hitler's soldiers stormed through the village, committing one *enormity* after another.

"Hugeness" or "great size" is not the main meaning of *enormity.* When you want to talk about the gigantic size of something, use *immensity* instead.

EPHEMERAL (i FEM ur al) *adj* lasting a very short time

Ephemeral comes from the Greek and means lasting a single day. The word is usually used more loosely to mean lasting a short time.

Youth and flowers are both *ephemeral*. They're gone before you know it. Some friendships are *ephemeral*.

• The tread on those used tires will probably turn out to be *ephemeral*.

Quick Quiz #38

Match each word in the first column with its definition in the second column. Check your answers in the back of the book.

1.	emulate	a.	cause to exist
2.	encroach	b.	mystery
3.	endemic	c.	remove voting rights
4.	enervate	d.	reduce the strength of
5.	enfranchise	e.	native
6.	disfranchise	f.	grant voting rights
7.	engender	g.	strive to equal
8.	enigma	h.	lasting a very short time
9.	enormity	i.	extreme evil
10.	ephemeral	j.	trespass

EPIGRAM (EP uh gram) *n* a brief and usually witty or satirical saying

People often find it difficult to remember the difference between an *epigram* and these similar-looking words:

> *epigraph:* an apt quotation placed at the beginning of a book or essay
>
> *epitaph:* a commemorative inscription on a grave
>
> *epithet:* a term used to characterize the nature of something; sometimes a disparaging term used to describe a person.

An *epigram* is *epigrammatic* (ep uh gruh MAT ik).

EPITOME (i PIT uh mee) *n* a brief summary that captures the meaning of the whole; the perfect example of something; a paradigm

• The first paragraph of the new novel is an *epitome* of the entire book; you can read it and understand what the author is trying to get across.

- Luke's freshman year was the *epitome* of a college experience; he made friends, joined a fraternity, and ate too much pizza.
- Eating corn dogs and drinking root beer is the *epitome* of the good life, as far as Kara is concerned.

> **Note carefully the pronunciation of this word.**

EQUANIMITY (ek wuh NIM uh tee) *n* composure; calm
- The entire apartment building was crumbling, but Rachel faced the disaster with *equanimity*. She ducked out of the way of a falling beam and continued searching for an exit.
- John's mother looked at the broken glass on the floor with *equanimity*; at least he didn't hurt himself when he knocked over the vase.

EQUITABLE (EK wuh tuh bul) *adj* fair
- King Solomon's decision was certainly *equitable;* each mother would receive half the child.
- The pirates distributed the loot *equitably* among themselves, so each one received the same share.
- The divorce settlement was quite *equitable.* Sheila got the right half of the house, and Tom got the left half.

Equity is fairness; *inequity* is unfairness. *Iniquity* and *inequity* both mean unfair, but *iniquity* implies wickedness as well. By the way, *equity* has a meaning in business. See our Finance chapter at the end of the book.

EQUIVOCAL (ih KWIV uh kul) *adj* ambiguous; intentionally confusing; capable of being interpreted in more than one way

Ambiguous means unclear. To be *equivocal* is to be intentionally ambiguous.
- Joe's response was *equivocal;* we couldn't tell whether he meant yes or no, which is precisely what Joe wanted.
- Dr. Festen's *equivocal* diagnosis made us think that she had no idea what Mrs. Johnson had.

To be *equivocal* is to *equivocate.* To *equivocate* is to mislead by saying confusing or ambiguous things.
- When we asked Harold whether that was his car that was parked in the middle of the hardware store, he *equivocated* and asked, "In which aisle?"

ERUDITE (ER yoo dyte) *adj* scholarly; deeply learned
- The professor said such *erudite* things that none of us had the slightest idea of what he was saying.

- The *erudite* biologist was viewed by many of her colleagues as a likely winner of the Nobel Prize.

To be *erudite* is to possess *erudition* (er yoo DISH un), or extensive knowledge.

- Mr. Fernicola's vast library was an indication of his *erudition*.

Note carefully the pronunciation of both forms of this word.

Quick Quiz #39

Match each word in the first column with its definition in the second column. Check your answers in the back of the book.

1.	epigram	a.	brief summary
2.	epigraph	b.	fair
3.	epitaph	c.	composure
4.	epithet	d.	intentionally confusing
5.	epitome	e.	apt quotation
6.	equanimity	f.	say confusing things
7.	equitable	g.	inscription on a gravestone
8.	equivocal	h.	scholarly
9.	equivocate	i.	brief, witty saying
10.	erudite	j.	characterizing term

ESOTERIC (es uh TER ik) *adj* **hard to understand; understood by only a select few; peculiar**

- Chicken wrestling and underwater yodeling were just two of Earl's *esoteric* hobbies.
- The author's books were so *esoteric* that even her mother didn't buy any of them.

ESPOUSE (eh SPOWZ) *v* **to support; to advocate**

- Some cultures used to *espouse* polygamy, or marriage to more than one woman.
- Alex *espoused* so many causes that he sometimes had trouble remembering which side he was on.
- The candidate for governor *espoused* a program in which all taxes would be abolished and all the state's revenues would be supplied by income from bingo and horse racing.

ETHEREAL (ih THIR ee ul) *adj* heavenly; as light and insubstantial as a gas or ether

- The *ethereal* music we heard turned out to be not angels plucking on their harps but the wind blowing through the slats of the metal awning.
- The *ethereal* mist on the hillside was delicate and beautiful.

EUPHEMISM (YOO fuh miz um) *n* a pleasant or inoffensive expression used in place of an unpleasant or offensive one

- Aunt Angie, who couldn't bring herself to say the word *death,* said that Uncle George had taken the big bus uptown. "Taking the big bus uptown" was her *euphemism* for dying.
- The sex-education instructor wasn't very effective. She was so embarrassed by the subject that she could only bring herself to speak *euphemistically* about it.

EVANESCENT (ev uh NES unt) *adj* fleeting; vanishing; happening for only the briefest period

- Meteors are *evanescent:* they last so briefly that it is hard to tell whether one has actually appeared.

EXACERBATE (ig ZAS ur bayt) *v* to make worse

- Dipping Austin in lye *exacerbated* his skin condition.
- The widow's grief was *exacerbated* by the minister's momentary inability to remember her dead husband's name.
- The fender-bender was *exacerbated* when two more cars plowed into the back of Margaret's car.

EXACTING (ig ZAK ting) *adj* extremely demanding; difficult; requiring great skill or care

- The *exacting* math teacher subtracted points if you didn't show every step of your work.
- The surgeon's *exacting* task was to reconnect the patient's severed eyelid.

EXALT (ig ZAWLT) *v* to raise high; to glorify

- The manager decided to *exalt* the lowly batboy by asking him to throw the first pitch in the opening game of the World Series.

The adjective *exalted* is used frequently. Being queen of England is an *exalted* occupation.

- Diamante felt *exalted* when he woke up to discover that his great-uncle had left him $100 million.
- Cleaning out a septic tank is not an *exalted* task.

Be careful not to confuse this word with *exult,* listed later.

EXASPERATE (ig ZAS puh rayt) *v* to annoy thoroughly; to make very angry; to try the patience of

- The child's insistence on hopping backward on one foot *exasperated* her mother, who was in a hurry.
- The algebra class's refusal to answer any questions was extremely *exasperating* to the substitute teacher.

EXEMPLIFY (ig ZEM pluh fye) *v* to illustrate by example; to serve as a good example

- Fred participated in every class discussion and typed all of his papers. His teacher thought Fred *exemplified* the model student; Fred's classmates thought he was sycophantic.

An *exemplar* (ig ZEM plahr) is an ideal model or a paradigm. *Exemplary* (ig ZEM plur ee) means outstanding or worthy of imitation.

EXHAUSTIVE (ig ZAWS tiv) *adj* thorough; rigorous; complete; painstaking

- Before you use a parachute, you should examine it *exhaustively* for defects. Once you jump, your decision is irrevocable.

EXHORT (ig ZORT) *v* to urge strongly; to give a serious warning to

- The coach used her bullhorn to *exhort* us to try harder.
- The fearful forest ranger *exhorted* us not to go into the cave, but we did so anyway and became lost in the center of the earth.

The adjective is *hortatory* (HOR tuh tor ee).

Quick Quiz #40

Match each word in the first column with its definition in the second column. Check your answers in the back of the book.

1.	esoteric	a.	peculiar
2.	espouse	b.	make worse
3.	ethereal	c.	extremely demanding
4.	euphemism	d.	raise high
5.	evanescent	e.	inoffensive substitute term
6.	exacerbate	f.	urge strongly
7.	exacting	g.	annoy thoroughly
8.	exalt	h.	heavenly
9.	exasperate	i.	advocate
10.	exemplify	j.	fleeting
11.	exhaustive	k.	illustrate by example
12.	exhort	l.	thorough

EXIGENCY (EK si jen see) *n* an emergency; an urgency

- An academic *exigency*: You haven't opened a book all term and the final is tomorrow morning.

Exigent means urgent.

EXISTENTIAL (eg zis TEN shul) *adj* having to do with existence; having to do with the body of thought called existentialism, which basically holds that human beings are responsible for their own actions

This word is overused but under-understood by virtually all of the people who use it. Unless you have a very good reason for throwing it around, you should probably avoid it.

EXONERATE (ig ZAHN uh rayt) *v* to free completely from blame; to exculpate

- The defendant, who had always claimed he wasn't guilty, expected to be *exonerated* by the testimony of his best friend.
- Our dog was *exonerated* when we discovered that it was in fact the cat that had eaten all the doughnuts.

EXPATRIATE (eks PAY tree ayt) *v* to throw (someone) out of his or her native land; to move away from one's native land; to emigrate

- The rebels were *expatriated* by the nervous general, who feared that they would cause trouble if they were allowed to remain in the country.
- Hugo was fed up with his native country, so he *expatriated* to America. In doing so, Hugo became an *expatriate* (eks PAY tree ut).

To *repatriate* (ree PAY tree ayt) is to return to one's native citizenship; that is, to become a *repatriate* (ree PAY tree it).

EXPEDIENT (ik SPEE dee unt) *adj* providing an immediate advantage; serving one's immediate self-interest; practical

- Because the basement had nearly filled with water, the plumber felt it would be *expedient* to clear out the drain.
- The candidate's position in favor of higher pay for teachers was an *expedient* one adopted for the national teachers' convention but abandoned shortly afterward.

Expedient can also be used as a noun for something *expedient*.

- The car repairman did not have his tool kit handy, so he used chewing gum as an *expedient* to patch a hole.

The noun *expedience* or *expediency* is practicality or being especially suited to a particular goal.

EXPEDITE (EK spi dyte) *v* to speed up or ease the progress of

- The post office *expedited* mail delivery by hiring more letter carriers.
- The lawyer *expedited* the progress of our case through the courts by bribing a few judges.
- Our wait for a table was *expedited* by a waiter who mistook Angela for a movie star.

EXPLICIT (ik SPLIS it) *adj* clearly and directly expressed

- The sexually *explicit* movie received an X rating.
- The machine's instructions were *explicit*—they told us exactly what to do.
- No one *explicitly* asked us to set the barn on fire, but we got the impression that that was what we were supposed to do.

Implicit means indirectly expressed or implied.

- Gerry's dissatisfaction with our work was *implicit* in his expression, although he never criticized us directly.

EXTOL (ik STOHL) *v* to praise highly; to laud

- The millionaire *extolled* the citizen who returned her gold watch but the only reward was a heartfelt handshake.

EXTRANEOUS (ik STRAY nee us) *adj* unnecessary; irrelevant; extra

- Extra ice cream would never be *extraneous,* unless everyone had already eaten so much that no one wanted any more.
- The book's feeble plot was buried in a lot of *extraneous* material about a talking dog.
- The salad contained several *extraneous* ingredients, including hair, sand, and a single dead fly.

To be *extraneous* is to be *extra* and always with the sense of being unnecessary.

EXTRAPOLATE (ik STRAP uh layt) *v* to project or deduce from something known; to infer

- George's estimates were *extrapolated* from last year's data; he simply took all the old numbers and doubled them.
- Emeril came up with a probable recipe by *extrapolating* from the taste of the cookies he had eaten at the store.
- By *extrapolating* from a handful of pottery fragments, the archaeologists formed a possible picture of the ancient civilization.

To *extrapolate,* a scientist uses the facts he or she has to project to facts outside; to *interpolate* (in TUR puh layt), the scientist tries to fill the gaps within data.

EXTRICATE (EK struh kayt) *v* to free from difficulty

- It took two and a half days to *extricate* the little girl from the abandoned well into which she had fallen.
- Yoshi had to pretend to be sick to *extricate* himself from the blind date with the ventriloquist who brought her puppet on the date with her.
- Monica had no trouble driving her car into the ditch, but she needed a tow truck to *extricate* it.

Something that is permanently stuck is *inextricable* (in EKS tri kuh bul).

EXTROVERT (EKS truh vurt) *n* an open, outgoing person; a person whose attention is focused on others rather than on himself or herself

- Maria was quite an *extrovert;* she walked boldly into the roomful of strange adults and struck up many friendly conversations.
- Damian was an *extrovert* in the sense that he was always more interested in other people's business than in his own.

An *introvert* (IN truh vurt) is a person whose attention is directed inward and who is concerned with little outside himself or herself.

- Ryan was an *introvert;* he spent virtually all his time in his room, writing in his diary and talking to himself.

An *introvert* is usually introspective.

EXULT (ig ZULT) *v* to rejoice; to celebrate
- The women's team *exulted* in its victory over the men's team at the badminton finals. They were *exultant.*

Quick Quiz #41

Match each word in the first column with its definition in the second column. Check your answers in the back of the book.

1.	exigency	a.	free from blame
2.	existential	b.	clearly expressed
3.	exonerate	c.	indirectly expressed
4.	expatriate	d.	having to do with existence
5.	expedient	e.	outgoing person
6.	expedite	f.	speed up
7.	explicit	g.	infer
8.	implicit	h.	free from difficulty
9.	extol	i.	immediately advantageous
10.	extraneous	j.	unnecessary
11.	extrapolate	k.	inwardly directed person
12.	extricate	l.	throw out of native land
13.	extrovert	m.	emergency
14.	introvert	n.	rejoice
15.	exult	o.	praise highly

F

FABRICATION (FAB ruh kay shun) *n* a lie; something made up
- My story about being the prince of Wales was a *fabrication.* I'm really the king of Denmark.
- The suspected murderer's alibi turned out to be an elaborate *fabrication;* in other words, he was lying when he said that he hadn't killed the victim.

To create a *fabrication* is to *fabricate.*

FACETIOUS (fuh SEE shus) *adj* humorous; not serious; clumsily humorous

- David was sent to the principal's office for making a *facetious* remark about the intelligence of the French teacher.
- Our proposal about shipping our town's garbage to the moon was *facetious,* but the first selectman took it seriously.

FACILE (FAS il) *adj* fluent; skillful in a superficial way; easy

To say that a writer's style is *facile* is to say both that it is skillful and that it would be better if the writer exerted himself or herself more. The word *facile* almost always contains this sense of superficiality.

- Paolo's poems were *facile* rather than truly accomplished; if you read them closely, you soon realized they were filled with clichés.
- The CEO of the company was a *facile* speaker. She could speak engagingly on almost any topic with very little preparation. She spoke with great *facility.*

Note carefully the pronunciation of this word.

FACTION (FAK shun) *n* a group, usually a small part of a larger group, united around some cause; disagreement within an organization

- At the Republican National Convention, the candidate's *faction* spent much of its time shouting at the other candidate's *faction.*
- The faculty was relatively happy, but there was a *faction* that called for higher pay.
- When the controversial topic of the fund drive came up, the committee descended into bitterness and *faction.* It was a *factious* topic.

FARCICAL (FARS i kul) *adj* absurd; ludicrous

- The serious play quickly turned *farcical* when the leading man's belt broke and his pants fell to his ankles.
- The formerly secret documents detailed the CIA's *farcical* attempt to discredit the dictator by sprinkling his shoes with a powder that was supposed to make his beard fall out.

Farcical means like a *farce,* which is a mockery or a ridiculous satire.

FASTIDIOUS (fa STID ee us) *adj* meticulous; demanding; finicky

- Mrs. O'Hara was a *fastidious* housekeeper; she cleaned up our crumbs almost before they hit the floor.
- Jeb was so *fastidious* in his work habits that he needed neither a wastebasket nor an eraser.
- The *fastidious* secretary was nearly driven mad by her boss, who used the floor as a file cabinet and her desk as a pantry.

FATALIST (FAYT uh list) *n* someone who believes that future events are already determined and that humans are powerless to change them

- The old man was a *fatalist* about his illness, believing there was no sense in worrying about something he could not control.
- Carmen was such a *fatalist* that she never wore a seatbelt; she said that if she were meant to die in a car accident, there was nothing she could do to prevent it.

Fatalist is closely related to the word *fate.* A *fatalist* is someone who believes that *fate* determines everything.

To be a *fatalist* is to be *fatalistic.*

FATUOUS (FACH oo us) *adj* foolish; silly; idiotic

- Pauline is so pretty that her suitors are often driven to *fatuous* acts of devotion. They are *infatuated* with her.

FAUNA (FAW nuh) *n* animals

- We saw little evidence of *fauna* on our walk through the woods. We did, however, see plenty of *flora,* or plants.

The phrase *flora* and *fauna* means plants and animals. The terms are used particularly in describing what lives in a particular region or environment.

Arctic *flora* are very different from tropical *flora.*

- In Jim's yard, the *flora* consists mostly of weeds.

It's easy to remember which of these words means what. Just replace *flora* and *fauna* with *flowers* and *fawns.*

FECUND (FEE kund) *adj* fertile; productive

- The *fecund* mother rabbit gave birth to hundreds and hundreds of little rabbits.
- The child's imagination was so *fecund* that dozens of stories hopped out of him like a bunch of baby rabbits.
- Our compost heap became increasingly *fecund* as it decomposed.

The state of being *fecund* is *fecundity* (fi KUN di tee).

This word can also be pronounced "FEK und."

Quick Quiz #42

Match each word in the first column with its definition in the
second column. Check your answers in the back of the book.

1.	fabrication	a.	plants
2.	facetious	b.	fertile
3.	facile	c.	absurd
4.	faction	d.	one who believes in fate
5.	farcical	e.	humorous
6.	fastidious	f.	animals
7.	fatalist	g.	superficially skillful
8.	fatuous	h.	group with a cause
9.	fauna	i.	lie
10.	flora	j.	meticulous
11.	fecund	k.	foolish

FELICITY (fuh LIS uh tee) *n* happiness; skillfulness, especially
at expressing things; adeptness
- Love was not all *felicity* for Judy and Steve; they argued all the
  time. In fact their relationship was characterized by *infelicity*.
- Shakespeare wrote with great *felicity*. His works are filled with *felic-
  itous* expressions.

FERVOR (FUR vur) *n* great warmth or earnestness; ardor; zeal
- Avid baseball fans frequently display their *fervor* for the game by
  throwing food at bad players.

FETTER (FET ur) *v* to restrain; to hamper
- In her pursuit of an Olympic gold medal, the runner was *fettered* by
  multiple injuries.

To be *unfettered* is to be unrestrained or free of hindrances.
- After the dictator was deposed, a novelist produced a fictional
  account of the dictatorship that was *unfettered* by the strict rules of
  censorship.

A *fetter* is literally a chain (attached to the foot) that is used to
restrain a criminal or, for that matter, an innocent person. A figurative *fetter* can be anything that hampers or restrains someone.
- The housewife's young children were the *fetters* that prevented her
  from pursuing a second master's degree.

The Words

FIDELITY (fuh DEL uh tee) *n* faithfulness; loyalty

- The motto of the United States Marine Corps is *semper fidelis,* which is Latin for always loyal.

A *high-fidelity* record player is one that is very faithful in reproducing the original sound of whatever was recorded.

- The crusader's life was marked by *fidelity* to the cause of justice.
- The soldiers couldn't shoot straight, but their *fidelity* to the cause of freedom was never in question.

Infidelity means faithlessness or disloyalty. Marital *infidelity* is another way of saying adultery. Early phonograph records were marked by *infidelity* to the original.

FIGURATIVE (FIG yur uh tiv) *adj* based on figures of speech; expressing something in terms usually used for something else; metaphorical

- When the mayor said that the housing market had sprouted wings, she was speaking *figuratively.* The housing market hadn't really sprouted wings; it had merely risen so rapidly that it had almost seemed to fly.

To say that the autumn hillside was a blaze of color is to use the word *blaze* in a *figurative* sense. The hillside wasn't really on fire, but the colors of the leaves made it appear (somewhat) as though it were.

A *figurative* meaning of a word is one that is not *literal.* A *literal* statement is one in which every word means exactly what it says. If the housing market had *literally* sprouted wings, genuine wings would somehow have popped out of it.

People very, very often confuse these words, using one when they really mean the other.

- Desmond could *literally* eat money if he chewed up and swallowed a dollar bill. Desmond's car eats money only *figuratively,* in the sense that it is very expensive to operate.

FINESSE (fi NES) *n* skillful maneuvering; subtlety; craftiness

- The doctor sewed up the wound with *finesse,* making stitches so small one could scarcely see them.
- The boxer moved with such *finesse* that his opponent never knew what hit him.

FLAGRANT (FLAY grunt) *adj* glaringly bad; notorious; scandalous

An example of a *flagrant* theft would be stealing a car from the parking lot of a police station. A *flagrant* spelling error is a very noticeable one. See the listing for *blatant*, as these two words are often confused.

FLAUNT (flawnt) *v* to show off; to display ostentatiously
- The brand-new millionaire annoyed all his friends by driving around his old neighborhood to *flaunt* his new Rolls-Royce.
- Colleen *flaunted* her engagement ring, shoving it in the face of almost anyone who came near her.

This word is very often confused with *flout*.

FLOUT (flowt) *v* to disregard something out of disrespect
- A driver *flouts* the traffic laws by driving through red lights and knocking down pedestrians.

To *flaunt* success is to make certain everyone knows that you are successful. To *flout* success is to be contemptuous of success or to act as though it means nothing at all.

FOIBLE (FOY bul) *n* a minor character flaw
- Patti's *foibles* included a tendency to prefer dogs to people.
- The delegates to the state convention ignored the candidates' positions on the major issues and concentrated on their *foibles*.

FOMENT (foh MENT) *v* to stir up; to instigate
- The bad news from abroad *fomented* pessimism among professional investors.
- The radicals spread several rumors in an effort to *foment* rebellion among the peasants.

Quick Quiz #43

Match each word in the first column with its definition in the second column. Check your answers in the back of the book.

1.	felicity	a.	loyalty
2.	fervor	b.	stir up
3.	fetter	c.	restrain
4.	fidelity	d.	meaning exactly what it says
5.	figurative		
6.	literal	e.	minor character flaw
7.	finesse	f.	show off
8.	flagrant	g.	based on figures of speech
9.	flaunt	h.	to disregard contemptuously
10.	flout		
11.	foible	i.	skillful maneuvering
12.	foment	j.	happiness
		k.	glaringly bad
		l.	zeal

FORBEAR (for BAYR) *v* to refrain from; to abstain

- Stephen told me I could become a millionaire if I joined him in his business, but his lack of integrity makes me nervous so I decided to *forbear.*
- Grace *forbore* to punch me in the nose, even though I told her that I thought she was a sniveling idiot.

The noun is *forbearance.*

A *forebear* (FOR bayr)—sometimes also spelled *forbear*—is an ancestor.

FOREGO (for GOH) *v* to do without; to forbear

- We had some of the chocolate cake, some of the chocolate mousse, and some of the chocolate cream pie. But we were worried about our weight, so we decided to *forego* the chocolate-covered potato chips. That is, we *forewent* them.

Can also be spelled *forgo.*

FORSAKE (for SAYK) *v* to abandon; to renounce; to relinquish

- We urged Buddy to *forsake* his life with the alien beings and return to his job at the drugstore.

- All the guru's followers had *forsaken* her, so she became a real estate developer and turned her temple into an apartment building.

FORTUITOUS (for TOO uh tus) *adj* accidental; occurring by chance
- The program's outcome was not the result of any plan but was entirely *fortuitous.*
- The object was so perfectly formed that its creation could not have been *fortuitous.*

FOUNDER (FOWN dur) *v* to fail; to collapse; to sink
- The candidate's campaign for the presidency *foundered* when it was revealed that she had once been married to a drug addict.
- Zeke successfully struggled through the first part of the course but *foundered* when the final examination was given.
- The ship *foundered* shortly after it hit the iceberg.

Be careful not to confuse this word with *flounder,* which means to move clumsily or in confusion.
- Our field hockey team *floundered* helplessly around the field while the opposing team scored goal after goal.
- The witness began to *flounder* as the attorney fired question after question.

If you want to remember the difference between the two words, think that when a person *flounders,* he is flopping around like a flounder.

FRATERNAL (fruh TUR nul) *adj* like brothers
- The *fraternal* feelings of the group were strengthened by monthly fishing trips.

A *fraternity* is an organization of men who have bound themselves together in a relationship analogous to that of real brothers.

FRENETIC (fruh NET ik) *adj* frantic; frenzied
- There was a lot of *frenetic* activity in the office, but nothing ever seemed to get accomplished.
- The bird's *frenetic* attempt to free itself from the thorn bush only made the situation worse.

FRUGAL (FROO gul) *adj* economical; penny-pinching
- Laura was so *frugal* that she even tried to bargain with the checkout girl at the discount store.

- We were as *frugal* as we could be, but we still ended up several thousand dollars in debt.
- Hannah's *frugality* annoyed her husband, who loved spending money on tech gadgets.

FURTIVE (FUR tiv) *adj* secretive; sly
- Cal wiggled his ears while the countess was talking to him in a *furtive* attempt to catch our attention.
- The burglars were *furtive,* but not *furtive* enough; the alert policeman grabbed them as they carried the TV through the Rubenstein's back door.

FUTILE (FYOOT ul) *adj* useless; hopeless
- A D+ average and no extracurricular interests to speak of meant that applying to Harvard was *futile,* but Lucinda hoped against hope.

Something *futile* is a *futility* (fyoo TIL uh tee).
- Lucinda doesn't know what a *futility* it is.

Quick Quiz #44

Match each word in the first column with its definition in the second column. Check your answers in the back of the book.

1.	forbear	a.	economical
2.	forebear	b.	ancestor
3.	forgo	c.	move in confusion
4.	forsake	d.	do without
5.	fortuitous	e.	refrain from
6.	founder	f.	sink
7.	flounder	g.	secretive
8.	frenetic	h.	accidental
9.	frugal	i.	abandon
10.	furtive	j.	frantic

G

GARRULOUS (GAR uh lus) *adj* talkative; chatty
- Gabriella is gregarious and *garrulous;* she loves to hang out with the gang and gab.

GAUCHE (gohsh) *adj* unskillful; awkward; maladroit

Remember *dextrous*? Well, *gauche* is pretty much the exact opposite. It is the French word for left—the connection is that left-handed people were once thought to be clumsy (this was clearly before the invention of left-handed scissors) and perverse, even evil. These days, *gauche* tends to describe social, rather than physical, ineptness.

- Smadar had a poor sense of comic timing, and her *gauche* attempts to mock her left-handed friends soon left her with none.

GENRE (ZHAHN ruh) *n* a type or category, especially of art or writing

The novel is one literary *genre*. Poetry is another.

- Daoyen displayed a great talent for a particular *genre:* the bawdy limerick.

GENTEEL (jen TEEL) *adj* refined; polite; aristocratic; affecting refinement

- The ladies at the ball were too *genteel* to accept our invitation to the wrestling match.

A person who is *genteel* has *gentility.*

GESTICULATE (jes TIK yuh layt) *v* to make gestures, especially when speaking or in place of speaking

- Massimo *gesticulated* wildly on the other side of the theater in an attempt to get our attention.
- The after-dinner speaker *gesticulated* in such a strange way that the audience paid more attention to her hands than to her words.

A person who *gesticulates* makes *gesticulations.*

GLUT (glut) *n* surplus; an overabundance

- The international oil shortage turned into an international oil *glut* with surprising speed.
- We had a *glut* of contributions but a dearth, or scarcity, of volunteers; it seemed that people would rather give their money than their time.

GRANDILOQUENT (gran DIL uh kwunt) *adj* pompous; using a lot of big, fancy words in an attempt to sound impressive

- The governor's speech was *grandiloquent* rather than eloquent; there were some six-dollar words and some impressive phrases, but she really had nothing to say.
- The new minister's *grandiloquence* got him in trouble with deacons, who wanted him to be more restrained in his sermons.

GRANDIOSE (GRAN dee ohs) *adj* absurdly exaggerated

- The scientist's *grandiose* plan was to build a huge shopping center on the surface of the moon.
- Their house was genuinely impressive, although there were a few *grandiose* touches: a fireplace the size of a garage, a kitchen with four ovens, and a computerized media center in every room.

To be *grandiose* is to be characterized by *grandiosity* (gran dee AHS uh tee).

GRATUITOUS (gruh TOO uh tus) *adj* given freely (said of something bad); unjustified; unprovoked; uncalled for

- The scathing review of the movie contained several *gratuitous* remarks about the love life of the director.
- Their attack against us was *gratuitous;* we had never done anything to offend them.

Gratuitous is often misunderstood because it is confused with *gratuity.* A *gratuity* is a tip, like the one you leave in a restaurant. A *gratuity* is a nice thing. *Gratuitous,* however, is not nice. Don't confuse these words.

GRAVITY (GRAV uh tee) *n* seriousness

- The newsanchor's nervous giggling was entirely inappropriate, given the *gravity* of the situation.
- No one realized the *gravity* of Myron's drug addiction until it was much too late to help him.

Gravity is the force that makes apples fall down instead of up, and the word also carries a different sort of weightiness.

At the heart of the word *gravity* is the word *grave,* which means serious.

GREGARIOUS (gruh GAR ee us) *adj* sociable; enjoying the company of others

- Dirk was too *gregarious* to enjoy the fifteen years he spent in solitary confinement.
- Kylie wasn't very *gregarious;* she went to the party, but she spent most of her time hiding in a closet.

In biology, *gregarious* is used to describe animals that live in groups. Bees, which live together in large colonies, are said to be *gregarious* insects.

GUILE (gyle) *n* cunning; duplicity; artfulness

- José used *guile,* not intelligence, to win the spelling bee; he cheated.

- Stuart was shocked by the *guile* of the automobile mechanic, who had poked a hole in his radiator and then told him that it had sprung a leak.

To be *guileless* is to be innocent or naive. *Guileless* and *artless* are synonyms.

The word *beguile* also means to deceive, but in a charming and not always bad way.

- Clarence found Mary's beauty so *beguiling* that he did anything she asked of him.

Quick Quiz #45

Match each word in the first column with its definition in the second column. Check your answers in the back of the book.

1.	futile	a.	chatty
2.	garrulous	b.	surplus
3.	gauche	c.	cunning
4.	genre	d.	unjustified
5.	genteel	e.	seriousness
6.	gesticulate	f.	make gestures
7.	glut	g.	hopeless
8.	grandiloquent	h.	refined
9.	grandiose	i.	sociable
10.	gratuitous	j.	pompous
11.	gravity	k.	absurdly exaggerated
12.	gregarious	l.	type of art
13.	guile	m.	awkward

H

HACKNEYED (HAK need) *adj* overused; trite; stale

- Michael's book was full of clichés and *hackneyed* phrases.
- The intelligent design issue had been discussed so much as to become *hackneyed*.

"As cold as ice" is a *hackneyed* expression.

HAPLESS (HAP lis) *adj* unlucky

- Joe's *hapless* search for fun led him from one disappointment to another.
- Beatriz led a *hapless* existence that made all her friends' lives seem fortunate by comparison.

HARBINGER (HAR bin jur) *n* a forerunner; a signal of

Warm weather is the *harbinger* of spring.

- A cloud of bad breath and body odor, which preceded him by several yards everywhere he went, was Harold's *harbinger.*

Note carefully the pronunciation of this word.

HEDONISM (HEED uh niz um) *n* the pursuit of pleasure as a way of life

A *hedonist* practices *hedonism* twenty-four hours a day.

- Yoshi's life of *hedonism* came to an end when his lottery winnings ran out; his massaging armchair and wide-screen TV were repossessed, he had to eat macaroni and cheese instead of champagne and lobster, and he could no longer pay to have models fan him with palm fronds and feed him grapes.

HEGEMONY (hi JEM uh nee) *n* leadership, especially of one nation over another

- America once held an unchallenged nuclear *hegemony.*
- Japan and Germany vie for *hegemony* in the foreign-car market.

Note carefully the pronunciation of this word.

HERESY (HER uh see) *n* any belief that is strongly opposed to established beliefs

Galileo was tried for the *heresy* of suggesting that the sun did not revolve around Earth. He was almost convicted of being a *heretic* (HER uh tik), but he recanted his *heretical* (huh RET i kul) view.

HERMETIC (hur MET ik) *adj* impervious to external influence; airtight

- The president led a *hermetic* existence in the White House, as her advisers attempted to seal her off from the outside world.
- The old men felt vulnerable and unwanted outside the *hermetic* security of their club.

- The poisonous substance was sealed *hermetically* inside a glass cylinder.

HEYDAY (HAY day) *n* golden age; prime
- In his *heyday,* Vernon was a world-class athlete; today he's just Vernon.
- The *heyday* of the British Navy ended a long, long time ago.

HIATUS (hye AY tus) *n* a break or interruption, often from work
- Spencer looked forward to spring break as a welcome *hiatus* from the rigors of campus parties.

Note carefully the pronunciation of this word.

HIERARCHY (HYE uh rahr kee) *n* an organization based on rank or degree; pecking order
- Kendra was very low in the State Department *hierarchy.* In fact, her phone number wasn't even listed in the State Department directory.
- There appeared to be no *hierarchy* in the newly discovered tribe; there were no leaders and, for that matter, no followers.

The adjective is *hierarchical* (hye uh RAHRK i kul).

HISTRIONIC (his tree AHN ik) *adj* overly dramatic; theatrical
- Adele's *histrionic* request for a raise embarrassed everyone in the office. She gesticulated wildly, jumped up and down, pulled out handfuls of hair, threw herself to the ground, and groaned in agony.
- The chairman's *histrionic* presentation persuaded no one.
- The young actor's *histrionics* made everyone in the audience squirm.

Histrionic behavior is referred to as *histrionics.*

HOMILY (HAHM uh lee) *n* a sermon
- The football coach often began practice with a lengthy *homily* on the virtues of clean living.

HOMOGENEOUS (hoh muh JEE nee us) *adj* uniform; made entirely of one thing
- The kindergarten class was extremely *homogeneous:* all the children had blond hair and blue eyes.

Homogenized (huh MAHJ uh nyzed) milk is milk in which the cream, which usually floats on top, has been permanently mixed with the rest of the milk. (Skim milk is milk from which the layer of cream has been skimmed off.) When milk is *homogenized,* it becomes a *homogeneous* substance—that is, it's the same throughout, or uniform.

To be *heterogeneous* (het ur uh JEE nee us) is to be mixed or varied.
  - On Halloween the children amassed a *heterogeneous* collection of candy, chewing gum, popcorn, and cookies.

The nouns are *homogeneity* (hoh muh juh NEE uh tee) and *heterogeneity* (het uh roh juh NEE uh tee), respectively.

HUSBANDRY (HUZ bun dree) *n* **thrifty management of resources; livestock farming**

Husbandry is the practice of conserving money or resources. To *husband* is to economize.
  - Everyone *husbanded* oil and electricity during the energy crisis of the 1970s.

HYPERBOLE (hye PUR buh lee) *n* **an exaggeration used as a figure of speech; exaggeration**
  - When Joe said, "I'm so hungry I could eat a horse," he was using *hyperbole* to convey the extent of his hunger.
  - The candidate was guilty of *hyperbole;* all the facts in her speech were exaggerated.

Note carefully the pronunciation of this word.

HYPOTHETICAL (hye puh THET uh kul) *adj* **uncertain; unproven**
  - There were several *hypothetical* explanations for the strange phenomenon, but no one could say for certain what had caused it.

A *hypothetical* explanation is a *hypothesis* (hye PAHTH uh sis), the plural of which is *hypotheses* (hye PAHTH uh seez).

Match each word in the first column with its definition in the second column. Check your answers in the back of the book.

1.	hackneyed	a.	leadership
2.	hapless	b.	uniform
3.	harbinger	c.	airtight
4.	hedonism	d.	forerunner
5.	hegemony	e.	pecking order
6.	heresy	f.	overused; trite
7.	hermetic	g.	exaggeration
8.	heyday	h.	golden age
9.	hiatus	i.	varied
10.	hierarchy	j.	unlucky
11.	histrionic	k.	uncertain; unproven
12.	homily	l.	overly dramatic
13.	homogeneous	m.	break
14.	heterogeneous	n.	sermon
15.	husbandry	o.	thrifty management of resources
16.	hyperbole	p.	lifelong pursuit of pleasure
17.	hypothetical	q.	strongly contrary belief

I

ICONOCLAST (eye KAHN uh klast) *n* one who attacks popular beliefs or institutions

Iconoclast comes from Greek words meaning image breaker. The original *iconoclasts* were opponents of the use of *icons*, or sacred images, in certain Christian churches. Today the word is used to refer to someone who attacks popular figures and ideas—a person to whom "nothing is sacred."

- The popular columnist was an inveterate *iconoclast,* avidly attacking public figures no matter what their party affiliations.
- To study and go to class is to be an *iconoclast* on that particular campus, which has a reputation for being the biggest party school in the country.
- Herbert's *iconoclastic* (eye kahn uh KLAS tik) views were not popular with the older members of the board.

IDEOLOGY (eye dee AHL uh jee) *n* a system of social or political ideas

Conservatism and liberalism are competing *ideologies.*

- The candidate never managed to communicate his *ideology* to the voters, so few people were able to grasp what he stood for.
- The senator's tax proposal had more to do with *ideology* than with common sense; her plan, though consistent with her principles, was clearly impractical.

A dogmatic person attached to an *ideology* is an *ideologue* (EYE dee uh lawg). An *ideologue* is doctrinaire.

Ideology is sometimes pronounced "ID ee ahl uh jee."

IDIOSYNCRASY (id ee oh SINK ruh see) *n* a peculiarity; an eccentricity

- Eating green beans drenched in ketchup for breakfast was one of Jordana's *idiosyncrasies.*
- The doctor's interest was aroused by an *idiosyncrasy* in Bill's skull: there seemed to be a coin slot in the back of his head.

A person who has an *idiosyncrasy* is said to be *idiosyncratic* (id ee oh sin KRAT ik).

- Tara's driving was somewhat *idiosyncratic;* she sometimes seemed to prefer the sidewalk to the street.

IDYLLIC (eye DIL ik) *adj* charming in a rustic way; naturally peaceful
- They built their house on an *idyllic* spot. There was a babbling brook in back and an unbroken view of wooded hills in front.
- Our vacation in the country was *idyllic;* we went for long walks down winding dirt roads and didn't watch television all week.

An *idyllic* time or place could also be called an *idyll* (EYE dul).

IGNOMINY (IG nuh min ee) *n* deep disgrace
- After the big scandal, the formerly high-flying investment banker fell into a life of shame and *ignominy.*
- The *ignominy* of losing the spelling bee was too much for Arnold, who decided to give up spelling altogether.

Something that is deeply disgraceful is *ignominious* (ig nuh MIN ee us).
- Lola's plagiarizing of Nabokov's work was an *ignominious* act that got her suspended from school for two days.

> Note carefully the pronunciation of both forms of the word.

ILLICIT (i LIS it) *adj* illegal; not permitted

Criminals engage in *illicit* activities.

Don't confuse this word with *elicit,* listed previously.
- The police interviewed hundreds of witnesses, trying to *elicit* clues that might help them stop an *illicit* business.

IMMIGRATE (IM i grayt) *v* to move permanently to a new country

It's easy to confuse this word with *emigrate.* To avoid this, just remember that *emigrate* means exit, and *immigrate* means come *in.*
- Edwin *immigrated* to Canada, thinking the move would give his two-year-old daughter a better shot at attending the University of Toronto preschool.

The noun form of the word is *immigration.*

IMMINENT (IM uh nunt) *adj* just about to happen
- The pink glow in the east made it clear that sunrise was *imminent.*
- Patrice had a strange feeling that disaster was *imminent,* and then her bathroom ceiling collapsed.

Don't confuse this word with *eminent,* listed previously.

IMMUTABLE (i MYOO tuh bul) *adj* unchangeable

- Jerry's mother had only one *immutable* rule: no dancing on the dinner table.
- The statue of the former principal looked down on the students with an *immutable* scowl.

Something that is changeable is said to be *mutable.*

- The *mutable* shoreline shifted continually as the tides moved sand first in one direction and then in another.
- Sonrisa's moods were *mutable;* one minute she was kind and gentle, the next minute she was screaming with anger.

Both *immutable* and *mutable* are based on a Latin root meaning change. So are *mutation* and *mutant.*

IMPARTIAL (im PAHR shul) *adj* fair; not favoring one side or the other; unbiased

- Jurors are supposed to be *impartial* rather than *partial;* they aren't supposed to make up their minds until they've heard all the evidence.
- Beverly tried to be an *impartial* judge at the beauty contest, but in the end she couldn't help selecting her own daughter to be the new Honeybee Queen.

The noun is *impartiality* (im pahr shee AL uh tee).

IMPECCABLE (im PEK uh bul) *adj* flawless; entirely without sin

- The children's behavior was *impeccable;* they didn't pour dye into the swimming pool.
- Hal's clothes were always *impeccable;* even the wrinkles were perfectly creased.

By the way, *peccable* means liable to sin. And while we're at it, a *peccadillo* is a minor sin.

IMPERIAL (im PEER ee ul) *adj* like an emperor or an empire

Imperial, emperor, and *empire* are all derived from the same root.

England's *imperial* days are over, now that the British Empire has broken apart.

- The palace was decorated with *imperial* splendor.
- George's *imperial* manner was inappropriate because he was nothing more exalted than the local dogcatcher.

A similar word is *imperious* (im PEER ee us), which means bossy and, usually, arrogant.

- The director's *imperious* style rubbed everyone the wrong way. She always seemed to be giving orders, and she never listened to what anyone said.

Match each word in the first column with its definition in the second column. Check your answers in the back of the book.

1.	iconoclast	a.	peculiarity
2.	ideology	b.	naturally peaceful
3.	idiosyncrasy	c.	like an emperor
4.	idyllic	d.	flawless
5.	ignominy	e.	attacker of popular beliefs
6.	illicit	f.	just about to happen
7.	imminent	g.	fair
8.	immutable	h.	system of social ideas
9.	impartial	i.	bossy
10.	impeccable	j.	deep disgrace
11.	imperial	k.	unchangeable
12.	imperious	l.	illegal

IMPERVIOUS (im PUR vee us) *adj* not allowing anything to pass through; impenetrable

- A raincoat, if it is any good, is *impervious* to water. It is made of an *impervious* material.
- David was *impervious* to criticism—he did what he wanted to do no matter what anyone said.

IMPETUOUS (im PECH oo wus) *adj* impulsive; extremely impatient

- *Impetuous* Dick always seemed to be running off to buy a new car, even if he had just bought one the month before.
- Samantha was so *impetuous* that she never took more than a few seconds to make up her mind.

IMPLEMENT (IM pluh munt) *v* to carry out

- Leo developed a plan for shortening the grass in his yard, but he was unable to *implement* it because he didn't have a lawn mower.
- The government was better at creating new laws than it was at *implementing* them.

IMPOTENT (IM puh tunt) *adj* powerless; helpless; unable to perform

Impotent means not *potent*—not powerful.
- Joe and Olga made a few *impotent* efforts to turn aside the steamroller, but it squished their vegetable garden anyway.
- We felt *impotent* in the face of their overpowering opposition to our plan.

Omnipotent (ahm NIP uh tunt) means all powerful. After winning a dozen games in a row, the football team began to feel *omnipotent*.

> **Note carefully the pronunciation of this word.**

IMPUGN (im PYOON) *v* to attack, especially to attack the truth or integrity of something
- The critic *impugned* the originality of Jacob's novel, claiming that long stretches of it had been lifted from the work of someone else.
- Fred said I was *impugning* his honesty when I called him a dirty liar, but I told him he had no honesty to *impugn*. This just seemed to make him angrier.

INANE (i NAYN) *adj* silly; senseless
- Their plan to make an indoor swimming pool by flooding their basement was *inane*.
- Mel made a few *inane* comments about the importance of chewing only on the left side of one's mouth and then he passed out beneath the table.

Something that is *inane* is an *inanity* (i NAN i tee).

INAUGURATE (in AW gyuh rayt) *v* to begin officially; to induct formally into office
- The mayor *inaugurated* the new no-smoking policy and then celebrated by lighting up a big cigar.
- The team's loss *inaugurated* an era of defeat that lasted for several years.

To *inaugurate* a U.S. president is to make him or her take the oath of office and then give him or her the keys to the White House.

Quick Quiz #48

Match each word in the first column with its definition in the second column. Check your answers in the back of the book.

1.	impervious	a.	begin officially
2.	impetuous	b.	carry out
3.	implement	c.	powerless
4.	impotent	d.	impenetrable
5.	impugn	e.	silly
6.	inane	f.	attack the truth of
7.	inaugurate	g.	impulsive

INCANDESCENT (in kun DES unt) *adj* **brilliant; giving off heat or light**

An *incandescent* light bulb is one containing a wire or filament that gives off light when it is heated. An *incandescent* person is one who gives off light or energy in a figurative sense.

- Jan's ideas were so *incandescent* that simply being near her made you feel as though you understood the subject for the first time.

INCANTATION (in kan TAY shun) *n* **a chant; the repetition of statements or phrases in a way reminiscent of a chant**

- Much to our delight, the wizard's *incantation* eventually caused the small stone to turn into a sleek black BMW.
- The students quickly became deaf to the principal's *incantations* about the importance of school spirit.

INCENSE (in SENS) *v* **to make very angry**

- Jeremy was *incensed* when I told him that even though he was stupid and loathsome, he would always be my best friend.
- My comment about the lovely painting of a tree *incensed* the artist, who said it was actually a portrait of her mother.

INCESSANT (in SES unt) *adj* **unceasing**

- I will go deaf and lose my mind if your children don't stop the *incessant* bickering.
- The noise from the city street was *incessant;* there always seemed to be a fire engine or a police car screaming by.

A *cessation* is a ceasing.

INCIPIENT (in SIP ee unt) *adj* beginning; emerging

- Sitting in class, Henrietta detected an *incipient* tingle of boredom that told her she would soon be asleep.
- Support for the plan was *incipient,* and the planners hoped it would soon grow and spread.

The *inception* of something is its start or formal beginning.

INCISIVE (in SYE siv) *adj* cutting right to the heart of the matter

When a surgeon cuts into you, he or she makes an *incision.* To be *incisive* is to be as sharp as a scalpel in a figurative sense.

- After hours of debate, Luisa offered a few *incisive* comments that made it immediately clear to everyone how dumb the original idea had been.
- Lloyd's essays were always *incisive:* he never wasted any words, and his reasoning was sharp and persuasive.

INCONGRUOUS (in KAHN groo us) *adj* not harmonious; not consistent; not appropriate; not fitting in

- The ultramodern kitchen seemed *incongruous* in the restored 18th-century farmhouse. It was an *incongruity* (in kun GROO uh tee).
- Bill's membership in the motorcycle gang was *incongruous* with his mild personality and his career as a management consultant.

INCORRIGIBLE (in KOR uh juh bul) *adj* incapable of being reformed

- The convict was an *incorrigible* criminal; as soon as he got out of prison, he said, he was going to rob another doughnut store.
- Bill is *incorrigible*—he eats three bags of potato chips every day even though he knows that eating two would be better for him.
- The ever-cheerful Annie is an *incorrigible* optimist.

Think of *incorrigible* as incorrectable. The word *corrigible* is rarely seen or used these days.

INCREMENT (IN cruh munt) *n* an increase; one in a series of increases

- Bernard received a small *increment* in his salary each year, even though he did less and less work with every day that passed.
- This year's fund-raising total represented an *increment* of 1 percent over last year's. This year's total represented an *incremental* change from last year's.
- Viola built up her savings account *incrementally,* one dollar at a time.

INDIFFERENT (in DIF ur unt) *adj* **not caring one way or the other; apathetic; mediocre**

- Pedro was *indifferent* about politics; he didn't care who was elected to office so long as no one passed a law against Monday Night Football.
- Henry's *indifference* was extremely annoying to Melissa, who loved to argue but found it difficult to do so with people who had no opinions.
- We planted a big garden, but the results were *indifferent*—only about half of the flowers came up.
- The painter did an *indifferent* job, but it was good enough for Susan, who was *indifferent* about painting.

Quick Quiz #49

Match each word in the first column with its definition in the second column. Check your answers in the back of the book.

1.	incandescent	a.	increase
2.	incantation	b.	make very angry
3.	incense	c.	beginning
4.	incessant	d.	chant
5.	incipient	e.	not harmonious
6.	incisive	f.	incapable of being reformed
7.	incongruous	g.	not caring; mediocre
8.	incorrigible	h.	cutting right to the heart
9.	increment	i.	unceasing
10.	indifferent	j.	brilliant

INDIGENOUS (in DIJ uh nus) *adj* **native; originating in that area**

- Fast-food restaurants are *indigenous* to America, where they were invented.
- The grocer said the corn had been locally grown, but it didn't appear to be *indigenous.*
- The botanist said that the small cactus was *indigenous* but that the large one had been introduced to the region by Spanish explorers.

INDIGENT (IN di junt) *adj* poor

- The *indigent* family had little to eat, nothing to spend, and virtually nothing to wear.
- Rusty had once been a lawyer but now was *indigent;* he spent most of his time sleeping on a bench in the park.

Don't confuse this word with *indigenous,* listed earlier.

INDIGNANT (in DIG nunt) *adj* angry, especially as a result of something unjust or unworthy; insulted

- Ted became *indignant* when the policewoman accused him of stealing the nuclear weapon.
- Isabel was *indignant* when we told her all the nasty things that Blake had said about her over the public address system.

INDOLENT (IN duh lunt) *adj* lazy

- The *indolent* teenagers slept late, moped around, and never looked for summer jobs.
- Inheriting a lot of money enabled Rodney to do what he loved most: pursue a life of *indolence.*

INDULGENT (in DUL junt) *adj* lenient; yielding to desire

- The nice mom was *indulgent* of her children, letting them have all the candy, cookies, and ice cream that they wanted, even for breakfast.
- Our *indulgent* teacher never punished us for not turning in our homework. He didn't want us to turn into ascetic automatons.

Someone who is *self-indulgent* yields to his or her every desire.

INEFFABLE (in EF uh bul) *adj* incapable of being expressed or described

- The simple beauty of nature is often so *ineffable* that it brings tears to our eyes.

The word *effable*—expressible—is rarely used.

INEPT (in EPT) *adj* clumsy; incompetent; gauche

- Joshua is an *inept* dancer; he is as likely to stomp on his partner's foot as he is to step on it.
- Julia's *inept* attempt at humor drew only groans from the audience.

To be *inept* is to be characterized by *ineptitude,* which is the opposite of aptitude.

- The woodworking class's *ineptitude* was broad and deep; there was little that they were able to do and nothing that they were able to do well.

The opposite of *inept* is *adept* (uh DEPT). *Adept* and *adroit* are synonyms.

INERT (in URT) *adj* **inactive; sluggish; not reacting chemically**
- The baseball team seemed strangely *inert;* it was as though they had lost the will to play.
- Having colds made the children *inert* and reluctant to get out of bed.
- Helium is an *inert* gas: it doesn't burn, it doesn't explode, and it doesn't kill you if you inhale it.

To be *inert* is to be characterized by *inertia.* As it is most commonly used, *inertia* means lack of get-up-and-go, or an inability or unwillingness to move.

In physics, *inertia* refers to an object's tendency to continue doing what it's doing (either moving or staying still) unless it's acted on by something else.

INEXORABLE (in EK sur uh bul) *adj* **relentless; inevitable; unavoidable**
- The *inexorable* waves pounded the shore, as they have always pounded it and as they always will pound it.
- Eliot drove his father's car slowly but *inexorably* through the grocery store, wrecking aisle after aisle despite the manager's anguished pleading.
- *Inexorable* death finds everyone sooner or later.

> **Note carefully the pronunciation of this word.**

INFAMOUS (IN fuh mus) *adj* **shamefully wicked; having an extremely bad reputation; disgraceful**

Be careful with the pronunciation of this word.

To be *infamous* is to be *famous* for being evil or bad. An *infamous* cheater is one whose cheating is well known.
- Deep within the prison was the *infamous* torture chamber, where hooded guards tickled their prisoners with feathers until they confessed.

Infamy is the state of being *infamous.*
- The former Nazi lived the rest of his life in *infamy* after the court convicted him of war crimes and atrocities.
- President Roosevelt said that the date of the Japanese attack on Pearl Harbor would "live in *infamy.*"

INFATUATED (in FACH oo ay tid) *adj* foolish; foolishly passionate or attracted; made foolish; foolishly in love

To be *infatuated* is to be *fatuous* or foolish.

- I was so *infatuated* with Polly that I drooled and gurgled whenever she was near.
- The *infatuated* candidate thought so highly of himself that he had the walls of his house covered with his campaign posters.
- My ride in Corinne's racing car *infatuated* me; I knew immediately that I would have to have a racing car, too.

Quick Quiz #50

Match each word in the first column with its definition in the second column. Check your answers in the back of the book.

1.	indigenous	a.	native
2.	indigent	b.	inactive
3.	indignant	c.	lazy
4.	indolent	d.	foolish
5.	indulgent	e.	shamefully wicked
6.	ineffable	f.	poor
7.	inept	g.	relentless
8.	inert	h.	angry
9.	inexorable	i.	clumsy
10.	infamous	j.	lenient
11.	infatuated	k.	inexpressible

INFER (in FUR) *v* to conclude; to deduce

- Raizel said she loved the brownies, but I *inferred* from the size of the piece left on her plate that she had actually despised them.
- She hadn't heard the score, but the silence in the locker room led her to *infer* that we had lost.

Infer is often confused with *imply*. To *imply* something is to hint at it, suggest it, or state it indirectly. To *infer* something is to figure out what it is without being told directly.

An *inference* is a deduction or conclusion.

INFINITESIMAL (in fin uh TES uh mul) *adj* very, very, very small; infinitely small

Infinitesimal does not mean huge, as some people incorrectly believe.

- An *infinitesimal* bug of some kind crawled into Heather's ear and bit her in a place she couldn't scratch.
- Our chances of winning were *infinitesimal,* but we played our hearts out anyway.

INGENUOUS (in JEN yoo us) *adj* frank; without deception; simple; artless; charmingly naive
- Young children are *ingenuous.* They don't know much about the ways of the world, and certainly not enough to deceive anyone.

An *ingenue* (AHN ji noo) is a somewhat naive young woman; generally a stock character in film or literature

Disingenuous means crafty or artful.
- The movie producer was being *disingenuous* when he said, "I don't care about making money on this movie. I just want every man, woman, and child in the country to see it."

INHERENT (in HAIR unt) *adj* part of the essential nature of something; intrinsic

Wetness is an *inherent* quality of water. (You could also say that wetness is *inherent* in water.)
- There is an *inherent* strength in steel that cardboard lacks.
- The man's *inherent* fatness, jolliness, and beardedness made it easy for him to play the part of Santa Claus.

INJUNCTION (in JUNGK shun) *n* a command or order, especially a court order
- Wendy's neighbors got a court *injunction* prohibiting her from playing her radio.
- Herbert, lighting up, disobeyed his doctor's *injunction* to stop smoking.

INNATE (i NAYT) *adj* existing since birth; inborn; inherent
- Joseph's kindness was *innate;* it was part of his natural character.
- Fiona has an apparently *innate* ability to throw a football. You just can't teach someone to throw a ball as well as she can.
- There's nothing *innate* about good manners; all children have to be taught to say "please" and "thank you."

INNOCUOUS (i NAHK yoo us) *adj* harmless; banal

Innocuous is closely related, in both origin and meaning, to *innocent.*

- The speaker's voice was loud but his words were *innocuous;* there was nothing to get excited about.
- Meredith took offense at Bruce's *innocuous* comment about the saltiness of her soup.

INORDINATE (in OR duh nit) *adj* excessive; unreasonable

- The math teacher paid an *inordinate* amount of attention to the grammar rather than algebra.
- The limousine was *inordinately* large, even for a limousine; there was room for more than a dozen passengers.
- Romeo's love for Juliet was perhaps a bit *inordinate,* given the outcome of their relationship.

INSATIABLE (in SAY shuh bul) *adj* hard or impossible to satisfy; greedy; avaricious

- Peter had an *insatiable* appetite for chocolate macadamia ice cream; he could never get enough. Not even a gallon of chocolate macadamia was enough to *sate* (sayt) or *satiate* (SAY shee ayt) his craving.
- Peter's addiction never reached *satiety* (suh TYE uh tee or SAY she uh tee).

Note carefully the pronunciation of both words.

Quick Quiz #51

Match each word in the first column with its definition in the second column. Check your answers in the back of the book.

1.	infer	a.	hard or impossible to satisfy
2.	imply		
3.	infinitesimal	b.	part of the nature of
4.	ingenuous	c.	hint at
5.	inherent	d.	artless
6.	injunction	e.	inborn
7.	innate	f.	conclude
8.	innocuous	g.	excessive
9.	inordinate	h.	harmless
10.	insatiable	i.	infinitely small
		j.	court order

INSIDIOUS (in SID ee us) *adj* treacherous; sneaky
- Winter was *insidious;* it crept in under the doors and through cracks in the windows.
- Cancer, which can spread rapidly from a small cluster of cells, is an *insidious* disease.

INSINUATE (in SIN yoo ayt) *v* to hint; to creep in
- When I told her that I hadn't done any laundry in a month, Valerie *insinuated* that I was a slob.
- He didn't ask us outright to leave; he merely *insinuated,* through his tone and his gestures, that it was time for us to go.
- Jessica *insinuated* her way into the conversation by moving her chair closer and closer to where we were sitting.

To *insinuate* is to make an *insinuation.*

INSIPID (in SIP id) *adj* dull; bland; banal
- Barney's jokes were so *insipid* that no one in the room managed to force out so much as a chuckle.

The Words

- We were bored to death at the party; it was full of *insipid* people making *insipid* conversation.
- The thin soup was so *insipid* that all the spices in the world could not have made it interesting.

INSOLENT (IN suh lunt) *adj* arrogant; insulting
- The ill-mannered four-year-old was so *insolent* that his parents had a hard time finding a babysitter.
- The *insolent* sales clerk clearly didn't like answering customers' questions.

INSTIGATE (IN stuh gayt) *v* to provoke; to stir up
- The strike was *instigated* by the ambitious union president, who wanted to get her name into the news.
- The CIA tried unsuccessfully to *instigate* rebellion in the tiny country by distributing pamphlets that, as it turned out, were printed in the wrong language.

INSULAR (IN suh lur) *adj* like an island; isolated
The Latin word for island is *insula*. From it we get the words *peninsula* ("almost an island"), *insulate* (*insulation* makes a house an island of heat), and *insular*, among others.
- The *insular* little community had very little contact with the world around it.

Something that is *insular* has *insularity*.
- The *insularity* of the little community was so complete that it was impossible to buy a big-city newspaper there.

INSURGENT (in SUR junt) *n* a rebel; someone who revolts against a government
- The heavily armed *insurgents* rushed into the presidential palace, but they paused to taste the fresh blueberry pie on the dinner table and were captured by the president's bodyguards.

This word can also be an adjective. A rebellion is an *insurgent* activity.

Insurgency is another word for rebellion; so is *insurrection*.

INTEGRAL (IN tuh grul) *adj* essential
- A solid offense was an *integral* part of our football team; so was a strong defense.
- Dave was *integral* to the organization; it could never have gotten along without him.

INTEGRATE (IN tuh grayt) *v* to combine two or more things into a whole

This word is related to *segregate, aggregate,* and *congregate,* all of which describe joining or separating. It has the same root as *integer,* which means a whole number.

- Marisol's school offered an *integrated* history and language curriculum so that students learned Roman history and Latin in the same classroom.

The noun form is *integration,* which often refers to the end of racial segregation.

INTRACTABLE (in TRAK tuh bul) *adj* uncontrollable; stubborn; disobedient

- The *intractable* child was a torment to his nursery school teacher.
- Lavanya was *intractable* in her opposition to pay increases for the library employees; she swore she would never vote to give them a raise.
- The disease was *intractable.* None of the dozens of medicines the doctor tried had the slightest effect on it.

The opposite of *intractable* is *tractable.*

INTRANSIGENT (in TRAN suh junt) *adj* uncompromising; stubborn

- Vijay was an *intransigent* hard-liner, and he didn't care how many people he offended with his views.
- The jury was unanimous except for one *intransigent* member, who didn't believe that anyone should ever be forced to go to jail.

The noun is *intransigence.*

INTRINSIC (in TRIN sik) *adj* part of the essential nature of something; inherent

- Larry's *intrinsic* boldness was always getting him into trouble.
- There was an *intrinsic* problem with Owen's alibi: it was a lie.

The opposite of *intrinsic* is *extrinsic*.

INTROSPECTIVE (in truh SPEC tiv) *adj* tending to think about oneself; examining one's feelings

- The *introspective* six-year-old never had much to say to other people but always seemed to be turning something over in her mind.
- Randy's *introspective* examination of his motives led him to conclude that he must have been at fault in the breakup of his marriage.

See *extrovert,* listed previously.

INUNDATE (IN un dayt) *v* to flood; to cover completely with water; to overwhelm

- The tiny island kingdom was *inundated* by the tidal wave. Fortunately, no one died from the deluge.
- The mother was *inundated* with telegrams and gifts after she gave birth to octuplets.

INVECTIVE (in VEK tiv) *n* insulting or abusive speech

- The critic's searing review was filled with bitterness and *invective*.
- Herman wasn't much of an orator, but he was brilliant at *invective*.

INVETERATE (in VET ur it) *adj* habitual; firm in habit; deeply rooted

- Erica was such an *inveterate* liar on the golf course that when she finally made a hole-in-one, she marked it on his score card as a zero.
- Larry's practice of spitting into the fireplace became *inveterate* despite his wife's protestations.

IRASCIBLE (i RAS uh bul) *adj* easily angered or provoked; irritable

A grouch is *irascible*.

- The CEO was so *irascible* that her employees were afraid to talk to her for fear she might hurl paperweights at them.

IRONIC (eye RAHN ik) *adj* meaning the opposite of what you seem to say; using words to mean something other than what they seem to mean

- Eddie was being *ironic* when he said he loved Peter like a brother; in truth, he hated him.
- Credulous Carol never realized that the speaker was being *ironic* as she discussed a plan to put a nuclear-missile silo in every backyard in America.

IRREVOCABLE (i REV uh kuh bul) *adj* irreversible

To *revoke* (ri VOHK) is to take back. Something *irrevocable* cannot be taken back.

- My decision not to wear a Tarzan costume and ride on a float in the Macy's Thanksgiving Day Parade is *irrevocable;* there is absolutely nothing you could do or say to make me change my mind.
- After his friend pointed out that the tattoo was spelled incorrectly, Tom realized that his decision to get a tattoo was *irrevocable.*

Something that can be reversed is *revocable* (REV uh kuh bul).

Note carefully the pronunciation of both words.

ITINERANT (eye TIN ur unt) *adj* moving from place to place

- The life of a traveling salesman is an *itinerant* one.
- The *itinerant* junk dealer passes through our neighborhood every month or so, pulling his wagon of odds and ends.
- The international banker's *itinerant* lifestyle began to seem less glamorous to her after her first child was born.

A closely related word is *itinerary*, which is the planned route or schedule of a trip.

- The tour guide handed the travelers an *itinerary* of the tour bus route so they would know what to expect throughout the day.

Quick Quiz #53

Match each word in the first column with its definition in the second column. Check your answers in the back of the book.

1.	intrinsic	a.	irreversible
2.	introspective	b.	insulting speech
3.	inundate	c.	planned trip route
4.	invective	d.	flood
5.	inveterate	e.	inherent
6.	irascible	f.	examining one's feelings
7.	ironic	g.	meaning other than what's said
8.	irrevocable		
9.	itinerant	h.	moving from place to place
10.	itinerary	i.	irritable
		j.	habitual

J

JUDICIOUS (joo DISH us) *adj* exercising sound judgment

- The judge was far from *judicious;* he told the jury that he thought the defendant looked guilty and said that anyone who would wear a red bow tie into a courtroom deserved to be sent to jail.
- The firefighters made *judicious* use of flame-retardant foam on the brush fire before it spread to nearby homes.
- The mother of twin boys *judiciously* used an electron microscope and a laser to divide the ice cream into equal parts.

The word *judicial* is obviously closely related, but there is a critically important difference in meaning between it and *judicious*. A judge is *judicial* simply by virtue of being a judge; *judicial* means having to do with judges, judgment, or justice. But a judge is *judicious* only if he or she exercises sound judgment.

JUXTAPOSE (JUK stuh pohz) *v* to place side by side

- Comedy and tragedy were *juxtaposed* in the play, which was alternately funny and sad.
- *Juxtaposing* the genuine painting and the counterfeit made it much easier to tell which was which.

The noun is *juxtaposition* (juk stuh puh ZISH un).

K

KINETIC (ki NET ik) *adj* having to do with motion; lively; active

Kinetic energy is energy associated with motion. A speeding bullet has a lot of *kinetic* energy.

Kinetic art is art with things in it that move. A mobile is an example of *kinetic* art.

A *kinetic* personality is a lively, active, and moving personality.

L

LABYRINTH (LAB uh rinth) *n* a maze; something like a maze

- Each of the fifty floors in the office building was a *labyrinth* of dark corridors and narrow passageways.
- The bill took many months to pass through the *labyrinth* of congressional approval.

A *labyrinth* is *labyrinthine* (lab uh RINTH in, lab uh RINTH ine, or lab uh RINTH een) or mazelike.

- Before beginning construction on the new house, the contractor had to weave his way through the *labyrinthine* bureaucracy in order to obtain a building permit.

LACONIC (luh KAHN ik) *adj* using few words, especially to the point of seeming rude

- The manager's *laconic* dismissal letter left the fired employees feeling angry and hurt.
- When she went backstage, June discovered why the popular rock musician was so *laconic* in public: her voice was high and squeaky.

LAMENT (luh MENT) v to mourn
- From the balcony of the bullet-pocked hotel, the foreign correspondents could hear hundreds of women and children *lamenting* the fallen soldiers.
- As the snowstorm gained in intensity, Stan *lamented* his decision that morning to dress in shorts and a T-shirt.

Lamentable (LAM en tuh bul) or (luh MEN tuh bul) means regrettable.

Note carefully the pronunciation of both parts of speech.

LAMPOON (lam POON) v to satirize; to mock; to parody
- The irreverent students mercilessly *lampooned* their Latin teacher's lisp in a skit at the school talent show.
- *The Harvard Lampoon,* the nation's oldest humor magazine, has *lampooned* just about everything there is to *lampoon.*

LANGUISH (LANG gwish) v to become weak, listless, or depressed
- The formerly eager and vigorous accountant *languished* in her tedious job at the international conglomerate.
- The longer Jill remained unemployed, the more she *languished* and the less likely it became that she would find another job.

To *languish* is to be *languid.*
- The child seemed so *languid* that his father thought he was sick and called the doctor. It turned out that the little boy had simply had an overdose of television.

LARGESS (lahr JES) n generous giving of gifts (or the gifts themselves); generosity; philanthropy
- Sam was marginally literate at best. Only the *largess* of his uncle got Sam into the Ivy League school.

Largess can also be spelled *largesse.*

Note carefully the pronunciation of this word.

LATENT (LAYT unt) adj present but not visible or apparent; potential
- At four, Maria was a *latent* shopaholic; she learned to read by browsing the descriptions in clothing catalogs.

LAUD (lawd) *v* to praise; to applaud; to extol; to celebrate

- The bank manager *lauded* the hero who trapped the escaping robber. The local newspaper published a *laudatory* editorial on this intrepid individual.

Laudatory means praising.

Giving several million dollars to charity is a *laudable* act of philanthropy. *Laudable* means praiseworthy.

LEGACY (LEG uh see) *n* something handed down from the past; a bequest

- The *legacy* of the corrupt administration was chaos, bankruptcy, and despair.
- A shoebox full of baseball cards was the dead man's only *legacy.*
- To be a *legacy* at a college sorority is to be the daughter of a former sorority member.

LETHARGY (LETH ur jee) *n* sluggishness; laziness; drowsiness; indifference

- After a busy week of sports, homework, and work, the student relished the *lethargy* of Saturday morning.
- The *lethargy* of the staff caused what should have been a quick errand to expand into a full day's work.

To be filled with *lethargy* is to be *lethargic.*

- The *lethargic* (luh THAR jik) teenagers took all summer to paint the Hendersons' garage.

LEVITY (LEV uh tee) *n* lightness; frivolity; unseriousness

To *levitate* something is to make it so light that it floats up into the air. *Levity* comes from the same root and has to do with a different kind of lightness.

- The speaker's *levity* was not appreciated by the convention of funeral directors, who felt that a convention of funeral directors was no place to tell jokes.
- The judge's attempt to inject some *levity* into the dreary court proceedings (by setting off a few firecrackers in the jury box) was entirely successful.

Quick Quiz #54

Match each word in the first column with its definition in the second column. Check your answers in the back of the book.

1.	judicious	a.	sluggishness
2.	juxtapose	b.	lightness
3.	kinetic	c.	using few words
4.	labyrinth	d.	maze
5.	laconic	e.	place side by side
6.	lament	f.	present but not visible
7.	lampoon	g.	bequest
8.	languish	h.	active
9.	latent	i.	become weak
10.	laud	j.	satirize
11.	legacy	k.	mourn
12.	lethargy	l.	praise
13.	levity	m.	exercising sound judgment

LIBEL (LYE bul) *n* a written or published falsehood that injures the reputation of, or defames, someone

- The executive said that the newspaper had committed *libel* when it called him a stinking, no-good, corrupt, incompetent, overpaid, lying, worthless moron. He claimed that the newspaper had *libeled* him, and that its description of him had been *libelous*. At the trial, the jury disagreed, saying that the newspaper's description of the executive had been substantially accurate.

Don't confuse this word with *liable*, which has an entirely different meaning.

Slander is just like *libel* except that it is spoken instead of written.

To *slander* someone is to say something untrue that injures that person's reputation.

LITIGATE (LIT uh gayt) *v* to try in court; to engage in legal proceedings

- His lawyer thought a lawsuit would be fruitless, but the client wanted to *litigate*. He was feeling *litigious* (li TIJ us); that is, he was feeling in a mood to go to court.
- When the company was unable to recover its money outside of court, its only option was to *litigate*.

To *litigate* is to engage in *litigation;* a court hearing is an example of *litigation.*

LOQUACIOUS (loh KWAY shus) *adj* talking a lot or too much
- The child was surprisingly *loquacious* for one so small.
- Mary is so *loquacious* that Belinda can sometimes put down the telephone receiver and run a load of laundry while Mary is talking.

A *loquacious* person is one who is characterized by *loquaciousness* or *loquacity* (loh KWAS uh tee).
- The English teacher's *loquacity* in class left little time for any of the students to speak, which was fine with most of them.

LUCID (LOO sid) *adj* clear; easy to understand
- The professor's explanation of the theory of relativity was so astonishingly *lucid* that even I could understand it.
- Hubert's remarks were few but *lucid:* he explained the complicated issue with just a handful of well-chosen words.
- The extremely old man was *lucid* right up until the moment he died; his body had given out but his mind was still going strong.

To *elucidate* something is to make it clear, to explain it.

LUGUBRIOUS (loo GOO bree us) *adj* exaggeratedly mournful

To be mournful is to be sad and sorrowful. To be *lugubrious* is to make a big show of being sad and sorrowful.
- Harry's *lugubrious* eulogy at the funeral of his dog eventually made everyone start giggling.
- The valedictorian suddenly turned *lugubrious* and began sobbing and tearing her hair at the thought of graduating from high school.

LUMINOUS (LOO muh nus) *adj* giving off light; glowing; bright
- The moon was a *luminous* disk in the cloudy nighttime sky.
- The snow on the ground appeared eerily *luminous* at night—it seemed to glow.
- The dial on my watch is *luminous;* it casts a green glow in the dark.

M

MACHINATION (mak uh NAY shun) *n* scheming activity for an evil purpose

This word is almost always used in the plural—*machinations*—in which form it means the same thing.

- The ruthless *machinations* of the mobsters left a trail of blood and bodies.
- The *machinations* of the conspirators were aimed at nothing less than the overthrow of the government.

This word is often used imprecisely to mean something like "machinelike activity." It should not be used in this way.

Note carefully the pronunciation of this word.

MAGNANIMOUS (mag NAN uh mus) *adj* forgiving; unresentful; noble in spirit; generous

- The boxer was *magnanimous* in defeat, telling the sports reporters that his opponent had simply been too talented for him to beat.
- Mrs. Jones *magnanimously* offered the little boy a cookie when he came over to confess that he had accidentally broken her window while playing baseball.

To be *magnanimous* is to have *magnanimity* (mag nuh NIM uh tee).
- The *magnanimity* of the conquering general was much appreciated by the defeated soldiers.

MAGNATE (MAG nayt) *n* **a rich, powerful, or very successful businessperson**
- John D. Rockefeller was a *magnate* who was never too cheap to give a shoeshine boy a dime for his troubles.

MALAISE (ma LAYZ) *n* **a feeling of depression, uneasiness, or queasiness**
- *Malaise* descended on the calculus class when the teacher announced a quiz.

MALFEASANCE (mal FEE zuns) *n* **an illegal act, especially by a public official**
- President Ford officially pardoned former president Nixon before the latter could be convicted of any *malfeasance*.

MALIGNANT (muh LIG nuhnt) *adj* **causing harm**

Many words that start with *mal-* connote evil or harm, just as words that begin with *ben-* generally have good connotations. *Malignant* and *benign* are often used to describe tumors or physical conditions that are either life-threatening or not.
- Lina has had recurring tumors since the operation; we're just glad that none of them have proved *malignant*.

MALINGER (muh LING ger) *v* **to pretend to be sick to avoid doing work**
- Indolent Leon always *malingered* when it was his turn to clean up the house.
- Angie is artful, and she always manages to *malinger* before a big exam.

MALLEABLE (MAL ee uh bul) *adj* **easy to shape or bend**
- Modeling clay is very *malleable*. So is Stuart. We can make him do whatever we want him to do.

MANDATE (MAN dayt) *n* **a command or authorization to do something; the will of the voters as expressed by the results of an election**
- Our *mandate* from the executive committee was to find the answer to the problem as quickly as possible.
- The newly elected president felt that the landslide vote had given her a *mandate* to do whatever she wanted to do.

Mandate can also be a verb. To *mandate* something is to command or require it.

A closely related word is *mandatory*, which means required or obligatory.

MANIFEST (MAN uh fest) *adj* visible; evident

- Daryl's anger at us was *manifest:* you could see it in his expression and hear it in his voice.

There is *manifest* danger in riding a pogo stick along the edge of a cliff.

Manifest can also be a verb, in which case it means to show, to make visible, or to make evident.

- Lee has been sick for a very long time, but it was only recently that he began to *manifest* symptoms.
- Rebecca *manifested* alarm when we told her that the end of her ponytail was dipped into the bucket of paint.

A visible sign of something is called a *manifestation* of it. A lack of comfort and luxury is the most obvious *manifestation* of poverty.

MANIFESTO (man uh FES toh) *n* a public declaration of beliefs or principles, usually political ones

The *Communist Manifesto* was a document that spelled out Karl Marx's critique of capitalistic society.

- Jim's article about the election was less a piece of reporting than a *manifesto* of his political views.

MARSHAL (MAHR shul) *v* to arrange in order; to gather together for the purpose of doing something

- The statistician *marshaled* her facts numerous times before making her presentation.
- The general *marshaled* his troops in anticipation of making an attack on the enemy fortress.
- We *marshaled* half a dozen local groups in opposition to the city council's plan to bulldoze our neighborhood.

MARTIAL (MAHR shul) *adj* warlike; having to do with combat

Martial is often confused with *marital* (MAR ih tul), which means having to do with marriage. Marriages are sometimes *martial*, but don't confuse these words.

Karate and judo are often referred to as *martial* arts.

- The parade of soldiers was *martial* in tone; the soldiers carried rifles and were followed by a formation of tanks.

- The school principal declared *martial* law when food riots erupted in the cafeteria.

MARTYR (MAHR tur) *n* **someone who gives up his or her life in pursuit of a cause, especially a religious one; one who suffers for a cause; one who makes a show of suffering in order to arouse sympathy**

Many of the saints were also *martyrs;* they were executed, often gruesomely, for refusing to renounce their religious beliefs.
- Jacob is a *martyr* to his job; he would stay at his desk 24 hours a day if his wife and the janitor would let him.
- Eloise played the *martyr* during hay-fever season, trudging wearily from room to room with a jumbo box of Kleenex in each hand.

MATRICULATE (muh TRIK yuh layt) *v* **to enroll, especially at a college**
- Benny told everyone he was going to Harvard, but he actually *matriculated* to the local junior college.

Quick Quiz #56

Match each word in the first column with its definition in the second column. Check your answers in the back of the book.

1.	machination	a.	forgiving
2.	magnanimous	b.	easy to shape
3.	magnate	c.	depression
4.	malaise	d.	command to do something
5.	malevolent	e.	scheming evil activity
6.	malfeasance	f.	public declaration
7.	malignant	g.	pretend to be sick
8.	malinger	h.	visible
9.	malleable	i.	one who dies for a cause
10.	mandate	j.	arrange in order
11.	manifest	k.	illegal act
12.	manifesto	l.	enroll
13.	marshal	m.	warlike
14.	martial	n.	rich businessperson
15.	martyr	o.	harmful
16.	matriculate	p.	wishing to do evil

MAUDLIN (MAWD lin) *adj* silly and overly sentimental

- The high school reunion grew more and more *maudlin* as the participants shared more and more memories.
- Magdalen had a *maudlin* concern for the worms in her yard; she would bang a gong before walking in the grass in order to give them a chance to get out of her way.

MAVERICK (MAV ur ik) *n* a nonconformist; a rebel

The word *maverick* originated in the Old West. It is derived from the name of Samuel A. Maverick, a Texas banker who once accepted a herd of cattle in payment of a debt. Maverick was a banker, not a rancher. He failed to confine or brand his calves, which habitually wandered into his neighbors' pastures. Local ranchers got in the habit of referring to any unbranded calf as a *maverick.* The word is now used for anyone who has refused to be "branded"—who has refused to conform.

- The political scientist was an intellectual *maverick;* most of her theories had no followers except herself.

Maverick can also be an adjective.

- The *maverick* police officer got in trouble with the department for using illegal means to track down criminals.

MAXIM (MAK sim) *n* a fundamental principle; an old saying

- We always tried to live our lives according to the *maxim* that it is better to give than to receive.
- No one in the entire world is entirely certain of the differences in meaning among the words *maxim, adage, proverb,* and *aphorism.*

MEDIATE (MEE dee ayt) *v* to help settle differences

- The United Nations representative tried to *mediate* between the warring countries, but the soldiers just kept shooting at one another.
- Joe carried messages back and forth between the divorcing husband and wife in the hope of *mediating* their differences.

To *mediate* is to engage in *mediation.* When two opposing groups, such as a trade union and the management of a company, try to settle their differences through *mediation,* they call in a *mediator* to listen to their cases and to make an equitable decision.

MELLIFLUOUS (muh LIF loo us) *adj* sweetly flowing

Mellifluous comes from Greek words meaning, roughly, "honey flowing." We use the word almost exclusively to describe voices, music, or sounds that flow sweetly, like honey.

- Melanie's clarinet playing was *mellifluous;* the notes flowed smoothly and beautifully.

MENDACIOUS (men DAY shus) *adj* lying; dishonest

Thieves are naturally *mendacious.* If you ask them what they are doing, they will automatically answer, "Nothing."

- The jury saw through the *mendacious* witness and convicted the defendant.

To be *mendacious* is to engage in *mendacity,* or lying. I have no flaws, except occasional *mendacity.* Don't confuse this word with *mendicant,* listed below.

MENDICANT (MEN di kunt) *n* a beggar

- The presence of thousands of *mendicants* in every urban area is a sad commentary on our national priorities.

MENTOR (MEN tur) *n* a teacher, tutor, counselor, or coach; especially in business, an experienced person who shows an inexperienced person the ropes

Mentor is too big a word to apply to just any teacher. A student might have many teachers but only one *mentor*—the person who taught him or her what was really important.

- Chris's *mentor* in the pole vault was a former track star who used to hang out by the gym and give the students pointers.
- Young men and women in business often talk about the importance of having a *mentor*—usually an older person at the same company who takes an interest in them and helps them get ahead by showing them the ropes.

MERCENARY (MUR suh ner ee) *n* a hired soldier; someone who will do anything for money

If an army can't find enough volunteers or draftees, it will sometimes hire *mercenaries.* The magazine *Soldier of Fortune* is aimed at *mercenaries* and would-be *mercenaries;* it even runs classified advertisements by soldiers looking for someone to fight.

You don't have to be a soldier to be a *mercenary.* Someone who does something strictly for the money is often called a *mercenary.*

- Our business contains a few dedicated workers and many, many *mercenaries,* who want to make a quick buck and then get out.

Mercenary can also be used as an adjective.

- Larry's motives in writing the screenplay for the trashy movie were strictly *mercenary*—he needed the money.

MERCURIAL (mur KYOOR ee ul) *adj* emotionally unpredictable; rapidly changing in mood

A person with a *mercurial* personality is one who changes rapidly and unpredictably between one mood and another.

• *Mercurial* Helen was crying one minute, laughing the next.

METAMORPHOSIS (met uh MOR fuh sis) *n* a magical change in form; a striking or sudden change

• When the magician passed her wand over Eileen's head, she underwent a bizarre *metamorphosis:* she turned into a hamster.

• Damon's *metamorphosis* from college student to Hollywood superstar was so sudden that it seemed a bit unreal.

To undergo a *metamorphosis* is to *metamorphose.*

Quick Quiz #57

Match each word in the first column with its definition in the second column. Check your answers in the back of the book.

1.	maudlin	a.	teacher
2.	maverick	b.	fundamental principle
3.	maxim	c.	lying
4.	mediate	d.	help settle differences
5.	mellifluous	e.	sweetly flowing
6.	mendacious	f.	nonconformist
7.	mendicant	g.	emotionally unpredictable
8.	mentor	h.	magical change in form
9.	mercenary	i.	overly sentimental
10.	mercurial	j.	hired soldier
11.	metamorphosis	k.	beggar

MICROCOSM (MYE kruh kahz um) *n* the world in miniature

The *cosmos* is the heavens, *cosmopolitan* means worldly, and a *microcosm* is a miniature version of the world. All three words are related.

• Our community, which holds so many different communities, institutions, businesses, and types of people, is a *microcosm* of the larger world.

The opposite of *microcosm* is a *macrocosm* (MAK ruh kahz um). A *macrocosm* is a large-scale representation of something, or the universe at large.

MILIEU (mil YOO) *n* environment; surroundings

- A caring and involved community is the proper *milieu* for raising a family.
- The farmer on vacation in the big city felt out of his *milieu*.

MINUSCULE (MIN uh skyool) *adj* very tiny

Be careful with the spelling of this word. People tend to spell it "miniscule." Think of *minus*.

- Hank's salary was *minuscule,* but the benefits were pretty good: he got to sit next to the refrigerator and eat all day long.

Minute (mye NOOT) is a synonym for *minuscule*. The small details of something are the *minutiae* (mi NOO shi ee).

MISANTHROPIC (mis un THRAHP ik) *adj* hating mankind

A *misogynist* (mis AH juh nist) hates women. A *misanthropic* person doesn't make distinctions; he or she hates everyone. The opposite of a *misanthrope* (MIS un throhp) is a *philanthropist* (fuh LAN thruh pist). Curiously, there is no word for someone who hates men only.

MITIGATE (MIT uh gayt) *v* to moderate the effect of something

- The sense of imminent disaster was *mitigated* by the guide's calm behavior and easy smile.
- The effects of the disease were *mitigated* by the experimental drug treatment.
- Nothing Joel said could *mitigate* the enormity of forgetting his mother-in-law's birthday.

Unmitigated means absolute, unmoderated, or not made less intense or severe.

MOLLIFY (MAHL uh fye) *v* to soften; to soothe; to pacify

- Lucy *mollified* the angry police officer by kissing his hand.
- My father was not *mollified* by my promise never to crash his car into a brick wall again.
- The babysitter was unable to *mollify* the cranky child, who cried all night.

MONOLITHIC (mah nuh LITH ik) *adj* massive, solid, uniform, and unyielding

A *monolith* is a huge stone shaft or column. Many other things can be said to be *monolithic*.

A huge corporation is often said to be *monolithic,* especially if it is enormous and powerful and all its parts are dedicated to the same purpose.

If the opposition to a plan were said to be *monolithic,* it would probably consist of a large group of people who all felt the same way.

MORIBUND (MOR uh bund) *adj* dying
- The steel industry in this country was *moribund* a few years ago, but now it seems to be reviving somewhat.
- The senator's political ideas were *moribund;* no one thinks that way anymore.

A dying creature could be said to be *moribund,* too, although this word is usually used in connection with things that die only figuratively.

MOROSE (muh ROHS) *adj* gloomy; sullen
- Louise was always so *morose* about everything that she was never any fun to be with.
- New Yorkers always seemed *morose* to the writer who lived in the country; she thought they seemed beaten down by the city.

MORTIFY (MOR tuh fye) *adj* to humiliate
- I was *mortified* when my father asked my girlfriend whether she thought I was a dumb, pathetic wimp.
- We had a *mortifying* experience at the opera; when Stanley's cell phone rang, the entire orchestra stopped playing and stared at him for several minutes.

MUNDANE (mun DAYN) *adj* ordinary; pretty boring; not heavenly and eternal
- My day was filled with *mundane* chores: I mowed the lawn, did the laundry, and fed the dog.
- Dee's job was so *mundane* she sometimes had trouble remembering whether she was at work or asleep.
- The monk's thoughts were far removed from *mundane* concerns; he was contemplating all the fun he was going to have in heaven.

MUNIFICENT (myoo NIF uh sunt) *adj* very generous; lavish
- The *munificent* millionaire gave lots of money to any charity that came to her with a request.
- Mrs. Bigelow was a *munificent* hostess; there was so much wonderful food and wine at her dinner parties that the guests had to rest between courses. She was known for her *munificence.*

MYOPIA (mye OH pee uh) *adj* nearsightedness; lack of foresight
Myopia is the fancy medical name for the inability to see clearly at a distance. It's also a word used in connection with people who lack other kinds of visual acuity.

- The president suffered from economic *myopia;* he was unable to see the consequences of his fiscal policies.
- The workers' dissatisfaction was inflamed by management's *myopia* on the subject of wages.

To suffer myopia is to be *myopic* (mye AHP ik). Some people who wear glasses are *myopic.* So are the people who can't see the consequences of their actions.

MYRIAD (MIR ee ud) *n* a huge number
- A country sky on a clear night is filled with a *myriad* stars.
- There are a *myriad* reasons why I don't like school.

This word can also be used as an adjective. *Myriad* stars is a lot of stars. The teenager was weighted down by the *myriad* anxieties of adolescence.

Note carefully the pronunciation of this word.

Quick Quiz #58

Match each word in the first column with its definition in the second column. Check your answers in the back of the book.

1.	microcosm	a.	a huge number
2.	milieu	b.	moderate the effect of
3.	minuscule	c.	massive and unyielding
4.	misanthropic	d.	humiliate
5.	mitigate	e.	ordinary
6.	mollify	f.	soften
7.	monolithic	g.	nearsightedness
8.	moribund	h.	very tiny
9.	morose	i.	gloomy
10.	mortify	j.	environment
11.	mundane	k.	very generous
12.	munificent	l.	dying
13.	myopia	m.	world in miniature
14.	myriad	n.	hating mankind

N

NARCISSISM (NAHR si siz um) *n* excessive love of one's body or oneself

In Greek mythology, Narcissus was a boy who fell in love with his own reflection. To engage in *narcissism* is to be like Narcissus.

Throwing a kiss to your reflection in the mirror is an act of *narcissism*—so is filling your living room with all your bowling trophies or telling everyone how smart and good-looking you are. You are a *narcissist* (NAHR suh sist).

Someone who suffers from *narcissism* is said to be *narcissistic* (nahr si SIS tik).

- The selfish students were bound up in *narcissistic* concerns and gave no thought to other people.

NEBULOUS (NEB yuh lus) *adj* vague; hazy; indistinct

- Oscar's views are so *nebulous* that no one can figure out what he thinks about anything.
- The community's boundaries are somewhat *nebulous;* where they are depends on whom you ask.
- Molly's expensive new hairdo was a sort of *nebulous* mass of wisps, waves, and hair spray.

A *nebula* (NEB yuh luh) is an interstellar cloud, the plural of which is *nebulae* (NEB yuh lee).

NEFARIOUS (ni FAR ee us) *adj* evil; flagrantly wicked

- The radicals' *nefarious* plot was to destroy New York by filling the reservoirs with strawberry Jell-O.
- The convicted murderer had committed myriad *nefarious* acts.

NEOLOGISM (nee OL uh jiz um) *n* a new word or phrase; a new usage of a word

Pedants don't like *neologisms.* They like the words we already have. But at one time every word was a *neologism.* Someone somewhere had to be the first to use it.

NEPOTISM (NEP uh tiz um) *n* showing favoritism to friends or family in business or politics

- Clarence had no business acumen, so he was counting on *nepotism* when he married the boss's daughter.

NIHILISM (NYE uh liz um) *n* the belief that there are no values or morals in the universe
- A *nihilist* does not believe in any objective standards of right or wrong.

Note carefully the pronunciation of this word.

NOMINAL (NOM uh nul) *adj* in name only; insignificant; A-OK (during rocket launches)
- Bert was the *nominal* chair of the committee, but Sue was the one who ran things.
- The cost was *nominal* in comparison with the enormous value of what you received.
- "All systems are *nominal*," said the NASA engineer as the space shuttle successfully headed into orbit.

NOSTALGIA (nahs TAL juh) *n* sentimental longing for the past; homesickness
- A wave of *nostalgia* overcame me when the song came on the radio; hearing it took me right back to 1997.
- Some people who don't remember what the decade was really like feel a misplaced *nostalgia* for the 1950s.

To be filled with *nostalgia* is to be *nostalgic.*
- As we talked about the fun we'd had together in junior high school, we all began to feel a little *nostalgic.*

NOTORIOUS (noh TOR ee us) *adj* famous for something bad

A well-known actor is famous; a well-known criminal is *notorious.*
- No one wanted to play poker with Jeremy because he was a *notorious* cheater.
- Rana's practical jokes were *notorious;* people always kept their distance when she came into the room.

To be *notorious* is to have *notoriety* (noh tuh RYE uh tee).
- Jesse's *notoriety* as a bank robber made it difficult for him to find a job in banking.

NOVEL (NAHV ul) *adj* new; original
- Ray had a *novel* approach to homework: he did the work before the teacher assigned it.
- There was nothing *novel* about the author's latest novel; the characters were old, and the plot was borrowed.

NOXIOUS (NAHK shus) *adj* harmful; offensive

- Smoking is a *noxious* habit in every sense.
- Poison ivy is a *noxious* weed.
- The mothers' committee believed that rock 'n' roll music exerted a *noxious* influence on their children.

NUANCE (NOO ahns) *n* a subtle difference or distinction

- The artist's best work explored the *nuance* between darkness and deep shadow.
- Harry was incapable of *nuance;* everything for him was either black or white.

In certain Chinese dialects, the difference between one word and its opposite is sometimes nothing more than a *nuance* of inflection.

Quick Quiz #59

Match each word in the first column with its definition in the second column. Check your answers in the back of the book.

1.	narcissism	a.	excessive love of self
2.	nebulous	b.	in name only
3.	nefarious	c.	harmful
4.	neologism	d.	original
5.	nepotism	e.	evil
6.	nihilism	f.	subtle difference
7.	nominal	g.	famous for something bad
8.	nostalgia	h.	vague
9.	notorious	i.	longing for the past
10.	novel	j.	favoritism
11.	noxious	k.	belief in the absence of all values and morals
12.	nuance	l.	new word

O

OBDURATE (AHB duh rit) *adj* stubborn and insensitive

Obdurate contains one of the same roots as *durable* and *endurance;* each word conveys a different sense of hardness.

- The committee's *obdurate* refusal to listen to our plan was heart-breaking to us because we had spent ten years coming up with it.
- The child begged and begged to have the bubble-gum machine installed in his bedroom, but his parents were *obdurate* in their insistence that it should go in the kitchen.

Note carefully the pronunciation of this word.

OBFUSCATE (AHB fuh skayt) *v* to darken; to confuse; to make confusing
- The spokesman's attempt to explain what the president had meant merely *obfuscated* the issue further. People had hoped the spokesman would elucidate the issue.
- Too much gin had *obfuscated* the old man's senses.
- The professor's inept lecture gradually *obfuscated* a subject that had been crystal clear to us before.

To *obfuscate* something is to engage in *obfuscation*.
- Lester called himself a used-car salesman, but his real job was *obfuscation:* he sold cars by confusing his customers.

OBLIQUE (oh BLEEK) *adj* indirect; at an angle

In geometry, lines are said to be *oblique* if they are neither parallel nor perpendicular to one another. The word has a related meaning outside of mathematics. An *oblique* statement is one that does not directly address the topic at hand, that approaches it as if from an angle.

An allusion could be said to be an *oblique* reference.

An *oblique* argument is one that does not directly confront its true subject.

To insult someone *obliquely* is to do so indirectly.
- Essence sprinkled her student council speech with *oblique* references to the principal's new toupee. The principal is so dense that he never figured out what was going on, but the rest of us were rolling on the floor.

OBLIVION (uh BLIV ee un) *n* total forgetfulness; the state of being forgotten
- A few of the young actors would find fame, but most were headed for *oblivion.*
- After tossing and turning with anxiety for most of the night, Marisol finally found the *oblivion* of sleep.

To be *oblivious* is to be forgetful or unaware.

- Old age had made the retired professor *oblivious* of all his old theories.
- The workers stomped in and out of the room, but the happy child, playing on the floor, was *oblivious* of all distraction.

It is also acceptable to say "*oblivious* to" rather than "*oblivious* of."

OBSCURE (ub SKYOOR) *adj* unknown; hard to understand; dark

- The comedy nightclub was filled with *obscure* comedians who stole one another's jokes and seldom got any laughs.
- The artist was so *obscure* that even her parents had trouble remembering her name.
- The noted scholar's dissertation was terribly *obscure;* it had to be translated from English into English before anyone could make head or tail of it.
- Some contemporary poets apparently believe that the only way to be great is to be *obscure.*
- The details of the forest grew *obscure* as night fell.

The state of being *obscure* in any of its senses is called *obscurity.*

OBSEQUIOUS (ub SEE kwee us) *adj* fawning; subservient; sucking up to

- Ann's assistant was so *obsequious* that she could never tell what he really thought about anything.
- My *obsequious* friend seemed to live only to make me happy and never wanted to do anything if I said I didn't want to do it.

OBTUSE (ahb TOOS) *adj* insensitive; blockheaded

- Karen was so *obtuse* that she didn't realize for several days that Caleb had asked her to marry him.
- The *obtuse* student couldn't seem to grasp the difference between addition and subtraction.

OFFICIOUS (uh FISH us) *adj* annoyingly eager to help or advise

- The *officious* officer could never resist sticking his nose into other people's business.
- The *officious* salesperson refused to leave us alone, so we finally left without buying anything.

Note carefully the pronunciation of this word.

ONEROUS (AHN ur us) *adj* burdensome; oppressive

- We were given the *onerous* task of cleaning up the fairgrounds after the carnival.

- The job had long hours, but the work wasn't *onerous*. Bill spent most of his time sitting with his feet on the desk.

This word can be pronounced "OH nur us."

OPAQUE (oh PAYK) *adj* impossible to see through; impossible to understand

- The windows in the movie star's house were made not of glass but of some *opaque* material intended to keep her fans from spying on her.
- We tried to figure out what Horace was thinking, but his expression was *opaque:* it revealed nothing.
- Jerry's mind, assuming he had one, was *opaque.*
- The statement was *opaque;* no one could make anything of it.

The noun form of *opaque* is *opacity* (oh PAS uh tee).

OPULENT (AHP yuh lunt) *adj* luxurious

- Everything in the *opulent* palace was made of gold—except the toilet-paper holder, which was made of platinum.
- The investment banker had grown so accustomed to an *opulent* lifestyle that he had trouble adjusting to the federal penitentiary.

Opulence is often ostentatious.

ORTHODOX (OR thuh dahks) *adj* conventional; adhering to established principles or doctrines, especially in religion; by the book

- The doctor's treatment for Lou's cold was entirely *orthodox:* plenty of liquids, aspirin, and rest.
- Austin's views were *orthodox;* there was nothing shocking about any of them.

The body of what is *orthodox* is called *orthodoxy.*

- The teacher's lectures were characterized by strict adherence to *orthodoxy.*

To be unconventional is to be *unorthodox.*

- "Swiss cheese" is an *unorthodox* explanation for the composition of the moon.

OSTENSIBLE (ah STEN suh bul) *adj* apparent (but misleading); professed

- Blake's *ostensible* mission was to repair a broken telephone, but his real goal was to eavesdrop on the boss's conversation.
- Tracee's *ostensible* kindness to squirrels belied her deep hatred of them.

OSTENTATIOUS (ahs ten TAY shus) *adj* excessively conspicuous; showy

- The designer's use of expensive materials was *ostentatious:* every piece of furniture was covered with silk or velvet, and every piece of hardware was made of silver or gold.
- The donor was *ostentatious* in making his gift to the hospital. He held a big press conference to announce it and then walked through the wards to give patients an opportunity to thank him personally.
- The young lawyer had *ostentatiously* hung her Harvard diploma on the door to her office.

To be *ostentatious* is to engage in *ostentation*.

- Lamar wore solid-gold shoes to the party; I was shocked by his *ostentation*.

Quick Quiz #60

Match each word in the first column with its definition in the second column. Check your answers in the back of the book.

1.	obdurate	a.	forgetfulness
2.	obfuscate	b.	hard to understand
3.	oblique	c.	stubborn
4.	oblivion	d.	insensitive
5.	obscure	e.	burdensome
6.	obsequious	f.	luxurious
7.	obtuse	g.	indirect
8.	officious	h.	misleadingly apparent
9.	onerous	i.	showing off
10.	opaque	j.	impossible to see through
11.	opulent	k.	confuse
12.	orthodox	l.	fawning
13.	ostensible	m.	conventional
14.	ostentatious	n.	annoyingly helpful

P

PACIFY (PAS uh fye) *v* to calm someone down; to placate

A parent gives a baby a *pacifier* to *pacify* him or her. A *pacifist* is someone who does not believe in war.

PAINSTAKING (PAYN stay king) *adj* extremely careful; taking pains

Painstaking = pains-taking = taking pains.
- The jeweler was *painstaking* in his effort not to ruin the $50 million diamond necklace.

PALLIATE (PAL ee ayt) *v* to relieve or alleviate something without getting rid of the problem; to assuage; to mitigate
- You take aspirin in the hope that it will *palliate* your headache.

Aspirin is a *palliative* (PAL yuh tiv).

PALPABLE (PAL puh bul) *adj* capable of being touched; obvious; tangible
- The tumor was *palpable;* the doctor could feel it with her finger.
- Harry's disappointment at being rejected by every college in America was *palpable;* it was so obvious that you could almost reach out and touch it.
- There was *palpable* danger in flying the kite in a thunderstorm.

The opposite of *palpable* is *impalpable.*

PALTRY (PAWL tree) *adj* insignificant; worthless
- The lawyer's efforts on our behalf were *paltry;* they didn't add up to anything.
- The *paltry* fee he paid us was scarcely large enough to cover our expenses.

PANACEA (pan uh SEE uh) *n* something that cures everything
- The administration seemed to believe that a tax cut would be a *panacea* for the country's economic ills.
- Granny believed that her "rheumatiz medicine" was a *panacea.* No matter what you were sick with, that was what she prescribed.

> Note carefully the pronunciation of this word.

PARADIGM (PAR uh dime) *n* a model or example

- Mr. Hufstader is the best teacher in the whole world; his classroom should be the *paradigm* for all classrooms.
- In selecting her wardrobe, messy Ana apparently used a scarecrow as her *paradigm*.

A *paradigm* is *paradigmatic* (par uh dig MAT ik).

- Virtually all the cars the company produced were based on a single, *paradigmatic* design.

Note carefully the pronunciation of this word.

PARADOX (PAR uh dahks) *n* a true statement or phenomenon that nonetheless seems to contradict itself; an untrue statement or phenomenon that nonetheless seems logical

- Mr. Cooper is a political *paradox;* he's a staunch Republican who votes only for Democrats.
- One of Xeno's *paradoxes* seems to prove the impossibility of an arrow's ever reaching its target: if the arrow first moves half the distance to the target, then half the remaining distance, then half the remaining distance, and so on, it can never arrive.

A *paradox* is *paradoxical*.

- Pasquale's dislike of ice cream was *paradoxical* considering that he worked as an ice-cream taster.

PAROCHIAL (puh ROH kee ul) *adj* narrow or confined in point of view; provincial

- The townspeople's concerns were entirely *parochial;* they worried only about what happened in their town and not about the larger world around it.
- The journalist's *parochial* point of view prevented her from becoming a nationally known figure.

A lot of people think a *parochial* school is a religious school. Traditionally, a *parochial* school is just the school of the parish or neighborhood. In other contexts *parochial* has negative connotations.

PARODY (PAR uh dee) *n* a satirical imitation

- At the talent show the girls sang a terrible *parody* of a Beatles song called "I Want to Hold Your Foot."

Some *parodies* are unintentional and not very funny.

- The unhappy student accused Mr. Benson of being not a teacher but a *parody* of one.

Parody can also be a verb. To *parody* something is to make a *parody* of it. A *parody* is *parodic* (puh ROD ik).

PARSIMONIOUS (pahr suh MOH nee us) *adj* stingy

- The widow was so *parsimonious* that she hung used teabags out to dry on her clothesline so that she would be able to use them again.
- We tried to be *parsimonious,* but without success. After just a few days at the resort we realized we had spent all the money we had set aside for our entire month-long vacation.

To be *parsimonious* is to practice *parsimony.*

PARTISAN (PAHR tuh zun) *n* one who supports a particular person, cause, or idea

- Henry's plan to give himself the award had no *partisan* except himself.
- I am the *partisan* of any candidate who promises not to make promises.
- The mountain village was attacked by *partisans* of the rebel chieftain.

Partisan can also be used as an adjective meaning biased, as in *partisan* politics. An issue that everyone agrees on regardless of the party he or she belongs to is a *nonpartisan* issue. *Bipartisan* means supported by two (bi) parties.

- Both the Republican and Democratic senators voted to give themselves a raise. The motion had *bipartisan* support.

Quick Quiz #61

Match each word in the first column with its definition in the second column. Check your answers in the back of the book.

1.	pacify	a.	obvious
2.	painstaking	b.	model
3.	palliate	c.	supporter of a cause
4.	palpable	d.	narrow in point of view
5.	paltry	e.	contradictory truth
6.	panacea	f.	stingy
7.	paradigm	g.	calm someone down
8.	paradox	h.	cure for everything
9.	parochial	i.	insignificant
10.	parody	j.	extremely careful
11.	parsimonious	k.	satirical imitation
12.	partisan	l.	alleviate

PATENT (PAYT unt) *adj* obvious

- To say that the earth is flat is a *patent* absurdity because the world is obviously spherical.
- It was *patently* foolish of Lee to think that she could sail across the Pacific Ocean in a washtub.

PATERNAL (puh TUR nul) *adj* fatherly; fatherlike

- Rich is *paternal* toward his niece.

Maternal (muh TUR nul) means motherly or momlike.

PATHOLOGY (puh THAHL uh jee) *n* the science of diseases

Pathology is the science or study of diseases, but not necessarily in the medical sense. *Pathological* means relating to *pathology*, but it also means arising from a disease. So if we say Brad is an inveterate, incorrigible, *pathological* (path uh LAHJ uh kul) liar, we are saying that Brad's lying is a sickness.

PATRIARCH (PAY tree ahrk) *n* the male head of a family or tribe

- The *patriarch* of the Murphy family, Jacob V. Murphy, made millions selling cobra fillets and established the Murphy family's empire in the snake meat business.

The adjective is *patriarchal* (pay tree AHRK ul).

- In the *patriarchal* country of Spambulia, the ruling monarch can never be a woman, though the current king is such a numbskull that his sister runs things behind the scenes.

A female head of a family is a *matriarch*, and such a family would be described as *matriarchal*.

- Spambulia is considering becoming a *matriarchy* (MAY tree ahr kee).

PATRICIAN (puh TRISH un) *n* a person of noble birth; an aristocrat

- Mr. Perno was a *patrician* and he was never truly happy unless his place at the dinner table was set with at least half a dozen forks.

Patrician can also be an adjective. Polo is a *patrician* sport.

- The noisy crowd on the luxury ocean liner was *patrician* in dress but not in behavior; rioters were wearing tuxedos and gowns but throwing deck chairs into the ocean.

PATRONIZE (PAY truh nyze) *v* to treat as an inferior; to condescend to

- Our guide at the art gallery was extremely *patronizing,* treating us as though we wouldn't be able to distinguish a painting from a piece of sidewalk without her help.
- We felt *patronized* by the waiter at the fancy restaurant; he ignored all our efforts to attract his attention and then pretended not to understand our accents.

Patronize also means to frequent or be a regular customer of. To *patronize* a restaurant is to eat there often, not to treat it as an inferior.

PAUCITY (PAW suh tee) *n* scarcity

- There was a *paucity* of fresh vegetables at the supermarket, so we had to buy frozen ones.
- The plan was defeated by a *paucity* of support.
- There is no *paucity* of water in the ocean.

PECCADILLO (pek uh DIL oh) *n* a minor offense

- The smiling defendant acted as though first-degree murder were a mere *peccadillo* rather than a hideous crime.
- The reporters sometimes seemed more interested in the candidates' sexual *peccadillos* than in their inane programs and proposals.

PEDANTIC (puh DAN tik) *adj* boringly scholarly or academic

- The discussion quickly turned *pedantic* as each participant tried to sound more learned than all the others.

- The professor's interpretation of the poem was *pedantic* and empty of genuine feeling.

A *pedantic* person is called a *pedant* (PED unt). A *pedant* is fond of *pedantry* (PED un tree).

PEDESTRIAN (puh DES tree un) *adj* unimaginative; banal

A *pedestrian* is someone walking, but to be *pedestrian* is to be something else altogether.
- Mary Anne said the young artist's work was brilliant, but I found it to be *pedestrian;* I've seen better paintings in kindergarten classrooms.
- The menu was *pedestrian.* I had encountered each of the dishes dozens of times before.

PEJORATIVE (pi JOR uh tiv) *adj* negative; disparaging

"Hi, stupid" is a *pejorative* greeting. "Loudmouth" is a nickname with a *pejorative* connotation.
- Abe's description of the college as "a pretty good school" was unintentionally *pejorative.*

PENCHANT (PEN chunt) *n* a strong taste or liking for something; a predilection
- Dogs have a *penchant* for chasing cats and mail carriers.

PENITENT (PEN uh tunt) *adj* sorry; repentant; contrite
- Julie was *penitent* when Kanye explained how much pain she had caused him.
- The two boys tried to sound *penitent* at the police station, but they weren't really sorry that they had herded the sheep into Mr. Ingersoll's house. They were *impenitent.*

PENSIVE (PEN siv) *adj* thoughtful and sad
- Norton became suddenly *pensive* when Jack mentioned his dead father.

PEREMPTORY (puh REMP tuh ree) *adj* final; categorical; dictatorial

Someone who is *peremptory* says or does something without giving
anyone a chance to dispute it.
- Asher's father *peremptorily* banished him to his room.

Note carefully the pronunciation of this word.

PERENNIAL (puh REN ee ul) *adj* continual; happening again
and again or year after year
- Mr. Lorenzo is a *perennial* favorite of students at the high school
  because he always gives everyone an A.
- Milton was a *perennial* candidate for governor; every four years he
  printed up another batch of his campaign bumper stickers.

Flowers called *perennials* are flowers that bloom year after year
without being replanted.

Biennial (bye EN ee ul) and *centennial* (sen TEN ee ul) are related words. *Biennial* means happening once every two years (biannual means happening twice a year). *Centennial* means happening once every century.

PERFIDY (PUR fuh dee) *n* treachery

- It was the criminals' natural *perfidy* that finally did them in, as each one became an informant on the other.
- I was appalled at Al's *perfidy*. He had sworn to me that he was my best friend, but then he asked my girlfriend to the prom.

To engage in *perfidy* is to be *perfidious* (pur FID ee us).

PERFUNCTORY (pur FUNGK tuh ree) *adj* unenthusiastic; careless

- John made a couple of *perfunctory* attempts at answering the questions on the test, but then he put down his pencil, laid down his head, and slept until the end of the period.
- Sandra's lawn mowing was *perfunctory* at best: she skipped all the difficult parts and didn't rake up any of the clippings.

PERIPATETIC (per uh peh TET ik) *adj* wandering; traveling continually; itinerant

- Groupies are a *peripatetic* bunch, traveling from concert to concert to follow their favorite rock stars.

PERIPHERY (puh RIF uh ree) *n* the outside edge of something

- José never got involved in any of our activities; he was always at the *periphery*.
- The professional finger painter enjoyed her position at the *periphery* of the art world.

To be at the *periphery* is to be *peripheral* (puh RIF uh rul). A *peripheral* interest is a secondary or side interest.

Your *peripheral* vision is your ability to see to the right and left while looking straight ahead.

PERJURY (PUR jur ee) *n* lying under oath

- The defendant was acquitted of bribery but convicted of *perjury* because he had lied on the witness stand during his trial.

To commit *perjury* is to *perjure* oneself.

- The former cabinet official *perjured* herself when she said that she had not committed *perjury* during her trial for bribery.

PERMEATE (PUR mee ayt) *v* to spread or seep through; to penetrate

- A horrible smell quickly *permeated* the room after Jock lit a cigarette.
- Corruption had *permeated* the company; every single one of its executives belonged in jail.

Something that can be *permeated* is said to be *permeable*. A *permeable* raincoat is one that lets water seep through.

PERNICIOUS (pur NISH us) *adj* deadly; extremely evil

- The drug dealers conducted their *pernicious* business on every street corner in the city.
- Lung cancer is a *pernicious* disease.

PERQUISITE (PUR kwuh zit) *n* a privilege that goes along with a job; a "perk"

- Free access to a photocopier is a *perquisite* of most office jobs.
- The big corporate lawyer's *perquisites* included a chauffeured limousine, a luxurious apartment in the city, and all the chocolate ice cream she could eat.

A *perquisite* should not be confused with a *prerequisite* (pree REK wuh zit), which is a necessity.

- Health and happiness are two *prerequisites* of a good life.
- A college degree is a *prerequisite* for many high-paying jobs.

PERTINENT (PUR tuh nunt) *adj* relevant; dealing with the matter at hand

- The suspect said that he was just borrowing the jewelry for a costume ball. The cop said he did not think that was *pertinent*.

By the way, *impertinent* means disrespectful.

PERTURB (pur TURB) *v* to disturb greatly

- Ivan's mother was *perturbed* by his aberrant behavior at the dinner table. Ivan's father was not bothered. Nothing bothered Ivan, Sr. He was *imperturbable*.

PERUSE (puh ROOZ) *v* to read carefully

This word is misused more often than it is used correctly. To *peruse* something is not to skim it or read it quickly. To *peruse* something is to study it or read it with great care.

- The lawyer *perused* the contract for many hours, looking for a loophole that would enable her client to back out of the deal.

To *peruse* something is to engage in *perusal*.

- My *perusal* of the ancient texts brought me no closer to my goal of discovering the meaning of life.

Quick Quiz #63

Match each word in the first column with its definition in the second column. Check your answers in the back of the book.

1.	peremptory	a.	outside edge of something
2.	perennial	b.	unenthusiastic
3.	perfidy	c.	penetrate
4.	perfunctory	d.	lying under oath
5.	peripatetic	e.	job-related privilege
6.	periphery	f.	continual
7.	perjury	g.	disturb greatly
8.	permeate	h.	necessity
9.	pernicious	i.	read carefully
10.	perquisite	j.	treachery
11.	prerequisite	k.	final
12.	pertinent	l.	wandering
13.	perturb	m.	relevant
14.	peruse	n.	deadly

PERVADE (pur VAYD) *v* to spread throughout

- A terrible smell *pervaded* the apartment building after the sewer main exploded.
- On examination day, the classroom was *pervaded* by a sense of imminent doom.

Something that *pervades* is *pervasive*.

- There was a *pervasive* feeling of despair on Wall Street on the day the Dow-Jones industrial average fell more than 500 points.
- There was a *pervasive* odor of mold in the house, and we soon discovered why: the basement was filled with the stuff.

PETULANT (PECH uh lunt) *adj* rude; cranky; ill-tempered

- Gloria became *petulant* when we suggested that she leave her pet cheetah at home when she came to spend the weekend; she said that we had insulted her cheetah and that an insult to her cheetah was an insult to her.
- The *petulant* waiter slammed down our water glasses and spilled a tureen of soup onto Roger's kilt.

To be *petulant* is to engage in *petulance,* or rudeness.

PHILANTHROPY (fi LAN thruh pee) *n* love of humankind, especially by doing good deeds

- His gift of one billion dollars to the local orphanage was the finest act of *philanthropy* I've ever seen.

A charity is a *philanthropic* (fi lun THRAH pik) institution. An *altruist* (AHL troo ist) is someone who cares about other people. A *philanthropist* (fi LAN thruh pist) is actively doing things to help, usually by giving time or money.

PHILISTINE (FIL i steen) *n* a smugly ignorant person with no appreciation of intellectual or artistic matters

- The novelist dismissed her critics as *philistines,* saying they wouldn't recognize a good book if it crawled up and bit them on the nose. The critics, in reply, dismissed the novelist as a *philistine* who wouldn't recognize a good book if it crawled up and rolled itself into her typewriter.

Philistine can also be an adjective. To be *philistine* is to act like a *philistine.*

PIOUS (PYE us) *adj* reverent or devout; outwardly (and sometimes falsely) reverent or devout; hypocritical

This is a sometimes confusing word with meanings that are very nearly opposite each other.

Pious Presbyterians go to church every Sunday and say their prayers every night before bed. *Pious* in this sense means something like religiously dutiful.

Pious can also be used to describe behavior or feelings that aren't religious at all but are quite hypocritical.

- The adulterous minister's sermon on marital fidelity was filled with *pious* disregard for his own sins.

The state of being *pious* is *piety* (PYE uh tee). The opposite of *pious* is *impious* (IM pee us).

Note carefully the pronunciation of this word.

PIVOTAL (PIV uh tul) *adj* crucial

Pivotal is the adjective form of the verb to *pivot.* To *pivot* is to turn on a single point or shaft. A basketball player *pivots* when he or she turns while leaving one foot planted in the same place on the floor.

A *pivotal* comment is a comment that turns a discussion. It is an important comment.

A *pivotal* member of a committee is a crucial or important member of a committee.

- Sofia's contribution was *pivotal;* without it, we would have failed.

PLACATE (PLAY kayt) *v* to pacify; to appease; to soothe

- The tribe *placated* the angry volcano by tossing a few teenagers into the raging crater.
- The beleaguered general tried to *placate* his fierce attacker by sending him a pleasant flower arrangement. His *implacable* (im PLAK uh bul) enemy decided to attack anyway.

PLAINTIVE (PLAYN tiv) *adj* expressing sadness or sorrow

- The lead singer's *plaintive* love song expressed his sorrow at being abandoned by his girlfriend for the lead guitarist.
- The chilly autumn weather made the little bird's song seem *plaintive.*

You could also say that there was *plaintiveness* in that bird's song.

Don't confuse *plaintive* with *plaintiff* (PLAYN tif). A *plaintiff* is a person who takes someone to court—who makes a legal complaint.

PLATITUDE (PLAT uh tood) *n* a dull or trite remark; a cliché

- The principal thinks he is a great orator, but his loud, boring speech was full of *platitudes.*
- Instead of giving us any real insight into the situation, the lecturer threw *platitudes* at us for the entire period. It was a *platitudinous* (plat uh TOOD i nus) speech.

PLEBEIAN (pluh BEE un) *adj* common; vulgar; low-class

Plebeian is the opposite of *aristocratic.*

- Sarah refused to eat frozen dinners, saying they were too *plebeian* for her discriminating palate.

Note carefully the pronunciation of this word.

PLETHORA (PLETH ur uh) *n* an excess

- We ate a *plethora* of candy on Halloween and a *plethora* of turkey on Thanksgiving.
- Letting the air force use our backyard as a bombing range created a *plethora* of problems.

POIGNANT (POYN yunt) *adj* painfully emotional; extremely moving; sharp or astute

The words *poignant* and *pointed* are very closely related, and they share much of the same range of meaning.

A *poignant* scene is one that is so emotional or moving that it is almost painful to watch.

- All the reporters stopped taking notes as they watched the old woman's *poignant* reunion with her daughter, whom she hadn't seen in 45 years.

Poignant can also mean pointed in the sense of sharp or astute.

A *poignant* comment might be one that shows great insight.

To be *poignant* is to have *poignancy*.

Quick Quiz #64

Match each word in the first column with its definition in the second column. Check your answers in the back of the book.

1.	pervade	a.	painfully emotional
2.	petulant	b.	spread throughout
3.	philanthropy	c.	pacify
4.	philistine	d.	smugly ignorant person
5.	pious	e.	excess
6.	pivotal	f.	expressing sadness
7.	placate	g.	reverent
8.	plaintive	h.	trite remark
9.	platitude	i.	rude
10.	plebeian	j.	crucial
11.	plethora	k.	love for mankind
12.	poignant	l.	low-class

POLARIZE (POH luh ryze) *v* to break up into opposing factions or groupings

- The issue of what kind of sand to put in the sandbox *polarized* the nursery school class; some students would accept nothing but wet, while others wanted only dry.
- The increasingly acrimonious debate between the two candidates *polarized* the political party.

POLEMIC (puh LEM ik) *n* a powerful argument often made to attack or refute a controversial issue

- The book was a convincing *polemic* that revealed the fraud at the heart of the large corporation.
- Instead of the traditional Groundhog Day address, the state senator delivered a *polemic* against the sales tax.

A *polemic* is *polemical*.

PONDEROUS (PAHN dur us) *adj* so large as to be clumsy; massive; dull

- The wedding cake was a *ponderous* blob of icing and jelly beans.
- The chairman, as usual, gave a *ponderous* speech that left half her listeners snoring in their plates.

PORTENT (POR tent) *n* an omen; a sign of something coming in the future

- The distant rumbling we heard this morning was a *portent* of the thunderstorm that hit our area this afternoon.
- Stock market investors looked for *portents* in their complicated charts and graphs; they hoped that the market's past behavior would give them clues as to what would happen in the future.

Portentous (por TENT uhs) is the adjective form of *portent*, meaning ominous or filled with *portent*. But it is very often used to mean pompous, or self-consciously serious or ominous sounding. It can also mean amazing or prodigious.

A *portentous* speech is not one that you would enjoy listening to.

A *portentous* announcement might be one that tried to create an inappropriate sense of alarm in those listening to it.

Portentous can also mean amazing or astonishing. A *portentous* sunset might be a remarkably glorious one rather than an ominous or menacing one.

POSTULATE (PAHS chuh lut) *n* **something accepted as true without proof; an axiom**

A *postulate* is taken to be true because it is convenient to do so.
- We might be able to prove a *postulate* if we had the time, but not now.

A *theorem* (THEER um) is something that is proven using *postulates*.

Postulate (PAHS chuh layt) can be used as a verb, too.
- Sherlock Holmes rarely *postulated* things, waiting for evidence before he made up his mind.

PRAGMATIC (prag MAT ik) *adj* **practical; down-to-earth; based on experience rather than theory**

A *pragmatic* person is one who deals with things as they are rather than as they might be or should be.
- Erecting a gigantic dome of gold over our house would have been the ideal solution to fix the leak in our roof, but the small size of our bank account forced us to be *pragmatic;* we patched the hole with a dab of tar instead.

Pragmatism (PRAG muh tiz um) is the belief or philosophy that the value or truth of something can be measured by its practical consequences.

PRECEDENT (PRES uh dunt) *n* **an earlier example or model of something**

Precedent is a noun form of the verb to *precede,* or go before. To set a *precedent* is to do something that sets an example for what may follow.
- Last year's million-dollar prom set a *precedent* that the current student council hopes will not be followed in the future. That is, the student council hopes that future proms won't cost a million dollars.

To be *unprecedented* is to have no *precedent,* to be something entirely new.
- Urvashi's consumption of 500 hot dogs was *unprecedented;* no one had ever eaten so many hot dogs before.

PRECEPT (PREE sept) *n* **a rule to live by; a principle establishing a certain kind of action or behavior; a maxim**
- "Love thy neighbor" is a *precept* we have sometimes found difficult to follow; our neighbor is a noisy oaf who painted his house electric blue and who throws his empty beer cans into our yard.

PRECIPITATE (pri SIP uh tayt) *v* to cause to happen abruptly

- A panic among investors *precipitated* last Monday's crisis in the stock market.
- The police were afraid that arresting the angry protestors might *precipitate* a riot.

Precipitate (pri SIP uh tit) can also be an adjective, meaning unwisely hasty or rash. A *precipitate* decision is one made without enough thought beforehand.

- The school counselor, we thought, was *precipitate* when she had the tenth grader committed to a mental hospital for saying that homework was boring.

PRECIPITOUS (pri SIP uh tus) *adj* steep

Precipitous means like a precipice, or cliff. It and *precipitate* are closely related, as you probably guessed. But they don't mean the same thing, even though *precipitous* is often used loosely to mean the same thing as *precipitate.*

A mountain can be *precipitous,* meaning either that it is steep or that it comprises lots of steep cliffs.

Precipitous can also be used to signify things that are only figuratively steep. For example, you could say that someone had stumbled down a *precipitous* slope into drug addiction.

Quick Quiz #65

Match each word in the first column with its definition in the second column. Check your answers in the back of the book.

1.	polarize	a.	massive and clumsy
2.	polemic	b.	rule to live by
3.	ponderous	c.	practical
4.	portent	d.	powerful refutation
5.	portentous	e.	steep
6.	postulate	f.	cause to happen abruptly
7.	pragmatic	g.	cause opposing positions
8.	precedent	h.	ominous
9.	precept	i.	earlier example
10.	precipitate	j.	omen
11.	precipitous	k.	axiom

PRECLUDE (pri KLOOD) *v* to prevent something from ever happening
- Ann feared that her abysmal academic career might *preclude* her becoming a brain surgeon.

PRECURSOR (pri KUR sur) *n* forerunner; something that goes before and anticipates or paves the way for whatever it is that follows
- The arrival of a million-dollar check in the mail might be the *precursor* of a brand-new car.
- A sore throat is often the *precursor* of a cold.
- Hard work on the practice field might be the *precursor* of success on the playing field.

PREDILECTION (pred uh LEK shun) *n* a natural preference for something
- The impatient judge had a *predilection* for well-prepared lawyers who said what they meant and didn't waste her time.
- Joe's *predilection* for saturated fats has added roughly a foot to his waistline in the past twenty years.

PREEMINENT (pree EM uh nunt) *adj* better than anyone else; outstanding; supreme
- The nation's *preeminent* harpsichordist would be the best harpsichordist in the nation.
- The Nobel Prize-winning physicist was *preeminent* in his field but he was still a lousy teacher.

See our listing for *eminent.*

PREEMPT (pree EMPT) *v* to seize something by prior right

When television show A *preempts* television show B, television show A is shown at the time usually reserved for television show B. The word *preempt* implies that television show A is more important than television show B and thus has a greater right to the time slot.

A *preemptive* action is one that is undertaken in order to prevent some other action from being undertaken.
- When the air force launched a *preemptive* strike against the missile base, the air force was attacking the missiles in order to prevent the missiles from attacking the air force.

PREMISE (PREM is) *n* an assumption; the basis for a conclusion
- In deciding to eat all the ice cream in the freezer, my *premise* was that if I didn't do it, you would.

- Based on the *premise* that two wrongs don't make a right, I forgave him for insulting me rather than calling him a nasty name.

PREPOSSESS (pree puh ZES) *v* to preoccupy; to influence beforehand or prejudice; to make a good impression on beforehand

This word has several common meanings. Be careful.

When a person is *prepossessed* by an idea, he or she can't get it out of his or her mind.

- My dream of producing energy from old chewing-gum wrappers *prepossessed* me, and I lost my job, my home, my wife, and my children.
- Experience had *prepossessed* Larry's mother not to believe him when he said that someone else had broken the window. Larry had broken it every other time, so she assumed that he had broken it this time.
- The new girl in the class was extremely *prepossessing*. The minute she walked into the room, her classmates rushed over to introduce themselves.

Unprepossessing means unimpressive, but the word is only mildly negative.

- The quaint farmhouse had an *unprepossessing* exterior, but a beautiful interior. Who would have imagined?

PREROGATIVE (pri RAHG uh tiv) *n* a right or privilege connected exclusively with a position, a person, a class, a nation, or some other group or classification

- Giving traffic tickets to people he didn't like was one of the *prerogatives* of Junior's job as a policeman.
- Sentencing people to death is a *prerogative* of many kings and queens.
- Big mansions and fancy cars are among the *prerogatives* of wealth.

PREVAIL (pri VAYL) *v* to triumph; to overcome rivals; (with *on*, *upon*, or *with*) to persuade

When justice *prevails,* it means that good defeats evil.

- The prosecutor *prevailed* in the murder trial; the defendant was found guilty.
- My mother *prevailed* on me to make my bed. She told me she would punish me if I didn't, so I did.

The adjective *prevailing* means most frequent or predominant. The *prevailing* opinion on a topic is the one that most people hold. If the *prevailing* winds are out of the north, then the wind is out of the north most of the time. A *prevailing* theory is the one most widely held at the time. It is *prevalent* (PREV uh lunt).

PRISTINE (PRIS teen) *adj* original; unspoiled; pure

An antique in *pristine* condition is one that hasn't been tampered with over the years. It's still in its original condition.

A *pristine* mountain stream is a stream that hasn't been polluted.

PRODIGAL (PRAHD uh gul) *adj* wastefully extravagant

- The chef was *prodigal* with her employer's money, spending thousands of dollars on ingredients for what was supposed to be a simple meal.
- The young artist was *prodigal* with his talents: he wasted time and energy on greeting cards that might have been devoted to serious paintings.
- The *prodigal* gambler soon found that she couldn't afford even a two-dollar bet.

To be *prodigal* is to be characterized by *prodigality*.

Quick Quiz #66

Match each word in the first column with its definition in the second column. Check your answers in the back of the book.

1.	preclude	a.	outstanding
2.	precursor	b.	triumph
3.	predilection	c.	seize by prior right
4.	preeminent	d.	wastefully extravagant
5.	preempt	e.	unspoiled
6.	premise	f.	natural preference
7.	prepossess	g.	preoccupy
8.	prerogative	h.	right or privilege
9.	prevail	i.	assumption
10.	pristine	j.	forerunner
11.	prodigal	k.	prevent

PRODIGIOUS (pruh DIJ us) *adj* extraordinary; enormous

- To fill the Grand Canyon with ping-pong balls would be a *prodigious* undertaking; it would be both extraordinary and enormous.

- The little boy caught a *prodigious* fish—it was ten times his size and might more easily have caught him had their situations been reversed.

See also *prodigy*.

PRODIGY (PRAHD uh jee) *n* an extremely talented child; an extraordinary accomplishment or occurrence

- The three-year-old *prodigy* could play all of Beethoven and most of Brahms on her harmonica.
- Barry was a mathematical *prodigy*; he had calculated *pi* to 100 decimal places almost before he could walk.
- Josephine's tower of dominoes and Popsicle sticks was a *prodigy* of engineering.

PROFANE (proh FAYN) *adj* not having to do with religion; irreverent; blasphemous

Profane is the opposite of sacred. Worshiping the almighty dollar is *profane*. *Profane* can also mean disrespectful of religion. Cursing in class would be *profane*.

Sticking out your tongue in church would be a *profane* gesture.

Profane can also be a verb.

- You *profaned* the classroom by cursing in it.
- Nick *profaned* his priceless Egyptian statue by using it as a doorstop.

The noun form of *profane* is *profanity* (proh FAN uh tee).

Spray painting the hallways at school would be an act of *profanity*.

PROFESS (pruh FES) *v* to declare; to declare falsely or pretend

- Jason *professed* to have taught himself calculus.
- No one in our town was fooled by the candidate's *professed* love for llama farmers; everyone knew she was just trying to win votes from the pro-llama faction.

PROFICIENT (pruh FISH unt) *adj* thoroughly competent; skillful; good (at something)

- Lillian was a *proficient* cabinetmaker. She could make a cabinet that would make you sit back and say, "Now, there's a cabinet."
- I fiddled around at the piano for many years but never became *proficient* at playing.
- Lucy was merely competent, but Molly was *proficient* at plucking canaries.

Proficiency is the state of being *proficient*.

PROFLIGATE (PRAHF luh git) *adj* extravagantly wasteful and, usually, wildly immoral

- The fraternity members were a *profligate* bunch; they held all-night parties on weeknights and nearly burned down their fraternity house with their shenanigans every weekend.
- The young heir was *profligate* with her fortune, spending millions on champagne and racehorses.

PROFOUND (pruh FOUND) *adj* deep (in several senses)

Profound understanding is deep understanding.

To say something *profound* is to say something deeply intelligent or discerning.

Profound respect is deep respect. *Profound* horror is deep horror.

The noun form of *profound* is *profundity* (pruh FUN duh tee).

PROFUSE (pruh FYOOS) *adj* flowing; extravagant

- When we gave Marian our house, our car, and all our clothes, her gratitude was *profuse.*
- My teacher said I had done a good job, but his praise was far from *profuse.* I got the feeling he hadn't really liked my epic poem about two dinosaurs who fall in love just before they become extinct.
- The grieving widow's tears were *profuse.* She had tears in *profusion.*

PROLETARIAT (proh luh TER ee ut) *n* the industrial working class

The *proletariat* is the laboring class—blue-collar workers or people who roll up their shirtsleeves to do an honest day's work.

PROLIFERATE (proh LIF uh rayt) *v* to spread or grow rapidly

- Honey bees *proliferated* when we filled our yard with flowering plants.
- Coughs and colds *proliferate* when groups of children are cooped up together during the winter.
- The police didn't know what to make of the *proliferation* of counterfeit money in the north end of town.

PROLIFIC (proh LIF ik) *adj* abundantly productive; fruitful or fertile

A *prolific* writer is a writer who writes a lot of books. A *prolific* artist is an artist who paints a lot of pictures.

- The old man had been extraordinarily *prolific;* he had thirty children and more than one hundred grandchildren.

Quick Quiz #67

Match each word in the first column with its definition in the second column. Check your answers in the back of the book.

1.	prodigious	a.	declare
2.	prodigy	b.	irreverent
3.	profane	c.	abundantly productive
4.	profess	d.	flowing
5.	proficient	e.	extremely talented child
6.	profligate	f.	extraordinary
7.	profound	g.	spread rapidly
8.	profuse	h.	deep
9.	proletariat	i.	thoroughly competent
10.	proliferate	j.	extravagantly wasteful
11.	prolific	k.	industrial working class

PROMULGATE (PRAHM ul gayt) *v* **to proclaim; to publicly or formally declare something**

- The principal *promulgated* a new dress code over the loudspeaker system: red, green, yellow, and blue were the only permissible artificial hair colors.

PROPENSITY (pruh PEN suh tee) *n* **a natural inclination or tendency; a predilection**

- Jessie has a *propensity* for saying stupid things: every time she opens her mouth, something stupid comes out.
- Edwin's *propensity* to sit around all day doing nothing came into conflict with his mother's *propensity* to kick him out of the house.

PROPITIOUS (pruh PISH us) *adj* **marked by favorable signs or conditions**

- Rush hour is not a *propitious* time to drive into the city.
- The early negotiations between the union and the company had been so *propitious* that no one was surprised when a new contract was announced well before the strike deadline.

PROPONENT (pruh POH nunt) *n* an advocate; a supporter of a position

Proponent and *opponent* are antonyms.

- The *proponents* of a tax increase will probably not be re-elected next fall.

PROPRIETARY (pruh PRYE uh ter ee) *adj* characteristic of an owner of property; constituting property

To take a *proprietary* interest in something is to act as though you own it.

- George felt *proprietary* about the chocolate cookie recipe; he had invented it himself.
- The company's design for musical toilet paper is *proprietary*. The company owns it, and outsiders are not allowed to examine it.

A *proprietor* (pruh PRYE uh tur) is an owner.

PROPRIETY (pruh PRYE uh tee) *n* properness; good manners

- The old lady viewed the little girl's failure to curtsy as a flagrant breach of *propriety.* She did not approve of or countenance such *improprieties.*
- *Propriety* prevented the young man from trashing the town in celebration of his unexpected acceptance by the college of his choice.

Propriety derives from *proper,* not *property,* and should not be confused with *proprietary.*

PROSAIC (proh ZAY ik) *adj* dull; unimaginative; like prose (as opposed to poetry)

- Her description of the battle was so *prosaic* that it was hard for her listeners to believe that any of the soldiers had even been wounded, much less blown to smithereens.
- The little boy's ambitions were all *prosaic:* he wanted to be an accountant, an auditor, or a claims adjuster.

PROSCRIBE (proh SKRYBE) *v* to outlaw; to prohibit

- Spitting on the sidewalk and shooting at road signs were both *proscribed* activities under the new administration.
- The young doctor *proscribed* smoking in the waiting room of his office.

The act of *proscribing* is *proscription;* an individual act of *proscribing* is also a *proscription.*

PROSELYTIZE (PRAHS uh luh tyze) *v* to convert (someone) from one religion or doctrine to another; to recruit converts to a religion or doctrine

- The former Methodist had been *proselytized* by a Lutheran deacon.
- The airport terminal was filled with *proselytizers* from a dozen different sects, cults, and religions. They were attempting to *proselytize* the passengers walking through the terminal.

PROTAGONIST (proh TAG uh nist) *n* the leading character in a novel, play, or other work; a leader or champion

- Martin Luther King Jr. was a *protagonist* in the long and continuing struggle for racial equality.
- The *protagonist* of the movie was an eleven-year-old boy who saved his hometown from destruction by eating all the doughnuts that the mad scientist had been using to fuel his nuclear reactor.
- The mad scientist was the boy's chief *antagonist*. An *antagonist* is an opponent or adversary.

PROTRACT (proh TRAKT) *v* to prolong

- The trial was so *protracted* that one of the jurors died of old age.
- The commencement speaker promised not to *protract* her remarks, but then she spoke for two solid hours. It was a *protracted* speech.

PROVIDENT (PRAHV uh dunt) *adj* preparing for the future; providing for the future; frugal

- We were *provident* with our limited food supplies, knowing that the winter ahead would be long and cold.
- The *provident* father had long ago set aside money for the college education of each of his children.

To be *improvident* is to fail to provide for the future.

- It was *improvident* of the grasshopper not to store any food for the winter, unlike his acquaintance the *provident* ant.

Quick Quiz #68

Match each word in the first column with its definition in the second column. Check your answers in the back of the book.

1.	promulgate	a.	natural inclination
2.	propensity	b.	good manners
3.	propitious	c.	advocate
4.	proponent	d.	prohibit
5.	proprietary	e.	prolong
6.	propriety	f.	leading character
7.	prosaic	g.	constituting property
8.	proscribe	h.	frugal
9.	proselytize	i.	dull
10.	protagonist	j.	marked by favorable signs
11.	protract	k.	convert
12.	provident	l.	proclaim

PROVINCIAL (pruh VIN shul) *adj* limited in outlook to one's own small corner of the world; narrow

- The farmers were *provincial;* they had no opinions about anything but the price of corn and no interest in anything except growing more of it.
- New Yorkers have reputations for being sophisticated and cosmopolitan, but most of them are actually *provincial;* they act as though nothing of interest had ever happened west of the Hudson River.

PROVISIONAL (pruh VIZH uh nul) *adj* conditional; temporary; tentative

- Louis had been accepted as a *provisional* member of the club. He wouldn't become a permanent member until the other members had had a chance to see what he was really like.
- The old woman's offer to donate $10,000 to the charity was *provisional;* she said that she would give the money only if the charity could manage to raise a matching sum.

PROXIMITY (prok SIM uh tee) *n* nearness

- I can't stand being in the *proximity* of a kid's birthday party. There is just too much noise.
- In a big city, one is almost always in the *proximity* of a restaurant.

PRUDENT (PROOD unt) *adj* careful; having foresight

- Joe is a *prudent* money manager. He doesn't invest heavily in racehorses, and he puts only a small part of his savings in the office football pool. Joe is the epitome of *prudence*.

The opposite of *prudent* is *imprudent*.

- It was *imprudent* of us to pour gasoline all over the floor of our living room and then light a fire in the fireplace.

PURPORTED (pur PORT id) *adj* rumored; claimed

- The heiress is *purported* to have been kidnapped by adventurers and buried in a concrete vault beneath the busiest intersection in Times Square. No one believes this story except the psychic who was consulted by the police.

To *purport* something is to claim or allege it.

PUTATIVE (PYOO tuh tiv) *adj* commonly accepted; supposed; reputed

- The *putative* reason for placing the monument downtown is that nobody had wanted it uptown.

When you use the word *putative,* you emphasize that the reason is only supposed, not proven.

Quick Quiz #69

Match each word in the first column with its definition in the second column. Check your answers in the back of the book.

1.	provincial	a.	commonly accepted
2.	provisional	b.	nearness
3.	proximity	c.	narrow in outlook
4.	prudent	d.	rumored
5.	purported	e.	careful
6.	putative	f.	conditional

Q

QUALIFY (KWAHL uh fye) *v* to modify or restrict

You already know the primary meaning of *qualify.* Here's another meaning.

- Susan *qualified* her praise of Judith by saying that her kind words applied only to Judith's skillful cooking and not to her abhorrent personality. Judith was upset by Susan's *qualification.*
- The library trustees rated their fund-raiser a *qualified* success: many more people than expected had come, but virtually no money had been raised.

An *unqualified* success is a complete, unrestricted success.

QUALITATIVE (KWAHL uh tay tiv) *adj* having to do with the quality or qualities of something (as opposed to the quantity)

If a school achieves a *qualitative* improvement in enrollment, it means the school is being attended by better students. If the school achieves a *quantitative* (KWAHN i tay tiv) improvement, it means the school is being attended by more students.

- The difference between the two restaurants was *quantitative* rather than *qualitative.* Both served the same dreadful food, but the second restaurant served more of it.

QUERULOUS (KWER uh lus) *adj* complaining; grumbling; whining

Although a *query* is a question, *querulous* does not mean questioning.

- The exasperated mother finally managed to hush her *querulous* child.
- The *querulous* voices of the students, who believed that their quizzes had been graded too harshly, could be heard all the way at the other end of the school building.

QUIXOTIC (kwik SAHT ik) *adj* romantic or idealistic to a foolish or impractical degree

The word *quixotic* is derived from the name of Don Quixote, the protagonist of Miguel de Cervantes's classic 17th-century novel. Don Quixote had read so many romances about the golden age of chivalry that he set out to become a knight himself and have chivalrous adventures. Instead, his romantic idealism almost invariably got him into trouble. To be *quixotic* is to be as foolish or impractical as Don Quixote in pursuing an ideal.

- For many years Mr. Morris had led a *quixotic* effort to repeal the federal income tax.
- The political organization had once been a powerful force in Washington. However, its membership had dwindled, and its causes had become increasingly *quixotic*.

Quick Quiz #70

Match each word in the first column with its definition in the second column. Check your answers in the back of the book.

1.	qualify	a.	having to do with quantity
2.	qualitative	b.	foolishly romantic
3.	quantitative	c.	complaining
4.	querulous	d.	modify or restrict
5.	quixotic	e.	having to do with quality

R

RAMIFICATION (ram uh fuh KAY shun) *n* a consequence; a branching out

A tree could be said to *ramify* (RAM i fye), or branch out, as it grows. A *ramification* is a consequence that grows out of something in the same way that a tree branch grows out of a tree trunk.
- The professor found a solution to the problem, but there are many *ramifications.* Some experts are afraid that she has created more problems than she has solved.

RANCOR (RANG kur) *n* bitter, long-lasting ill will or resentment
- The mutual *rancor* felt by the two nations eventually led to war.
- Jeremy's success produced such feelings of *rancor* in Jessica, his rival, that she was never able to tolerate being in the same room with him again.

To feel *rancor* is to be *rancorous*.
- The *rancorous* public exchanges between the two competing boxers are strictly for show; outside the ring, they are the best of friends.

RAPACIOUS (ruh PAY shus) *adj* greedy; plundering; avaricious
- Wall Street investment bankers are often accused of being *rapacious,* but they claim they are performing a valuable economic function.

The noun form is *rapacity* (ruh PAS uh tee).

REBUKE (ri BYOOK) *v* to criticize sharply

- We trembled as Mr. Solomon *rebuked* us for flipping over his car and taking off the tires.

A piece of sharp criticism is called a *rebuke*.

- When the students got caught cheating on their French test, the principal delivered a *rebuke* that made their ears twirl.

REBUT (ri BUT) *v* to contradict; to argue in opposition to; to prove to be false

- They all thought I was crazy, but none of them could *rebut* my argument.
- The defense attorney attempted to *rebut* the prosecutor's claim that the defendant's fingerprints, hair, clothing, signature, wallet, wristwatch, credit cards, and car had been found at the scene of the crime.

An act or instance of *rebutting* is called a *rebuttal* (ri BUT ul). *Rebut* and *refute* are synonyms.

RECALCITRANT (ri KAL suh trunt) *adj* stubbornly defiant of authority or control; disobedient

- The *recalcitrant* cancer continued to spread through the patient's body despite every therapy and treatment the doctors tried.
- The country was in turmoil, but the *recalcitrant* dictator refused even to listen to the pleas of the international representatives.

RECANT (ri KANT) *v* to publicly take back and deny (something previously said or believed); to openly confess error

- The chagrined scientist *recanted* his theory that mice originated on the moon; it turned out that he had simply mixed up the results of two separate experiments.
- The secret police tortured the intellectual for a week, by tickling her feet with a feather duster, until she finally *recanted*.

An act of *recanting* is called a *recantation*.

RECIPROCAL (ri SIP ruh kul) *adj* mutual; shared; interchangeable

- The Rochester Club had a *reciprocal* arrangement with the Duluth Club. Members of either club had full privileges of membership at the other.
- Their hatred was *reciprocal;* they hated each other.

To *reciprocate* (ri SIP ro kayt) is to return in kind, to interchange, or to repay.

- Our new neighbors had us over for dinner several times, but we were unable to *reciprocate* immediately because our dining room was being remodeled.

Reciprocity (res uh PRAHS uh tee) is a *reciprocal* relation between two parties, often whereby both parties gain.

RECLUSIVE (ri KLOOS iv) *adj* hermitlike; withdrawn from society

- The crazy millionaire led a *reclusive* existence, shutting herself up in her labyrinthine mansion and never setting foot in the outside world.
- Our new neighbors were so *reclusive* that we didn't even meet them until a full year after they had moved in.

A *reclusive* person is a *recluse* (REK loos).

- After his wife's death, the grieving old man turned into a *recluse* and seldom ventured out of his house.
- Emily Dickinson, one of America's most creative poets, became a *recluse* after her father's death in 1874—she kept in contact with friends and family through cards and letters.

RECONDITE (REK un dyte) *adj* hard to understand; over one's head

- The philosopher's thesis was so *recondite* that I couldn't get past the first two sentences.
- Every now and then the professor would lift his head from his desk and deliver some *recondite* pronouncement that left us scratching our heads and trying to figure out what he meant.
- The scholarly journal was so *recondite* as to be utterly incomprehensible.

Note carefully the pronunciation of this word.

Quick Quiz #71

Match each word in the first column with its definition in the second column. Check your answers in the back of the book.

1.	ramification	a.	hard to understand
2.	rancor	b.	criticize sharply
3.	rapacious	c.	consequence
4.	rebuke	d.	mutual
5.	rebut	e.	hermitlike
6.	recalcitrant	f.	bitter resentment
7.	recant	g.	stubbornly defiant
8.	reciprocal	h.	publicly deny
9.	reclusive	i.	contradict
10.	recondite	j.	greedy

RECRIMINATION (ri krim uh NAY shun) *n* a bitter counteraccusation, or the act of making a bitter counteraccusation

- Melissa was full of *recrimination*. When I accused her of stealing my pen, she angrily accused me of being careless, evil, and stupid.

The word is often used in the plural.

- The courtroom echoed with the *recriminations* of the convicted defendant as he was taken off to the penitentiary.

To make a *recrimination* is to *recriminate*. The adjective is *recriminatory* (ruh KRIM uh nuh tor ee).

REDOLENT (RED uh lunt) *adj* fragrant

- The air in autumn is *redolent* of wood smoke and fallen leaves.
- The flower arrangements on the tables were both beautiful and *redolent*.

Something that is *redolent* has *redolence*.

Redolent also means suggestive.

- The new play was *redolent* of one I had seen many years ago.

REDUNDANT (ri DUN dunt) *adj* unnecessarily repetitive; excessive; excessively wordy

- Erica had already bought paper plates, so our purchase of paper plates was *redundant*.
- Shawn's article was *redundant*—he kept saying the same thing over and over again.

An act of being *redundant* is a *redundancy*. The title "Department of *Redundancy* Department" is *redundant.*

REFUTE (ri FYOOT) *v* to prove to be false; to disprove

- His expensive suit and imported shoes clearly *refuted* his claim that he was poor.
- I *refuted* Billy's mathematical proof by showing him that it depended on two and two adding up to five.

An act of *refuting* is called a *refutation.*

- The audience enjoyed the panelist's humorous *refutation* of the main speaker's theory about the possibility of building an antigravity airplane.

Something that is indubitable, something that cannot be disproven, is *irrefutable.*

- Claudia's experiments with jelly beans and pencil erasers offered *irrefutable* proof that jelly beans taste better than pencil erasers.

REITERATE (ree IT uh rayt) *v* to say again; to repeat

- The candidate had *reiterated* his position so many times on the campaign trail that he sometimes even muttered it in his sleep.
- To *reiterate,* let me say once again that I am happy to have been invited to the birthday celebration of your adorable Pekingese.

An act of *reiterating* is called a *reiteration.*

RELEGATE (REL uh gayt) *v* to banish; to send away

- The most junior of the junior executives was *relegated* to a tiny, windowless office that had once been a broom closet.
- The new dad's large collection of jazz records was *relegated* to the cellar to make room for the new baby's larger collection of stuffed animals. The father objected to the *relegation* of his record collection to the cellar, but his objection did no good.

RELENTLESS (ri LENT lis) *adj* continuous; unstoppable

To *relent* is to stop or give up. *Relentless,* or *unrelenting,* means not stopping.

- The insatiable rabbit was *relentless;* it ate and ate until nothing was left in the botanical garden.
- The torrential rains were *relentless,* eventually creating a deluge.

RELINQUISH (ri LING kwish) *v* to release or let go of; to surrender; to stop doing

- The hungry dog refused to *relinquish* the enormous beef bone that he had stolen from the butcher's shop.

- The retiring president *relinquished* control of the company only with the greatest reluctance.
- Sandra was eighty-five years old before she finally *relinquished* her view of herself as a glamorous teenaged beauty.

REMONSTRATE (ri MAHN strayt) *v* to argue against; to protest; to raise objections
- My boss *remonstrated* with me for telling all the secretaries they could take off the rest of the week.
- The manager *remonstrated,* but the umpire continued to insist that the base runner had been out at third. When the manager continued to *remonstrate,* the umpire threw her out of the game.

An act of *remonstrating* is a *remonstration.*

RENAISSANCE (REN uh sahns) *n* a rebirth or revival

The *Renaissance* was a great blossoming of art, literature, science, and culture in general that transformed Europe between the 14th and 17th centuries. The word is also used in connection with lesser rebirths.
- The declining neighborhood underwent a *renaissance* when a group of investors bought several crumbling tenements and turned them into attractive apartment buildings.
- The small college's football team had endured many losing seasons but underwent a dramatic *renaissance* when the new coach recruited half a dozen 400-pound freshmen.

Renaissance can also be spelled *renascence* (ri NAY suns).

RENOUNCE (ri NOWNSE) *v* to give up formally or resign; to disown; to have nothing to do with anymore
- Despite the pleadings and protestations of her parents, Deborah refused to *renounce* her love for the leader of the motorcycle gang.
- The presidential candidate *renounced* his manager after it was revealed that the zealous manager had tried to murder the candidate's opponent in the primary.

To *renounce* is to make a *renunciation* (ri nun see AY shun).

REPARATION (rep uh RAY shun) *n* **paying back; making amends; compensation**

To make a *reparation* is to *repair* some damage that has occurred.

This word is often used in the plural.

- The defeated country demanded *reparations* for the destruction it had suffered at the hands of the victorious army.
- After the accident we sought *reparation* in court. Unfortunately, our lawyer was not competent, so we didn't win a cent.

Something that cannot be *repaired* is *irreparable* (i REP uh ruh bul).

Note carefully the pronunciation of these words.

REPERCUSSION (ree pur KUSH un) *n* **a consequence; an indirect effect**

- One *repercussion* of the new tax law was that accountants found themselves with a lot of new business.
- The declaration of war had many *repercussions,* including a big increase in production at the bomb factory.

REPLENISH (ri PLEN ish) *v* **to fill again; to resupply; to restore**

- The manager of the hardware store needed to *replenish* his stock; quite a few of the shelves were empty.

- The commanding general *replenished* his army with a trainload of food and other supplies.
- After the big Thanksgiving meal, everyone felt *replenished*.

An act of *replenishing* is a *replenishment*.

- The *replenishment* of our firewood supply was our first thought after the big snowstorm.

REPLETE (ri PLEET) *adj* completely filled; abounding

- The once-polluted stream was now *replete* with fish of every description.
- The bride wore a magnificent sombrero *replete* with fuzzy dice and campaign buttons.
- Tim ate all nine courses at the wedding banquet. He was filled to the point of *repletion*.

REPREHENSIBLE (rep ri HEN suh bul) *adj* worthy of severe blame or censure

- He put the cat in the laundry chute, tied the dog to the chimney, and committed several other *reprehensible* acts.
- Malcolm's manners were *reprehensible:* he ate his soup by drinking it from his empty wineglass and flipped his peas into his mouth with the back of his salad fork.

REPRISAL (ri PRYE zul) *n* a military action undertaken in revenge for another; an act of taking "an eye for an eye"

- The raid on the Iranian oil-drilling platform was a *reprisal* for the Iranians' earlier attack on the American tanker.
- Fearing *reprisals,* the CIA beefed up its security after capturing the insurgent leader.

REPROACH (ri PROHCH) *v* to scold, usually in disappointment; to blame; to disgrace

- The police officer *reproached* me for leaving my car parked overnight in a no-standing zone.

Reproach can also be a noun. To look at someone with *reproach* is to look at that person critically or accusingly. To be filled with *self-reproach* can mean to be ashamed.

Impeccable behavior that's beyond fault is *irreproachable* (ir ri PROHCH uh bul).

- Even though Jerome did hit Mabel on the head, his motive was *irreproachable:* he had merely been trying to kill a fly perched on her hairnet.

REPROVE (ri PROOV) *v* to criticize mildly

- Aunt May *reproved* us for eating too much, but we could tell she was actually thrilled that we had enjoyed the meal.
- My friend *reproved* me for leaving my dirty dish in the sink.

An act of *reproving* is called a *reproof.*

- The judge's decision was less a sentence than a gentle *reproof;* she put Jerry on probation and told him never to get in trouble again.

REPUDIATE (ri PYOO dee ayt) *v* to reject; to renounce; to disown; to have nothing to do with

- Hoping to receive a lighter sentence, the convicted gangster *repudiated* his former connection with the mob.

REQUISITE (REK wuh zit) *adj* required; necessary

- Howard bought a hunting rifle and the *requisite* ammunition.
- As the *requisite* number of members was not in attendance, the chairperson adjourned the meeting just after it had begun.

Requisite can also be a noun, meaning a requirement or a necessity. A hammer and a saw are among the *requisites* of the carpenter's trade.

A *prerequisite* is something required before you can get started. A high school diploma is usually a *prerequisite* to entering college.

RESOLUTE (REZ uh loot) *adj* determined; firm; unwavering

- Uncle Ted was *resolute* in his decision not to have a good time at our Christmas party; he stood alone in the corner and muttered to himself all night long.
- The other team was strong, but our players were *resolute.* They kept pushing and shoving until, in the final moments, they won the roller-derby tournament.

Someone who sticks to his New Year's *resolution* is *resolute. Resolute* and *resolved* are synonyms.

To be *irresolute* is to be wavering or indecisive.

- Our *irresolute* leader led us first one way and then the other way in the process of getting us thoroughly and completely lost.

Quick Quiz #73

Match each word in the first column with its definition in the second column. Check your answers in the back of the book.

1.	reparation	a.	act of revenge
2.	repercussion	b.	determined
3.	replenish	c.	worthy of blame
4.	replete	d.	consequence
5.	reprehensible	e.	scold
6.	reprisal	f.	completely filled
7.	reproach	g.	paying back
8.	reprove	h.	necessary
9.	repudiate	i.	criticize mildly
10.	requisite	j.	fill again
11.	resolute	k.	reject

RESPITE (RES pit) *n* a period of rest or relief
- We worked without *respite* from five in the morning until five in the afternoon.
- The new mother fell asleep when her baby stopped crying. However, the *respite* was brief; the baby started up again almost immediately.

Note carefully the pronunciation of this word.

RETICENT (RET uh sint) *adj* quiet; restrained; reluctant to speak, especially about oneself
- Luther's natural *reticence* made him an ideal speaker: his speeches never lasted more than a few minutes.
- Kaynard was *reticent* on the subject of his accomplishments; he didn't like to talk about himself.

To be *reticent* is to be characterized by *reticence.*

REVERE (ri VEER) *v* to respect highly; to honor
- Einstein was a preeminent scientist who was *revered* by everyone, even his rivals. Einstein enjoyed nearly universal *reverence* (REV uh rins).

To be *irreverent* is to be mildly disrespectful.
- Peter made jokes about his younger sister's painting. She was perturbed at his *irreverence* and began to cry.

RHETORIC (RET ur ik) *n* the art of formal speaking or writing; inflated discourse

A talented public speaker might be said to be skilled in *rhetoric.*

The word is often used in a pejorative sense to describe speaking or writing that is skillfully executed but insincere or devoid of meaning.

A political candidate's speech that was long on drama and promises but short on genuine substance might be dismissed as "mere *rhetoric.*"

To use *rhetoric* is to be *rhetorical* (ruh TOR ik uhl). A *rhetorical* question is one the speaker intends to answer himself or herself—that is, a question asked only for *rhetorical* effect.

RIGOROUS (RIG ur us) *adj* strict; harsh; severe

To be *rigorous* is to act with *rigor.*
- Our exercise program was *rigorous* but effective; after just a few months, our eighteen minutes of daily exercise had begun to pay off.
- The professor was popular largely because he wasn't *rigorous;* there were no tests in his course and only one paper, which was optional.

ROBUST (roh BUST) *adj* strong and healthy; vigorous
- The ninety-year-old woman was still *robust.* Every morning she ran several miles down to the ocean and jumped in.
- The tree we planted last year isn't looking *robust.* Most of the leaves have fallen off, and the bark has begun to peel.

ROGUE (rohg) *n* a criminally dishonest person; a scoundrel

A *rogue* is someone who can't be trusted. This word is often used, however, to characterize a playfully mischievous person.
- Huckleberry Finn is a bit of a *rogue;* while his actions are technically criminal, he performs them with noble intentions and a humorous spirit.

RUDIMENTARY (roo duh MEN tuh ree) *adj* basic; crude; unformed or undeveloped
- The boy who had lived with wolves for fifteen years lacked even the most *rudimentary* social skills.
- The strange creature had small bumps on its torso that appeared to be *rudimentary* limbs.

RUMINATE (ROO muh nayt) *v* to contemplate; to ponder; to mull over

Ruminate comes from a Latin word meaning to chew cud.

Cows, sheep, and other cud-chewing animals are called *ruminants*. To *ruminate* is to quietly chew on or ponder your own thoughts.
- The teacher's comment about the causes of weather set me to *ruminating* about what a nice day it was and to wishing that I were outside.

An act of *ruminating* is called a *rumination*.
- Serge was a private man; he kept his *ruminations* to himself.

RUSTIC (RUS tik) *adj* rural; lacking urban comforts or sophistication; primitive
- Life in the log cabin was too *rustic* for Leah; she missed hot showers, electricity, and ice.

Rustic can be used as a noun. A *rustic* is an unsophisticated person from the country.
- We enjoyed the *rustic* scenery as we traveled through the countryside.

To *rusticate* is to spend time in the country.

Quick Quiz #74

Match each word in the first column with its definition in the second column. Check your answers in the back of the book.

1.	respite	a.	basic
2.	reticent	b.	contemplate
3.	revere	c.	vigorous
4.	rhetoric	d.	formal writing or speaking
5.	rigorous	e.	restrained
6.	robust	f.	rural
7.	rogue	g.	period of rest
8.	rudimentary	h.	strict
9.	ruminate	i.	honor
10.	rustic	j.	scoundrel

S

SACCHARINE (SAK uh rin) *adj* sweet; excessively or disgustingly sweet

Saccharin is a calorie-free sweetener; *saccharine* means sweet. Except for the spelling, this is one of the easiest-to-remember words out there.

Saccharine can be applied to things that are literally sweet, such as sugar, *saccharin,* fruit, and so on. It can also be applied to things that are sweet in a figurative sense, such as children, personalities, and sentiments—especially things that are *too* sweet, or sweet in a sickening way.

- We wanted to find a nice card for Uncle Mo, but the cards in the display at the drugstore all had such *saccharine* messages that we would have been too embarrassed to send any of them.
- The love story was so *saccharine* that I vowed never to see another sappy, predictable movie again.

SACRILEGE (SAK ruh lij) *n* a violation of something sacred; blasphemy

- The minister committed the *sacrilege* of delivering his sermon while wearing his golf shoes; he didn't want to be late for his tee-off time, which was just a few minutes after the scheduled end of the service.
- The members of the fundamentalist sect believed that dancing, going to movies, and watching television were *sacrileges.*

To commit a *sacrilege* is to be *sacrilegious.*

Be careful with the spelling of these words.

SACROSANCT (SAK roh sangkt) *adj* sacred; held to be inviolable

A church or temple is *sacrosanct.* So, for Christians, is belief in the divinity of Jesus. *Sacrosanct* is also used loosely, and often ironically, outside of religion.

- Mr. Peters's lunchtime trip to his neighborhood bar was *sacrosanct;* he would no sooner skip it than he would skip his mother's funeral.

SAGACIOUS (suh GAY shus) *adj* discerning; shrewd; keen in judgment; wise

- Edgar's decision to move the chickens into the barn turned out to be *sagacious;* about an hour later, the hailstorm hit.
- The announcer's *sagacious* commentary made the baseball game seem vastly more profound than we had expected it to be.

To be *sagacious* is to have *sagacity* (suh GAS uh tee). A similar word is *sage,* which means wise or possessing wisdom derived from experience or learning.

- When we were contemplating starting our own popcorn business, we received some *sage* advice from a man who had lost all his money selling candied apples.
- The professor's critique, which comprised a few *sage* comments, sent me back to my room feeling pretty stupid.

Sage can also be a noun. A wise person, especially a wise old person, is often called a *sage.*

SALIENT (SAYL yunt) *adj* sticking out; conspicuous; leaping

A *salient* characteristic is one that leaps right out at you.

- Ursula had a number of *salient* features including, primarily, her nose, which stuck out so far that she was constantly in danger of slamming it in doors and windows.

Note carefully the pronunciation of this word.

SALUTARY (SAL yuh ter ee) *adj* healthful; remedial; curative

- Lowered blood pressure is among the *salutary* effects of exercise.
- The long sea voyage was *salutary;* when Elizabeth landed, she looked ten years younger than she had when she set sail.

SANCTIMONIOUS (sangk tuh MOH nee us) *adj* pretending to be devout; affecting religious feeling

- The *sanctimonious* old bore pretended to be deeply offended when Lucius whispered a mild swear word after dropping the hammer on his bare foot.
- Simon is an egoist who speaks about almost nothing but caring for one's fellow man. His altruism is *sanctimonious.*

SANGUINE (SANG gwin) *adj* cheerful; optimistic; hopeful

- Miguel was *sanguine* about his chances of winning the Nobel Peace Prize, even though, as an eighth grader, he hadn't yet done anything to deserve it.
- The ebullient checkers champion remained *sanguine* in defeat; he was so sure of himself that he viewed even catastrophe as merely a temporary setback.

Don't confuse *sanguine* (a nice word) with *sanguinary* (not a nice word). *Sanguinary* means bloodthirsty.

SARDONIC (sahr DAHN ik) *adj* mocking; scornful

- Isabella's weak attempts at humor were met by nothing but a few scattered pockets of *sardonic* laughter.
- Even George's friends found him excessively *sardonic:* he couldn't discuss anything without mocking it, and there was almost nothing about which he could bring himself to say two nice words in a row.

Quick Quiz #75

Match each word in the first column with its definition in the second column. Check your answers in the back of the book.

1. saccharine	a.	blasphemy
2. sacrilege	b.	wise
3. sacrosanct	c.	sweet
4. sagacious	d.	pretending to be devout
5. sage	e.	healthful
6. salient	f.	mocking
7. salutary	g.	cheerful
8. sanctimonious	h.	sacred
9. sanguine	i.	sticking out
10. sardonic	j.	discerning

SCINTILLATE (SIN tuh layt) *v* to sparkle, either literally or figuratively

- Stars and diamonds *scintillate*—so do witty comments, charming personalities, and anything else that can be said to sparkle.
- Stefan was a quiet drudge at home, but at a party he could be absolutely *scintillating,* tossing off witty remarks and charming everyone in the room.
- Jenny's grades last term weren't *scintillating,* to put it mildly; she had four Ds and an F.

The act of *scintillating* is called *scintillation.*

SCRUPULOUS (SKROO pyuh lus) *adj* strict; careful; hesitant for ethical reasons

- Leela was *scrupulous* in keeping her accounts; she knew where every penny came from and where every penny went.
- We tried to be *scrupulous* about not dripping paint, but by the time the day was over there was nearly as much paint on the floor as there was on the walls.

- Philip was too *scrupulous* to make a good used-car dealer; every time he started to lie, he was overcome by ethical doubts.

A *scruple* is a qualm or moral doubt. To have no *scruples*—to be *unscrupulous*—is to have no conscience.

SCRUTINIZE (SKROOT uh nyze) *v* to examine very carefully

- I *scrutinized* the card catalog at the library but couldn't find a single book on the topic I had chosen for my term paper.
- The rocket scientists *scrutinized* thousands of pages of computer printouts, looking for a clue to why the rocket had exploded.
- My mother *scrutinized* my clothes and my appearance before I left for the evening, but even after several minutes of careful analysis, she was unable to find anything to complain about.

To *scrutinize* something is to subject it to *scrutiny*.

- The clever forgery fooled the museum curator but did not withstand the *scrutiny* of the experts; after studying for several weeks, the experts pronounced the painting to be a fake.

Something that cannot be examined is *inscrutable* (in SKROOT uh bul). *Inscrutable* means mysterious, impossible to understand.

- We had no idea what Bill was thinking because his smile was *inscrutable*. Poker players try to be *inscrutable* to their opponents.

SECULAR (SEK yuh lur) *adj* having nothing to do with religion or spiritual concerns

- The group home had several nuns on its staff, but it was an entirely *secular* operation, run by the city, not the church.
- The priest's *secular* interests include German food and playing the trombone.

SEDITION (si DISH un) *n* treason; the incitement of public disorder or rebellion

- The political group was charged with *sedition* because it had advocated burning the capital to the ground.

SEGREGATE (SEG ruh gayt) *v* to separate

- Rico kept his prize-winning poodle, Fluffy, *segregated* from his other two dogs, which were mixed breeds.

The noun form is *segregation*, which can also refer to periods in history when people of different races were kept apart by social norms or law. In other nations, *segregation* has been called by other names. See *apartheid*.

Integrate, congregate, segregate, and *aggregate*—all words about joining and separating—share a common root.

SENSORY (SEN suh ree) *adj* having to do with the senses or sensation
- Babies enjoy bright colors, moving objects, pleasant sounds, and other forms of *sensory* stimulation.

Your ears, eyes, and tongue are all *sensory* organs. It is through them that your *senses* operate.

Extrasensory perception is the supposed ability of some people to perceive things without using the standard senses of sight, hearing, smell, touch, or taste.

Two similar-sounding and often confusing words are *sensual* and *sensuous*. To be *sensual* is to be devoted to gratifying one's senses through physical pleasure, especially sexual pleasure; to be *sensuous* is to delight the senses. A *sensual* person is one who eagerly indulges his or her physical desires. A *sensuous* person is one who stimulates the senses of others.

SENTIENT (SEN shunt) *adj* able to perceive by the senses; conscious

Human beings are *sentient*. Rocks are not.
- While trees are not, strictly speaking, *sentient* beings, many credible people claim to have communicated with them.

Note carefully the pronunciation of this word.

SEQUESTER (si KWES tur) *v* to set or keep apart
- Because much of the rest of the city had become a battle zone, the visiting entertainers were *sequestered* in the international hotel.
- The struggling writer *sequestered* herself in her study for several months, trying to produce the next Great American Novel.
- Juries are sometimes *sequestered* during trials to prevent them from talking to people or reading newspapers.

Quick Quiz #76

Match each word in the first column with its definition in the second column. Check your answers in the back of the book.

1. scintillate
2. scrupulous
3. scrutinize
4. secular
5. sedition
6. segregate
7. sensory
8. sensual
9. sensuous
10. sentient
11. sequester

a. sparkle
b. having nothing to do with religion
c. treason
d. having to do with the senses
e. set apart
f. strict
g. delighting the senses
h. examine very carefully
i. devoted to pleasure
j. conscious
k. separate

SERENDIPITY (ser un DIP uh tee) *n* accidental good fortune; discovering good things without looking for them

- It was *serendipity* rather than genius that led the archaeologist to his breathtaking discovery of the ancient civilization. While walking his dog in the desert, he tripped over the top of a buried tomb.

Something that occurs through *serendipity* is *serendipitous*.

- Our arrival at the airport *serendipitously* coincided with that of the queen, and she offered us a ride to our hotel in her carriage.

SERVILE (SUR vyle) *adj* submissive and subservient; like a servant

- Cat lovers sometimes say that dogs are too *servile* because they follow their owners everywhere and slobber all over them at every opportunity.
- The horrible boss demanded *servility* from his employees; when he said, "Jump!" he expected them to ask, "How high?"

A similar word is *slavish* (SLAY vish), which means even more subservient than *servile*. *Slavish* devotion to a cause is devotion in spite of everything. An artist's *slavish* imitator would be an imitator who imitated everything about the artist.

SINGULAR (SING gyuh lur) *adj* unique; superior; exceptional; strange
- Darren had the *singular* ability to stand on one big toe for several hours at a time.
- The man on the train had a *singular* deformity: both of his ears were on the same side of his head.

A *singularity* is a unique occurrence. *Singularity* is also the quality of being unique.

SINISTER (SIN ih stur) *adj* evil, wicked; foreshadowing evil, trouble, or wickedness
- The house on the hill is pretty by day, but at night it casts *sinister* shadows and emits frightening moans.

SLANDER (SLAN dur) *v* to speak badly about someone publicly; to defame; to spread malicious rumor
- Jonathan *slandered* Mr. Perriwinkle by telling everyone in school that the principal was a thief; Mr. Perriwinkle resented this *slander*. Because he was the principal, he expelled the *slanderous* student.

SLOTH (slawth) *n* laziness; sluggishness

You may have seen a picture of an animal called a *sloth*. It hangs upside down from tree limbs and is never in a hurry to do anything. To fall into *sloth* is to act like a *sloth*.
- Yusuke's weekends were devoted to *sloth*. He never arose before noon and seldom left the house before Monday morning.

To be lazy and sluggish is to be *slothful*.
- Ophelia's *slothful* husband virtually lived on the couch in the living room, and the television remote-control device was in danger of becoming grafted to his hand.

SOBRIETY (suh BRYE uh tee) *n* the state of being sober; seriousness

A *sober* person is a person who isn't drunk. A *sober* person can also be a person who is serious, solemn, or not ostentatious. *Sobriety* means both "undrunkness" and seriousness or solemnity.
- *Sobriety* was such an unfamiliar condition that the reforming alcoholic didn't recognize it at first.

Sobriety of dress is one characteristic of the hardworking Amish.

> **Note carefully the pronunciation of this word.**

SOLICITOUS (suh LIS uh tus) *adj* eager and attentive, often to the point of hovering; anxiously caring or attentive

- Every time we turned around, we seemed to step on the foot of the *solicitous* salesman, who appeared to feel that if he left us alone for more than a few seconds, we would decide to leave the store.
- When the sick movie star sneezed, half-a-dozen *solicitous* nurses came rushing into her hospital room.

The noun is *solicitude.*

SOLVENT (SAHL vunt) *adj* not broke or bankrupt; able to pay one's bills

- Jerry didn't hope to become a millionaire; all he wanted to do was remain *solvent.*

To be broke is to be *insolvent.* An *insolvent* company is one that can't cover its debts.

The state of being *solvent* is called *solvency;* the state of being *insolvent* is called *insolvency.*

SOPORIFIC (sahp uh RIF ik) *adj* sleep inducing; boring; sleepy

- The doctor calmed his hysterical patient by injecting him with some sort of *soporific* medication.
- Sam's *soporific* address was acknowledged not by applause but by a chorus of snores.
- The *soporific* creature from the bottom of the sea lay in a gigantic blob on the beach for several days and then roused itself enough to consume the panic-stricken city.

SORDID (SOR did) *adj* vile; filthy; squalid

- The college roommates led a *sordid* existence, surrounded by dirty laundry, rotting garbage, and filthy dishes.
- The conspirators plotted their *sordid* schemes at a series of secret meetings in an abandoned warehouse.
- The leprosy blight had turned a once-pretty neighborhood into a *sordid* outpost of despair and crime.

SPAWN (spawn) *v* to bring forth; to produce a large number

- A best-selling book or blockbuster movie will *spawn* dozens of imitators.

SPECIOUS (SPEE shus) *adj* deceptively plausible or attractive

- The charlatan's *specious* theories about curing baldness with used tea bags charmed the studio audience but did not convince the experts, who believed that fresh tea bags were more effective.
- The river's beauty turned out to be *specious;* what had looked like churning rapids from a distance was, on closer inspection, some sort of foamy industrial waste.

To be *specious* is to be characterized by *speciousness.*

SPORADIC (spuh RAD ik) *adj* stopping and starting; scattered; occurring in bursts every once in a while

- Kyle's attention to his schoolwork was *sporadic* at best; he tended to lose his concentration after a few minutes of effort.

SPURIOUS (SPYOOR ee us) *adj* false; fake

An apocryphal story is one whose truth is uncertain. A *spurious* story, however, is out-and-out false, no doubt about it.
- The political candidate attributed his loss to numerous *spurious* rumors that had hounded him throughout his campaign.

SQUALOR (SKWAHL ur) *n* filth; wretched, degraded, or repulsive living conditions
- If people live in *squalor* for too long, the ruling elite can count on an insurgency.

SQUANDER (SKWAHN dur) *v* to waste
- Jerry failed to husband his inheritance; instead, he *squandered* it on trips to Las Vegas.

STAGNATION (stag NAY shun) *n* motionlessness; inactivity
- The company grew quickly for several years; then it fell into *stagnation.*
- Many years of carelessly dumping garbage next to the river led to the gradual *stagnation* of the water because the trash covered the bottom and made an impromptu dam.

To fall into *stagnation* is to *stagnate.* To be in a state of *stagnation* is to be *stagnant.*

STATIC (STAT ik) *adj* stationary; not changing or moving
- Sales of the new book soared for a few weeks then became *static.*
- The movie was supposed to be a thriller, but we found it tediously *static;* nothing seemed to happen from one scene to the next.

STAUNCH (stawnch) *adj* firmly committed; firmly in favor of; steadfast

A *staunch* Republican is someone who always votes for Republican candidates.

A *staunch* supporter of tax reform would be someone who firmly believes in tax reform.

To be *staunch* in your support of something is to be unshakable.

STEADFAST (STED fast) *adj* loyal; faithful
- *Steadfast* love is love that never wavers. To be *steadfast* in a relationship is to be faithfully committed.

To be *steadfast* is to be like a rock: unchanging, unwavering, and unmoving.

STIGMATIZE (STIG muh tyze) *v* to brand with disgrace; to set a mark of disgrace upon

- Steve once went into the girls' bathroom by accident, and this mistake *stigmatized* him for the rest of his high school career.

A *stigma* (STIG muh) is a mark of disgrace.

STIPULATE (STIP yuh layt) *v* to require something as part of an agreement

- You are well-advised to *stipulate* the maximum amount you will pay in any car-repair contract.

Guarantees often *stipulate* certain conditions that must be met if the guarantee is to be valid.

STOIC (STOH ik) *adj* indifferent (at least outwardly) to pleasure or pain, to joy or grief, to fortune or misfortune

- Nina was *stoic* about the death of her canary; she went about her business as though nothing sad had happened.
- We tried to be *stoic* about our defeat, but as soon as we got into the locker room, we all began to cry and bang our foreheads on our lockers.

STRATUM (STRAT um) *n* a layer; a level

The middle class is one *stratum* of society.

The plural of *stratum* is *strata.* A hierarchy is composed of *strata.*

To *stratify* is to make into layers.

This word can also be pronounced "STRAY tum."

STRICTURE (STRIK chur) *n* a restriction; a limitation; a negative criticism

- Despite the *strictures* of apartment living, we enjoyed the eight years we spent in New York City.
- The unfavorable lease placed many *strictures* on how the building could be used.
- The poorly prepared violinist went home trembling after her concert to await the inevitable *strictures* of the reviewers.

STRIFE (stryfe) *n* **bitter conflict; discord; a struggle or clash**

- Marital *strife* often leads to divorce.

STRINGENT (STRIN junt) *adj* **strict; restrictive**

- The restaurant's *stringent* dress code required male diners to wear a suit coat and tie or they had to leave.
- The IRS accountant was quite *stringent* in her interpretation of the tax code; she disallowed virtually all of Leslie's deductions.

STYMIE (STYE mee) *v* **to thwart; to get in the way of; to hinder**

Stymie is a golfing term. A golfer is *stymied* when another player's ball lies on the direct path between his or her own ball and the cup.

Off the golf course, one might be *stymied* by one's boss.

- In my effort to make a name for myself in the company, I was *stymied* by my boss, who always managed to take credit for all the good things I did and to blame me for his mistakes.

SUBJUGATE (SUB juh gayt) *v* to subdue and dominate; to enslave

- I bought the fancy riding lawn mower because I thought it would make my life easier, but it quickly *subjugated* me. All summer long, it seems, I did nothing but change its oil, sharpen its blades, and drive it back and forth between my house and the repair shop.
- The tyrant *subjugated* all the peasants living in the kingdom; once free, they were now forced to do her bidding.

SUBLIME (suh BLYME) *adj* awesome; extremely exalted; lofty; majestic

- After winning $70 million in the lottery and quitting our jobs as sewer workers, our happiness was *sublime.*
- Theodore was a *sublime* thinker; after pondering even a difficult problem for just a few minutes, he would invariably arrive at a concise and elegant solution.
- The soup at the restaurant was *sublime.* I've never tasted anything so good.

The noun form of *sublime* is *sublimity* (suh BLIM i tee). Don't confuse *sublime* with *subliminal* (suh BLIM uh nuhl), which means subconscious, or *sublimate* (SUB li mayt), which means to suppress one's subconscious mind.

SUBORDINATE (suh BOR duh nit) *adj* lower in importance, position, or rank; secondary

- My desire to sit on the couch and watch television all night long was *subordinate* to my desire to stand in the kitchen eating junk food all night long, so I did the latter instead of the former.

A vice president is *subordinate* to a president.

Subordinate (suh BOR duh nayt) can also be a verb. To *subordinate* something in relation to something else is to make it secondary or less important.

To be *insubordinate* (in suh BOR duh nit) is not to acknowledge the authority of a superior. An army private who says, "Bug off!" when ordered to do something by a general is guilty of being *insubordinate* or of committing an act of *insubordination.*

SUBSTANTIVE (SUB stan tiv) *adj* having substance; real; essential; solid; substantial

- The differences between the two theories were not *substantive;* in fact, the two theories said the same thing with different words.
- The gossip columnist's wild accusations were not based on anything *substantive*—her source was a convicted perjurer, and she had made up all the quotations.

SUBTLE (SUT ul) *adj* not obvious; able to make fine distinctions; ingenious; crafty

- The alien beings had created a shrewd replica of Mr. Jenson, but his wife did notice a few *subtle* differences, including the fact that the new Mr. Jenson had no pulse.
- Jim's *subtle* mind enables him to see past problems that confuse the rest of us.
- The burglar was *subtle;* she had come up with a plan that would enable her to steal all the money in the world without arousing the suspicions of the authorities.

Something *subtle* is a *subtlety* (SUT ul tee).

Note carefully the pronunciation of this word.

SUBVERSIVE (sub VUR siv) *adj* corrupting; overthrowing; undermining; insurgent

- The political group destroyed the Pentagon's computer files, hijacked *Air Force One,* and engaged in various other *subversive* activities.
- Madeline's efforts to teach her first-grade students to read were thwarted by that most *subversive* of inventions, the television set.

SUCCINCT (suk SINGKT) *adj* brief and to the point; concise

- Aaron's *succinct* explanation of why the moon doesn't fall out of the sky and crash into the earth quickly satisfied even the most skeptical of the seventh graders.
- We were given so little room in which to write on the examination that we had no choice but to keep our essays *succinct.*

Note carefully the pronunciation of this word.

Quick Quiz #79

Match each word in the first column with its definition in the second column. Check your answers in the back of the book.

1.	strife	a.	not obvious
2.	stringent	b.	awesome
3.	stymie	c.	brief and to the point
4.	subjugate	d.	thwart
5.	sublime	e.	subdue
6.	subordinate	f.	corrupting
7.	insubordinate	g.	not respectful of authority
8.	substantive	h.	strict
9.	subtle	i.	lower in importance
10.	subversive	j.	having substance
11.	succinct	k.	bitter conflict

SUCCUMB (suh KUM) *v* to yield or submit; to die

- I had said I wasn't going to eat anything at the party, but when Ann held the tray of imported chocolates under my nose, I quickly *succumbed* and ate all of them.
- The Martians in *The War of the Worlds* survived every military weapon known to man but *succumbed* to the common cold.
- When Willard reached the age of 110, his family began to think that he would live forever, but he *succumbed* not long afterward.

SUPERCILIOUS (soo pur SIL ee us) *adj* haughty; patronizing

- The *supercilious* Rolls-Royce salesman treated us like peasants until we opened our suitcase full of one-hundred-dollar bills.
- The newly famous author was so *supercilious* that she pretended not to recognize members of her own family, whom she now believed to be beneath her.

SUPERFICIAL (soo pur FISH ul) *adj* on the surface only; shallow; not thorough

- Tom had indeed been shot, but the wound was *superficial*—the bullet had merely creased the tip of his nose.
- The mechanic, who was in a hurry, gave my car what appeared to be a *superficial* tune-up. In fact, if he checked the oil, he did it without opening the hood.

A person who is *superficial* can be accused of *superficiality*.

- The *superficiality* of the editor's comments made us think that she hadn't really read the manuscript.

SUPERFLUOUS (soo PUR floo us) *adj* extra; unnecessary; redundant

- Andrew's attempt to repair the light bulb was *superfluous* because the light bulb had already been repaired.
- Roughly 999 of the book's 1,000 pages were *superfluous.*

The noun is *superfluity* (soo pur FLOO uh tee).

Note carefully the pronunciation of this word.

SURFEIT (SUR fit) *n* excess; an excessive amount; excess or over-indulgence in eating or drinking

- Thanksgiving meals are usually a *surfeit* for everyone involved.

Note carefully the pronunciation of this word.

SURREPTITIOUS (sur up TISH us) *adj* sneaky; secret

- The babysitter made herself a *surreptitious* meal of lobster as soon as Mr. and Mrs. Robinson had driven away.

The word is sometimes used as an adverb.

- The dinner guest *surreptitiously* slipped a few silver spoons into his jacket as he was leaving the dining room.

SURROGATE (SUR uh git) *adj* substitute

A *surrogate* mother is a woman who bears a child for someone else.

This word is often a noun. A *surrogate* is a substitute.

- A kind parent offered to go to prison as a *surrogate* for his son, who had been convicted of extortion.

SYCOPHANT (SIK uh funt) *n* one who sucks up to others

- The French class seemed to be full of *sycophants;* the students were always bringing apples to the teacher and telling her how nice she looked.

A *sycophant* is *sycophantic* (sik uh FAN tik).

- The exasperated boss finally fired her *sycophantic* secretary because she couldn't stand being around someone who never had anything nasty to say.

Note carefully the pronunciation of this word.

SYNTHESIS (SIN thuh sis) *n* the combining of parts to form a whole

- It seemed as though the meeting might end in acrimony and confusion until Raymond offered his brilliant *synthesis* of the two diverging points of view.
- A hot fudge sundae is the perfect *synthesis* of hot fudge and vanilla ice cream.

Quick Quiz #80

Match each word in the first column with its definition in the second column. Check your answers in the back of the book.

1.	succumb	a.	haughty
2.	supercilious	b.	yield
3.	superficial	c.	flatterer
4.	superfluous	d.	substitute
5.	surfeit	e.	unnecessary
6.	surreptitious	f.	on the surface only
7.	surrogate	g.	sneaky
8.	sycophant	h.	excess
9.	synthesis	i.	combining of parts

T

TACIT (TAS it) *adj* implied; not spoken

- Mrs. Rodgers never formally asked us to murder her husband, but we truly believed that we were acting with her *tacit* consent.

Tacit is related to *taciturn*.

TACITURN (TAS i turn) *adj* untalkative by nature

- The chairman was so *taciturn* that we often discovered that we had absolutely no idea what he was thinking.
- The *taciturn* physicist was sometimes thought to be brilliant simply because no one had ever heard him say anything that wasn't intelligent. Everyone misconstrued his *taciturnity;* he was actually quite dumb.

Taciturn is related to *tacit*.

TANGENTIAL (tan JEN shul) *adj* only superficially related to the matter at hand; not especially relevant; peripheral
- The vice president's speech bore only a *tangential* relationship to the topic that had been announced.
- Stuart's connection with our organization is *tangential.* He once made a phone call from the lobby of our building, but he never worked here.

When a writer or speaker "goes off on a *tangent,*" he or she is making a digression or straying from the original topic.

Note carefully the pronunciation of this word.

TANGIBLE (TAN juh bul) *adj* touchable; palpable
- A mountain of cigarette butts was the only *tangible* evidence that Luke had been in our house.
- There was no *tangible* reason I could point to, but I did have a sneaking suspicion that Ernest was a rodeo fan.

The opposite of *tangible* is *intangible.*

TANTAMOUNT (TAN tuh mownt) *adj* equivalent to
- Waving a banner for the visiting team at that football game would be *tantamount* to committing suicide; the home-team fans would tear you apart in a minute.
- Yvonne's method of soliciting donations from her employees was *tantamount* to extortion; she clearly implied that she would fire them if they didn't pitch in.

TAUTOLOGICAL (tawt uh LAH juh kul) *adj* redundant; circular
"When everyone has a camera, cameras will be universal" is a *tautological* statement, because "everyone having a camera" and "cameras being universal" mean the same thing.
- The testing company's definition of intelligence—"that which is measured by intelligence tests"—is *tautological.*

A *tautology* (taw TAHL uh jee) is a needless repetition of words, or saying the same thing using different words. Here's an example:
- The trouble with bachelors is that they aren't married.

TEMERITY (tuh MER uh tee) *n* boldness; recklessness; audacity
- Our waiter at the restaurant had the *temerity* to tell me he thought my table manners were atrocious.
- The mountain climber had more *temerity* than skill or sense. She tried to climb a mountain that was much too difficult and ended up in a heap at the bottom.

TEMPERATE (TEM pur it) *adj* mild; moderate; restrained
- Our climate is *temperate* during the spring and fall but nearly unbearable during the summer and winter.
- The teacher's *temperate* personality lent a feeling of calm and control to the kindergarten class.

The opposite of *temperate* is *intemperate,* which means not moderate.
- Becky's *intemperate* use of oregano ruined the chili.

To *temper* something is to make it milder.
- Anna laughed and shrieked so loudly at every joke that even the comedian wished she would *temper* her appreciation.

Temperance is moderation, especially with regard to alcoholic drinks.

TENABLE (TEN uh bul) *adj* defensible, as in one's position in an argument; capable of being argued successfully; valid
- Members of the Flat Earth Society continue to argue that the earth is flat, although even children dismiss their arguments as *untenable.*

Untenable means unable to be defended.

TENACIOUS (tuh NAY shus) *adj* persistent; stubborn; not letting go
- The foreign student's *tenacious* effort to learn English won him the admiration of all the teachers at our school.
- Louise's grasp of geometry was not *tenacious.* She could handle the simpler problems most of the time, but she fell apart on quizzes and tests.
- The ivy growing on the side of our house was so *tenacious* that we had to tear the house down to get rid of it.

To be *tenacious* is to have *tenacity* (tuh NAS us tee).

TENET (TEN it) *n* a shared principle or belief

- The *tenets* of his religion prohibited him from dancing and going to movies.
- One of the most important *tenets* of our form of government is that people can be trusted to govern themselves.

TENTATIVE (TEN tuh tiv) *adj* experimental; temporary; uncertain

- George made a *tentative* effort to paint his house by himself; he slapped some paint on the front door and his clothes, tipped over the bucket, and called a professional.
- Our plans for the party are *tentative* at this point, but we are considering hiring a troupe of accordionists to play polkas while our guests are eating dessert.
- Hugo believed himself to be a great wit, but his big joke was rewarded by nothing more than a very *tentative* chuckle from his audience.

TENUOUS (TEN yoo us) *adj* flimsy; extremely thin

- The organization's financial situation has always been *tenuous;* the balance of the checking account is usually close to zero.

To *attenuate* is to make thin. *Extenuating* circumstances are those that lessen the magnitude of something, especially a crime.

- Cherrie admitted that she stole the Cracker Jacks, but claimed that there were *extenuating* circumstances: she had no money to buy food for her dog.

TERSE (turs) *adj* using no unnecessary words; succinct

- The new recording secretary's minutes were so *terse* that they were occasionally cryptic.
- *Terseness* is not one of Rex's virtues; he would talk until the crack of dawn if someone didn't stop him.

THEOLOGY (thee AHL uh jee) *n* the study of God or religion

- Ralph was a paradox: he was an atheist, yet he passionately studied *theology*.

TIRADE (TYE rayd) *n* a prolonged, bitter speech

- Preston launched into a *tirade* against imitation cheese on the school lunch menu.

TORPOR (TOR pur) *n* sluggishness; inactivity; apathy

- After consuming the guinea pig, the boa constrictor fell into a state of contented *torpor* that lasted several days.
- The math teacher tried to reduce the *torpor* of his students by banging on his desk, but the students scarcely blinked.

To be in a state of *torpor* is to be *torpid*.

TOUCHSTONE (TUCH stohn) *n* a standard; a test of authenticity or quality

- The size of a student's vocabulary is a useful *touchstone* for judging the quality of his or her education.
- A candidate's pronouncements about the economy provided a *touchstone* by which his or her fitness for office could be judged.

In its original usage, a *touchstone* was a dark stone against which gold and other precious metals were rubbed in order to test their purity. Now the word is used more loosely to describe a broad range of standards and tests.

TOUT (towt) *v* to praise highly; to brag publicly about

- Advertisements *touted* the chocolate-flavored toothpaste as getting rid of your sweet tooth while saving your teeth.

TRANSCEND (tran SEND) *v* to go beyond or above; to surpass

- The man who claimed to have invented a perpetual motion machine believed that he had *transcended* the laws of physics.
- The basketball player was so skillful that she seemed to have *transcended* the sport altogether; she was so much better than her teammates that she seemed to be playing an entirely different game.

To be *transcendent* is to be surpassing or preeminent. Something *transcendent* is *transcendental* (tran sen DEN tul).

TRANSGRESS (trans GRES) *v* to violate (a law); to sin

- The other side had *transgressed* so many provisions of the treaty that we had no choice but to go to war.
- We tried as hard as we could not to *transgress* their elaborate rules, but they had so many prohibitions that we couldn't keep track of all of them.

An act of *transgressing* is a *transgression.*

- The bully's innumerable *transgressions* included breaking all the windows in the new gymnasium and pushing several first graders off the jungle gym.

TRANSIENT (TRAN shunt) *adj* not staying for a long time; temporary

- The *transient* breeze provided some relief from the summer heat, but we were soon perspiring again.
- The child's smile was *transient;* it disappeared as soon as the candy bar was gone.
- A hotel's inhabitants are *transient;* the population changes every night as they come and go.

Transient can also be a noun. A *transient* person is sometimes called a *transient.* Hoboes, mendicants, and other homeless people are often called *transients.*

A very similar word is *transitory,* which means not lasting long. A *transient* breeze might provide *transitory* relief from the heat.

This word can also be pronounced "TRAN zee unt."

TREPIDATION (trep uh DAY shun) *n* fear; apprehension; nervous trembling

- The nursery school students were filled with *trepidation* when they saw the other children in their class dressed in their Halloween costumes.
- The *trepidation* of the swimming team was readily apparent: their knees were knocking as they lined up along the edge of the pool.

To be fearless is to be *intrepid.*

- The *intrepid* captain sailed her ship around the world with only a handkerchief for a sail.

TURPITUDE (TUR puh tood) *n* shameful wickedness; depravity

- Paul was sacked by his boss because of a flagrant act of *turpitude:* he was caught stealing office supplies.

Quick Quiz #82

Match each word in the first column with its definition in the second column. Check your answers in the back of the book.

1.	tenet	a.	without unnecessary words
2.	tentative	b.	go beyond
3.	tenuous	c.	brag publicly about
4.	terse	d.	fearless
5.	torpor	e.	experimental
6.	theology	f.	not lasting long
7.	tirade	g.	bitter speech
8.	touchstone	h.	shared principle
9.	tout	i.	wickedness
10.	transcend	j.	sluggishness
11.	transgress	k.	flimsy
12.	transient	l.	fear
13.	transitory	m.	study of religion
14.	trepidation	n.	standard
15.	intrepid	o.	violate
16.	turpitude		

U

UBIQUITOUS (yoo BIK wuh tus) *adj* **being everywhere at the same time**

- The new beer commercial was *ubiquitous*—it seemed to be on every television channel at once.
- Personal computers, once a rarity, have become *ubiquitous*.

To be *ubiquitous* is to be characterized by *ubiquity* (yoo BIK wuh tee). The *ubiquity* of fast-food restaurants is one of the more depressing features of American culture.

Note carefully the pronunciation of both parts of speech.

UNCONSCIONABLE (un KAHN shuh nuh bul) *adj* not controlled by conscience; unscrupulous

- Leaving a small child unattended all day long is an *unconscionable* act.
- Stealing money from every citizen of that town was *unconscionable.* Bert should be ashamed of himself for doing it.

Don't confuse this word with *unconscious.*

UNCTUOUS (UNGK choo us) *adj* oily, both literally and figuratively; insincere

Salad oil is literally *unctuous.* A used-car salesman might be figuratively *unctuous*—that is, oily in the sense of being slick, sleazy, and insincere.

UNIFORM (YOO nuh form) *adj* consistent; unchanging; the same for everyone

- Traffic laws are similar from one state to the next, but they aren't *uniform.* Each state has its own variations.
- The school did not have a *uniform* grading policy; each teacher was free to mark students according to any system that he or she thought appropriate.

Something that is *uniform* has *uniformity* (yoo nuh FOR muh tee).

Uniforms are suits of clothing that are *uniform* in appearance from one person to the next.

UNREMITTING (un ri MIT ing) *adj* unceasing; unabated; relentless

- Superman waged an *unremitting* battle against evildoers everywhere.

UNWITTING (un WIT ing) *adj* unintentional; ignorant; not aware

- When Leo agreed to hold open the door of the bank, he became an *unwitting* accomplice to the bank robbery.
- My theft was *unwitting.* I hadn't meant to steal the car, but had absentmindedly driven it away from the automobile dealership and parked it in my garage.
- On the camping trip, Josephine *unwittingly* stepped into a bear trap and remained stuck in it for several days.

URBANE (ur BAYN) *adj* poised; sophisticated; refined

- The British count was witty and *urbane;* all the hosts and hostesses wanted to have him at their parties.
- The new magazine was far too *urbane* to appeal to a wide audience outside the big city.

Urbanity (ur BAN uh tee) is a quality more often acquired in an *urban* setting than in a rural one.

USURP (yoo SURP) *v* to seize wrongfully

- The children believed that their mother's new boyfriend had *usurped* their father's rightful place in their family.
- The founder's scheming young nephew *usurped* a position of power in the company.

The noun is *usurpation* (yoo sur PAY shun).

UTILITARIAN (yoo til uh TAR ee un) *adj* stressing usefulness or utility above all other qualities; pragmatic

- Jason's interior-decorating philosophy was strictly *utilitarian;* if an object wasn't genuinely useful, he didn't want it in his home.

Utilitarian can also be a noun. Jason, just aforementioned, could be called a *utilitarian*.

UTOPIA (yoo TOH pee uh) *n* an ideal society

- A country where nobody had to work would be Quentin's idea of *utopia*.
- The little town wasn't just a nice place to live, as far as Edith was concerned; it was *utopia*.

A *utopian* is someone with unrealistic or impractical plans or expectations for society. Such plans or expectations are *utopian* plans or expectations.

The opposite of a *utopia* is a *dystopia*.

Quick Quiz #83

Match each word in the first column with its definition in the second column. Check your answers in the back of the book.

1.	ubiquitous	a.	oily; slick
2.	unconscionable	b.	poised and sophisticated
3.	unctuous	c.	everywhere at once
4.	uniform	d.	pragmatic
5.	unremitting	e.	seize wrongfully
6.	unwitting	f.	unscrupulous
7.	urbane	g.	an ideal society
8.	usurp	h.	unintentional
9.	utilitarian	i.	consistent
10.	utopia	j.	unceasing

V

VACILLATE (VAS uh layt) *v* to be indecisive; to waver
- We invited James to spend Thanksgiving with us, but he *vacillated* for so long that we finally became annoyed and disinvited him.
- Tiffany *vacillated* about buying a new car. She couldn't decide whether to get one.

The act of *vacillating* is called *vacillation.*

VAPID (VAP id) *adj* without liveliness; dull; spiritless

An apathetic person just doesn't care about anything, and everything he or she does is *vapid.*
- The novelist's prose was so *vapid* that Mary couldn't get beyond the first page.

VEHEMENT (VEE uh munt) *adj* intense; forceful; violent
- Shaking his fist and stomping his foot, Gerry was *vehement* in his denial.

The noun is *vehemence.*

VENAL (VEEN ul) *adj* capable of being bribed; willing to do anything for money; corrupt

- The *venal* judge reversed his favorable ruling when the defendant refused to make good on his promised bribe.
- The young man's interest in helping the sick old woman was strictly *venal*. He figured that if he was kind to her, she would leave him a lot of money in her will.

A *venal* person is a person characterized by *venality* (vee NAL uh tee).

Don't confuse this word with *venial* (VEE nee ul), which means trivial or pardonable. A peccadillo is a *venial,* harmless sin.

VENERATE (VEN uh rayt) *v* to revere; to treat as something holy, especially because of great age

- Lester *venerated* his grandfather; he worshiped the ground the old man limped on.
- The members of the curious religion *venerated* Elvis Presley and hoped that the pope would declare him a saint.

A person who is worthy of being *venerated* is said to be *venerable.*

VERACITY (vuh RAS uh tee) *n* truthfulness

- The *veracity* of young George Washington is apocryphal.

Veracious (vuh RAY shus) means truthful.

VERBOSE (vur BOHS) *adj* using too many words; not succinct; circumlocutory

Someone who is *verbose* uses too many words when fewer words would suffice.

- Lee handed in a 178-word final assignment; no one ever accused him of being *verbose*.

VERISIMILITUDE (ver uh si MIL uh tood) *n* similarity to reality; the appearance of truth; looking like the real thing

- They used pine cones and old truck tires to make statues of Hollywood celebrities that were remarkable for their *verisimilitude.*
- The *verisimilitude* of counterfeit eleven-dollar bills did not fool the eagle-eyed treasury officer, who recognized them immediately for what they were.

VERNACULAR (vur NAK yuh lur) *n* everyday speech; slang; idiom

- Our teacher said that we should save our *vernacular* for the street; in the classroom we should use proper grammar.

VESTIGE (VES tij) *n* a remaining bit of something; a last trace

- The unhappy young man found *vestiges* of his fiancée in the rubble, but the explosion had effectively ended their romance.
- An old uniform and a tattered scrapbook were the only *vestiges* of the old man's career as a professional athlete.

Your appendix is a *vestige:* it used to have a function, but now this organ does nothing.

The adjective form of *vestige* is *vestigial* (vuh STIJ ee ul). The appendix is referred to as a *vestigial* organ. It is still in our bodies, although it no longer has a function. It is a mere *vestige* of some function our digestive systems no longer perform.

> Note carefully the pronunciation of both parts of speech.

VEX (veks) *v* to annoy; to pester; to confuse

- Margaret *vexed* me by poking me with a long, sharp stick.
- Stuck at the bottom of a deep well, I found my situation extremely *vexing.*

The act of *vexing,* or the state of being *vexed,* is *vexation.* A *vexed* issue is one that is troubling or puzzling.

VIABLE (VYE uh bul) *adj* capable of living; workable

- When a doctor says that an organ is no longer *viable,* it means it can't be used as a transplant organ.
- A fetus is said to be *viable* when it has developed to the point when it is capable of surviving outside the womb.
- Lupe's plan for storing marshmallows in the dome of the Capitol just wasn't *viable.*

Something that is *viable* has *viability* (vye uh BIL uh tee).

VICARIOUS (vye KAR ee us) *adj* experienced, performed, or suffered through someone else; living through the experiences of another as though they were one's own experiences

To take *vicarious* pleasure in someone else's success is to enjoy that person's success as though it were your own.

- We all felt a *vicarious* thrill when the mayor's daughter won fourth prize in the regional kickboxing competition.

VICISSITUDE (vi SIS uh tood) *n* upheaval; natural change; change in fortune

- The *vicissitudes* of the stock market were too much for Karen; she decided to look for a job that would stay the same from one day to the next.
- The *vicissitudes* of the local political machine were such that one could never quite be certain whom one was supposed to bribe.

VILIFY (VIL uh fye) *v* to say vile things about; to defame

- The teacher was reprimanded for *vilifying* the slow student in front of the rest of the class.
- Our taxi driver paused briefly on the way to the airport to *vilify* the driver of the car that had nearly forced him off the road.
- The political debate was less a debate than a *vilification* contest. At first the candidates took turns saying nasty things about one another; then they stopped taking turns.

Quick Quiz #84

Match each word in the first column with its definition in the second column. Check your answers in the back of the book.

1.	vacillate	a.	annoy
2.	vapid	b.	be indecisive
3.	vehement	c.	defame
4.	venal	d.	capable of living
5.	venerate	e.	experienced through
6.	veracity		another
7.	verbose	f.	dull
8.	verisimilitude	g.	upheaval
9.	vernacular	h.	revere
10.	vestige	i.	last trace
11.	vex	j.	similarity to reality
12.	viable	k.	truthfulness
13.	vicarious	l.	corrupt
14.	vicissitude	m.	wordy
15.	vilify	n.	slang
		o.	intense

VINDICATE (VIN duh kayt) *v* to clear from all blame or suspicion; to justify

- Divya, having been accused of stealing money from the cash register, was *vindicated* when the store manager counted the money again and found that none was missing after all.
- Tom's claim of innocence appeared to be *vindicated* when several dozen inmates at the state mental hospital confessed to the crime of which he had been accused.

A person who has been *vindicated* is a person who has found *vindication*.

VINDICTIVE (vin DIK tiv) *adj* seeking revenge

- Jeremy apologized for denting the fender of my car. However, I was feeling *vindictive,* so I made him buy me a new car.
- Samantha's *vindictive* ex drove all the way across the country just to put a stink bomb in her car.

To feel *vindictive* is to be filled with *vindictiveness*.

VIRTUOSO (vur choo WOH soh) *n* a masterful musician; a masterful practitioner in some other field

- The concert audience fell silent when the *virtuoso* stepped forward to play the sonata on her electric banjo.
- As an artist, he was a *virtuoso;* as a husband, he was a chump.

Virtuoso can also be an adjective. A *virtuoso* performance is a performance worthy of a *virtuoso*.

VIRULENT (VIR uh lunt) *adj* extremely poisonous; malignant; full of hate

- The *virulent* disease quickly swept through the community, leaving many people dead and many more people extremely ill.
- The snake was a member of a particularly *virulent* breed; its bite could kill an elephant.
- Jonathan is a *virulent* antifeminist; he says that all women should sit down and shut up.

To be *virulent* is to be characterized by *virulence*. *Virulent* is related to *virus,* not to *virile* (VI ruhl), which means manly.

VISIONARY (VIZH uh ner ee) *n* a dreamer; someone with impractical goals or ideas about the future

- My uncle was a *visionary,* not a businessman; he spent too much time tinkering with his antigravity generator and not enough time working for his plumbing business.
- The candidate was a *visionary;* she had a lot of big ideas but no realistic plan for putting them into practice.

Visionary can also be an adjective. A *visionary* proposal is an idealistic and usually impractical proposal.

VITIATE (VISH ee ayt) *v* to make impure; to pollute

- For years a zealous group of individuals has campaigned against the use of fluoride in water, claiming that it has *vitiated* our bodies as well as our morals.

VITRIOLIC (vi tree AHL ik) *adj* caustic; full of bitterness

Vitriol (VI tree ahl) is another name for sulfuric acid. To be *vitriolic* is to say or do something so nasty that your words or actions burn like acid.

- The review of the new book was so *vitriolic* that we all wondered whether the reviewer had some personal grudge against the author.

VOCATION (voh KAY shun) *n* an occupation; a job

Your *vocation* is what you do for a living.

- If Stan could figure out how to make a *vocation* out of watching television and eating potato chips, he would be one of the most successful people in the world.

Vocational training is job training. Because your *vocation* is your job, your *avocation* (a vuh KAY shun) is your hobby.

- The accountant's *vocation* bored her, but her *avocation* of mountain climbing did not.

VOCIFEROUS (voh SIF ur us) *adj* loud; noisy

- Randy often becomes *vociferous* during arguments. He doesn't know what he believes, but he states it loudly nevertheless.

VOLATILE (VAHL uh tul) *adj* quick to evaporate; highly unstable; explosive

- A *volatile* liquid is one that evaporates readily. Gasoline is a *volatile* liquid. It evaporates readily, and then the vapor poses a great danger of explosion.
- The *volatile* crowd seemed to be in imminent danger of getting out of control.
- The situation in the Middle East was highly *volatile;* the smallest incident could have set off a war.

To be *volatile* is to be characterized by *volatility.*

VOLITION (voh LISH un) *n* will; conscious choice

- Insects, lacking *volition,* simply aren't as interesting to the aspiring anthropologist as humans are.
- The question the jury had to answer was whether the killing had been an accident or an act of *volition.*

W

WANTON (WAHN tun) *adj* **malicious; unjustifiable; unprovoked; egregious**

- Terrorists commit *wanton* acts on a helpless populace to make their point.

Wanton also means intemperate.

- A hedonist lives a *wanton* life in the relentless, unremitting pursuit of pleasure; an ascetic does not.

WILLFUL (WIL ful) *adj* **deliberate; obstinate; insistent on having one's way**

- The mother insisted that the killing committed by her son had not been *willful,* but the jury apparently believed that he had known what he was doing.
- When her mother told her she couldn't have a cookie, the *willful* little girl simply snatched the cookie jar and ran out of the room with it. She had stolen the cookies *willfully.*

Note carefully the spelling of this word.

WISTFUL (WIST ful) *adj* yearning; sadly longing

- I felt *wistful* when I saw Steve's fancy new car. I wished that I had enough money to buy one for myself.
- The boys who had been cut from the football team watched *wistfully* as the team put together an undefeated season and won the state championship.

Z

ZEALOUS (ZEL us) *adj* enthusiastically devoted to something; fervent

- The *zealous* young policeman made so many arrests that the city jail soon became overcrowded.
- The dictator's followers were so *zealous* that if he had asked them all to jump off a cliff, most of them would have done so.

To be *zealous* is to be full of zeal, or fervent enthusiasm. An overly *zealous* person is a *zealot*.

Quick Quiz #86

Match each word in the first column with its definition in the second column. Check your answers in the back of the book.

1.	wanton	a.	fervent
2.	willful	b.	yearning
3.	wistful	c.	deliberate
4.	zealous	d.	malicious

CHAPTER 3

The Final Exam

The following final exam drills contain every word in the *Word Smart* core list. If you get a question wrong, look up all the answer choices for that question and review the definitions. The answers to these drills are found in Chapter 13.

Final Exam Drill #1: Completions

For each question below, choose the word that best completes the meaning of the sentence.

1. Because Stan had been preoccupied during his dynamite-juggling demonstration, the jury felt that he was not _____ for the destruction of the property.
   a. decorous
   b. decimated
   c. indiscreet
   d. culpable
   e. indiscrete

2. Sally was sad because Mr. Reeves, our English teacher, filled the margins of her term paper with _____ remarks about her spelling, grammar, and writing style.
   a. fatuous
   b. heretical
   c. ineffable
   d. prepossessing
   e. derogatory

3. The fans were _____ when the football team lost its fiftieth game in a row.
   a. irascible
   b. despondent
   c. rapacious
   d. stigmatized
   e. precipitous

4. Da-Shawn and Harry were given jobs on the stage crew because their _____ voices ruined the sound of the chorus.

a. unremitting
b. paternal
c. wanton
d. laconic
e. dissonant

5. The baby kittens were so _____ that the nursery school children were able to pick them up, carry them around by the scruffs of their necks, and dress them up in doll clothes.

a. abashed
b. peripatetic
c. docile
d. agrarian
e. nefarious

Final Exam Drill #2: Synonyms

For each question below, match the word on the left with the word most similar in meaning on the right.

1. litigious	a. ingenuous
2. artless	b. querulous
3. taciturn	c. auspicious
4. refute	d. perennial
5. perjure	e. avow
6. allege	f. reticent
7. gauche	g. delude
8. officious	h. rebut
9. chronic	i. inept
10. propitious	j. solicitous

Final Exam Drill #3: Odd Man Out

Each question below consists of four words. Three of them are related in meaning. Find the word that does not fit.

1. address   infer   construe   extrapolate
2. rigorous   punctilious   integral   painstaking
3. consecrate   revere   venerate   delineate
4. abstain   relegate   forbear   forgo
5. insubordinate   willful   didactic   intransigent
6. labyrinthine   profane   secular   atheistic
7. acrid   amoral   sardonic   virulent
8. analogous   perfunctory   cursory   desultory
9. decadent   degenerate   profligate   magnanimous
10. connoisseur   virtuoso   malleable   aesthete

Final Exam Drill #4: Relationships

For each question below, decide whether the pair of words are roughly similar (S) in meaning, roughly opposite (O) in meaning, or unrelated (U) to each other.

1. sporadic   incessant
2. beget   spawn
3. malaise   subversion
4. coerce   compel
5. peccadillo   enormity
6. charismatic   insipid
7. countenance   condone
8. usurp   appropriate
9. espouse   extricate
10. arbitrate   mediate

Final Exam Drill #5: Completions

For each question below, choose the word that best completes the meaning of the sentence.

1. The applicant's credentials were _____, but I didn't like the color of his necktie so I didn't hire him.
   a. irreproachable
   b. aloof
   c. domestic
   d. vitriolic
   e. histrionic

2. Walter's skin took on a(n) _____ cast after his exposure to the pool of radioactive wastes.
   a. artful
   b. squalid
   c. luminous
   d. nebulous
   e. garrulous

3. The police spent seven months working on the crime case but were never able to determine the identity of the _____.
   a. demagogue
   b. dilettante
   c. egotist
   d. malefactor
   e. patriarch

4. The portions at the restaurant were so _____ that immediately after dessert we drove to another restaurant and ordered a second full meal.
   a. pertinent
   b. minuscule
   c. exhaustive
   d. futile
   e. misanthropic

5. Xavier thought that throwing some scraps to the bear would
_____ it, but instead the beast tore apart our campsite in search
of more to eat.

    a. accost
    b. mollify
    c. preclude
    d. efface
    e. tout

Final Exam Drill #6: Relationships

For each question below, decide whether the pair of words are
roughly similar (S) in meaning, roughly opposite (O) in meaning, or
unrelated (U) to each other.

1.	debacle	coup
2.	amenity	injunction
3.	cognizant	unwitting
4.	emigrate	expatriate
5.	concurrent	anachronistic
6.	blithe	morose
7.	disinterested	partial
8.	anachronism	archaism
9.	collusion	complicity
10.	insular	hermetic

Final Exam Drill #7: Odd Man Out

Each question below consists of four words. Three of them are
related in meaning. Find the word that does not fit.

1.	sacrilege	renaissance	blasphemy	desecration
2.	ambiguous	equivocal	cryptic	requisite
3.	apprehensive	martial	contentious	belligerent
4.	arcane	esoteric	sacrosanct	recondite
5.	incense	replenish	foment	antagonize
6.	exacting	onerous	ponderous	arbitrary
7.	circumspect	eclectic	scrupulous	fastidious
8.	introverted	aloof	reclusive	elliptical
9.	allocate	relinquish	capitulate	succumb
10.	effusive	histrionic	avuncular	gesticulating

Word Smart

Final Exam Drill #8: Relationships

For each question below, decide whether the pair of words are roughly similar (S) in meaning, roughly opposite (O) in meaning, or unrelated (U) to each other.

1. abyss   chasm
2. substantive   ethereal
3. loquacious   taciturn
4. doctrinaire   dogmatic
5. colloquial   pedantic
6. encroach   transgress
7. amorphous   nebulous
8. domestic   endemic
9. cogent   incisive
10. lethargic   capricious

Final Exam Drill #9: Completions

For each question below, choose the word or phrase that best completes the meaning of the sentence.

1. Mei _____ her daughter for putting the cat in the washing machine.
   a. expropriated
   b. disfranchised
   c. coerced
   d. broached
   e. chastised

2. David's salary was _____ his limited skills; he was paid nothing.
   a. as vapid as
   b. tenable despite
   c. vehement in view of
   d. commensurate with
   e. acerbic notwithstanding

3. After several decades of peace, the little country grew _____ about defense and let its army slowly drift away.

a. dissolute
b. partisan
c. catholic
d. adamant
e. complacent

4. None of us had enough money to undertake the project alone, so we had to depend on the _____ of our parents.

a. postulate
b. vilification
c. largess
d. hedonism
e. veracity

5. The court ruled that Ursula's covert discussions with the Russian ambassador did not _____ treason.

a. comprise
b. abnegate
c. libel
d. broach
e. constitute

Final Exam Drill #10: Relationships

For each question below, decide whether the pair of words are roughly similar (S) in meaning, roughly opposite (O) in meaning, or unrelated (U) to each other.

1.	bureaucracy	hierarchy
2.	extrapolate	infer
3.	mercurial	volatile
4.	impeccable	culpable
5.	corroborate	refute
6.	expedient	utilitarian
7.	censure	approbation
8.	propriety	decorum
9.	emulate	peruse
10.	mandate	touchstone

Final Exam Drill #11: Relationships

For each question below, decide whether the pair of words are roughly similar (S) in meaning, roughly opposite (O) in meaning, or unrelated (U) to each other.

1.	ameliorate	exacerbate
2.	candor	equivocation
3.	caricature	parody
4.	scrupulous	mendacious
5.	apartheid	mentor
6.	bane	panacea
7.	facile	arduous
8.	philistine	erudite
9.	absolute	commensurate
10.	kinetic	stagnant

Final Exam Drill #12: Odd Man Out

Each question below consists of four words. Three of them are related in meaning. Find the word that does not fit.

1.	awry	overt	salient	manifest
2.	duplicity	ascendancy	guile	chicanery
3.	contrition	remorse	cadence	penitence
4.	temperance	sobriety	celibacy	oblivion
5.	nominal	amiable	affable	congenial
6.	choleric	querulous	petulant	equitable
7.	dormant	latent	nostalgic	inert
8.	astute	bereft	sagacious	prudent
9.	copious	bourgeois	profuse	myriad
10.	ascetic	austere	frugal	pejorative

Final Exam Drill #13: Relationships

For each question below, decide whether the pair of words are roughly similar (S) in meaning, roughly opposite (O) in meaning, or unrelated (U) to each other.

1.	serendipitous	hapless
2.	lugubrious	facetious
3.	espouse	appease
4.	qualitative	pejorative
5.	exigency	periphery
6.	harbinger	precursor
7.	profound	desecrated
8.	despotic	autocratic
9.	engender	decimate
10.	pristine	unalloyed

Final Exam Drill #14: Completions

For each question below, choose the word that best completes the meaning of the sentence.

1. Jarel was as clever as he was unscrupulous, and he knew what he could not obtain by legitimate means he could always obtain through _____.

   a. chicanery
   b. burlesque
   c. nihilism
   d. strife
   e. theology

2. The visiting professor was so _____ in her field that many of our faculty members became nervous in her presence.

   a. antithetical
   b. archetypal
   c. eminent
   d. plebeian
   e. pathological

3. The orator _____ a bizarre economic program whose central tenet was the abolition of all forms of money.
a. scintillated
b. espoused
c. vacillated
d. emulated
e. inundated

4. "Kicking the bucket" is a humorous _____ for "dying."
a. dictum
b. stipulation
c. incantation
d. conjecture
e. euphemism

5. The actor, pretending to be inebriated, made a(n) _____ attempt to open his umbrella in a telephone booth.
a. viable
b. enigmatic
c. farcical
d. cognitive
e. aphoristic

Final Exam Drill #15: Synonyms

For each question below, match the word on the left with the word most similar in meaning on the right.

1. opaque	a. obscure
2. ostensible	b. secular
3. avaricious	c. mellifluous
4. mundane	d. prudent
5. judicious	e. venal
6. mercenary	f. specious
7. ramification	g. rapacious
8. saccharine	h. repercussion
9. archaic	i. dearth
10. paucity	j. anachronism

Final Exam Drill #16: Relationships

For each question below, decide whether the pair of words are roughly similar (S) in meaning, roughly opposite (O) in meaning, or unrelated (U) to each other.

1.	belie	aggregate
2.	legacy	bequest
3.	aptitude	propensity
4.	matriculate	purport
5.	fatalist	cynic
6.	fecund	desiccated
7.	exhort	admonish
8.	polarize	prevail
9.	condescension	adulation
10.	discreet	blatant

Final Exam Drill #17: Odd Man Out

Each question below consists of four words. Three of them are related in meaning. Find the word that does not fit.

1.	uniform	monolithic	existential	homogeneous
2.	flaunt	malign	slander	libel
3.	felicity	audacity	temerity	impetuosity
4.	meager	tenuous	pivotal	paltry
5.	indulgent	salutary	prodigal	profligate
6.	disparate	incongruous	heterogeneous	ubiquitous
7.	apprehensive	diffident	succinct	circumspect
8.	cogent	eminent	potent	robust
9.	farcical	affected	contrived	ostentatious
10.	ennui	satiety	languor	volition

Final Exam Drill #18: Relationships

For each question below, decide whether the pair of words are roughly similar (S) in meaning, roughly opposite (O) in meaning, or unrelated (U) to each other.

1.	zealous	catholic
2.	aloof	nefarious
3.	mitigate	assuage
4.	agnostic	atheist
5.	clique	consensus
6.	coalition	faction
7.	husbandry	itinerary
8.	coalesce	dissipate
9.	slavish	subservient
10.	flaunt	reproach

Final Exam Drill #19: Completions

For each question below, choose the word that best completes the meaning of the sentence.

1. The Sandersons viewed the flaming image of the devil, which hovered above their house for thirteen days, as a(n) _____ of evil to come.

   a. stratum
   b. portent
   c. periphery
   d. infidelity
   e. aberration

2. There was nothing _____ about Herbert's scientific theories; in fact, they were quite shallow.

   a. sentient
   b. vociferous
   c. peremptory
   d. profound
   e. nepotistic

3. The _____ author turned out a new book every week of her adult life.
   a. prolific
   b. canine
   c. dialectical
   d. implicit
   e. contiguous

4. The _____ girls stubbornly refused to call off their rock fight, despite the pleadings of their mothers.
   a. recalcitrant
   b. pacific
   c. egalitarian
   d. exemplary
   e. fervent

5. Hal's disappointed wife _____ him for being a lazy, foul-smelling, obnoxious slob.
   a. instigated
   b. reproached
   c. flaunted
   d. desecrated
   e. belied

Final Exam Drill #20: Relationships

For each question below, decide whether the pair of words are roughly similar (S) in meaning, roughly opposite (O) in meaning, or unrelated (U) to each other.

1.	profess	espouse
2.	extrovert	introspective
3.	foible	hiatus
4.	caricature	touchstone
5.	debilitate	enervate
6.	placid	frenetic
7.	depravity	debauchery
8.	infinitesimal	grandiose
9.	grandiloquent	rhetorical
10.	malefactor	benefactor

Final Exam Drill #21: Odd Man Out

Each question below consists of four words. Three of them are related in meaning. Find the word that does not fit.

1.	avaricious	covetous	officious	parsimonious
2.	reprove	scrutinize	censure	rebuke
3.	reprehensible	transient	ephemeral	transitory
4.	belittle	depreciate	disparage	founder
5.	palpable	resolute	tenacious	steadfast
6.	absolve	condone	qualify	exculpate
7.	civil	culinary	aristocratic	genteel
8.	stricture	reproach	admonishment	corollary
9.	fidelity	proximity	steadfastness	resolution
10.	circumlocutory	redundant	tautological	vicarious

Final Exam Drill #22: Relationships

For each question below, decide whether the pair of words are roughly similar (S) in meaning, roughly opposite (O) in meaning, or unrelated (U) to each other.

1.	elude	circumvent
2.	rustic	urbane
3.	circuitous	oblique
4.	beset	beleaguered
5.	imperial	servile
6.	pedestrian	prosaic
7.	reprisal	reparation
8.	daunt	stymie
9.	apotheosis	epitome
10.	inaugurate	abort

Final Exam Drill #23: Completions

For each question on the next page, choose the word that best completes the meaning of the sentence.

1. Sally had already eaten all her cookies, so she _____ mine.
   a. permeated
   b. mortified
   c. protracted
   d. appropriated
   e. defamed

2. The country's _____ ruler required her citizens to receive official permission before changing channels on their television sets.
   a. definitive
   b. dubious
   c. indigenous
   d. autocratic
   e. redolent

3. I don't enjoy oysters myself, but I'm not _____ to letting others eat them.
   a. innate
   b. averse
   c. opaque
   d. adverse
   e. oblique

4. The president was so _____ by international crises that he found it difficult to watch an entire baseball game without being interrupted.
   a. beset
   b. belittled
   c. bereaved
   d. bequeathed
   e. bemused

5. The representative had _____ so many losing causes that she fainted dead away when her proposal was unanimously adopted by the legislature.
   a. championed
   b. caricatured
   c. misappropriated
   d. flouted
   e. mediated

Final Exam Drill #24: Relationships

For each question below, decide whether the pair of words are roughly similar (S) in meaning, roughly opposite (O) in meaning, or unrelated (U) to each other.

1.	preempt	usurp
2.	turpitude	confluence
3.	incipient	culminating
4.	burgeon	arbitrate
5.	belittle	stymie
6.	dictum	paradigm
7.	luminous	incandescent
8.	mortified	chagrined
9.	precipitate	prudent
10.	inscrutable	obscure

Final Exam Drill #25: Odd Man Out

Each question below consists of four words. Three of them are related in meaning. Find the word that does not fit.

1.	intrinsic	innate	omnipotent	inherent
2.	fortuitous	gregarious	convivial	amicable
3.	cliché	verisimilitude	maxim	epigram
4.	belligerent	indignant	pertinent	contentious
5.	inane	hackneyed	platitudinous	conducive
6.	vitriolic	acrimonious	choleric	prolific
7.	gravity	austerity	vicissitude	sobriety
8.	noxious	obsequious	pernicious	deleterious
9.	finesse	competence	proficiency	euphemism
10.	incorrigible	recalcitrant	diffident	obdurate

Final Exam Drill #26: Relationships

For each question below, decide whether the pair of words are roughly similar (S) in meaning, roughly opposite (O) in meaning, or unrelated (U) to each other.

1.	catalyst	coherence
2.	concord	dissonance
3.	discord	consonant
4.	ingenuous	urbane
5.	infatuated	beguiled
6.	categorical	contingent
7.	novel	banal
8.	parsimony	munificence
9.	permeate	pervade
10.	tentative	definitive

Final Exam Drill #27: Completions

For each question below, choose the word that best completes the meaning of the sentence.

1. The trees, vines, and other plants in the tropical forest were truly remarkable, but it was the exotic _____ that caught the zoologist's attention.

   a. accolade

   b. compendium

   c. acumen

   d. fauna

   e. surfeit

2. Ernesto hated to pay extra for a fancy name, but he had discovered that he greatly preferred expensive brand-name products to the cheaper _____ ones.

   a. generic

   b. hypothetical

   c. supercilious

   d. amorphous

   e. contentious

3. After several years of disappointing crops, the enormous harvest left the farmers confronting a(n) _____ of soybeans.

a. alacrity
b. blight
c. glut
d. chasm
e. debacle

4. The previously undefeated team found it difficult to cope with the _____ of defeat.

a. attrition
b. ignominy
c. prerequisite
d. penchant
e. neologism

5. The darkening sky indicated to all of us that a thunderstorm was _____.

a. ambivalent
b. imminent
c. conciliatory
d. inherent
e. lugubrious

Final Exam Drill #28: Relationships

For each question below, decide whether the pair of words are roughly similar (S) in meaning, roughly opposite (O) in meaning, or unrelated (U) to each other.

1.	hegemony	heyday
2.	fortuitous	nominal
3.	deride	venerate
4.	deduce	infer
5.	supercilious	servile
6.	placid	nonchalant
7.	reverence	insolence
8.	extraneous	extrinsic
9.	levity	irony
10.	onerous	exacting

Final Exam Drill #29: Odd Man Out

Each question below consists of four words. Three of them are related in meaning. Find the word that does not fit.

1.	comprise	placate	appease	mollify
2.	beguile	bemuse	cajole	delude
3.	provident	egregious	flagrant	unconscionable
4.	adept	adroit	anecdotal	dexterous
5.	iconoclast	insurgent	maverick	prodigy
6.	cadence	incisiveness	acumen	acuity
7.	gratuitous	superfluous	soporific	inordinate
8.	incongruous	staunch	anomalous	eccentric
9.	vacillate	incense	foment	instigate
10.	aberration	vestige	anomaly	singularity

Final Exam Drill #30: Relationships

For each question below, decide whether the pair of words are roughly similar (S) in meaning, roughly opposite (O) in meaning, or unrelated (U) to each other.

1.	mandate	martyr
2.	laud	defame
3.	belabor	complement
4.	disdain	supercilious
5.	distinguish	distend
6.	eulogize	censure
7.	apocalypse	covenant
8.	segregate	sequester
9.	quixotic	utopian
10.	microcosm	magnate

Final Exam Drill #31: Completions

For each question below, choose the word that best completes the meaning of the sentence.

1. The _____ salesperson bowed deeply and said, "Yes, ma'am, of course, ma'am," whenever I requested anything.
   a. verbose
   b. incumbent
   c. evanescent
   d. malingering
   e. obsequious

2. Because he had never lost a tennis match, Luther believed himself to be _____ on the court.
   a. ascetic
   b. deleterious
   c. omnipotent
   d. inane
   e. amorous

3. Our teacher was so _____ in his interpretation of the novel that it was difficult to believe he had taken any pleasure in reading it.
   a. pedantic
   b. laudable
   c. intrepid
   d. inveterate
   e. coherent

4. The prisoners were all _____ as they were led off to the firing squad, but they were shot all the same.
   a. perfunctory
   b. concise
   c. virulent
   d. prosaic
   e. penitent

5. The divisive issue _____ the community; half the residents seemed to be strongly for it, and half strongly against.
   a. circumscribed
   b. polarized
   c. assuaged
   d. castigated
   e. disseminated

Final Exam Drill #32: Relationships

For each question below, decide whether the pair of words are roughly similar (S) in meaning, roughly opposite (O) in meaning, or unrelated (U) to each other.

1.	reverence	disdain
2.	conjure	incant
3.	profound	superficial
4.	protract	curtail
5.	fauna	glut
6.	deprecate	lament
7.	abridge	augment
8.	eccentric	orthodox
9.	iconoclast	maverick
10.	idiosyncratic	conventional

Final Exam Drill #33: Odd Man Out

Each question below consists of four words. Three of them are related in meaning. Find the word that does not fit.

1.	infamous	abhorrence	innocuous	nefarious
2.	assimilate	abate	mitigate	alleviate
3.	laconic	unctuous	concise	terse
4.	relinquish	renounce	forsake	exult
5.	axiom	maxim	surrogate	precept
6.	virulent	tantamount	adverse	baneful
7.	catharsis	abhorrence	rancor	animosity
8.	idiosyncrasy	eccentricity	complacency	affectation
9.	antecedent	precursor	precedent	recrimination
10.	exonerate	patronize	exculpate	vindicate

Final Exam Drill #34: Relationships

For each question below, decide whether the pair of words are roughly similar (S) in meaning, roughly opposite (O) in meaning, or unrelated (U) to each other.

1.	slothful	assiduous
2.	affluent	opulent
3.	consummate	rudimentary
4.	chastisement	amnesty
5.	sycophant	cajoler
6.	implication	allusion
7.	quantitative	qualitative
8.	agenda	itinerary
9.	pragmatic	quixotic
10.	paradox	anomaly

Final Exam Drill #35: Synonyms

For each question below, match the word on the left with the word most similar in meaning on the right.

1.	torpid	a.	subservient
2.	sublime	b.	astuteness
3.	recapitulate	c.	ingenuous
4.	acuity	d.	subtlety
5.	replete	e.	provincial
6.	subordinate	f.	inert
7.	parochial	g.	transcendent
8.	credulous	h.	reiterate
9.	recant	i.	satiated
10.	nuance	j.	repudiate

Final Exam Drill #36: Relationships

For each question below, decide whether the pair of words are roughly similar (S) in meaning, roughly opposite (O) in meaning, or unrelated (U) to each other.

1. colloquial   contiguous
2. auspicious   portentous
3. moribund   viable
4. aristocratic   patrician
5. perquisite   prerogative
6. stagnation   metamorphosis
7. ebullient   roguish
8. turpitude   sordidness
9. cosmopolitan   urbane
10. denizen   lampoon

Final Exam Drill #37: Completions

For each question below, choose the word that best completes the meaning of the sentence.

1. The _____ spring weather was a great relief to all of us who had struggled through the long, harsh winter.
   a. abortive
   b. volatile
   c. temperate
   d. pragmatic
   e. intrinsic

2. I made a(n) _____ effort to repair the leak, but my improvised patch didn't hold. I soon realized that I would have to call a plumber.
   a. vindictive
   b. tentative
   c. pristine
   d. acrid
   e. caustic

3. The adoring members of the tribe _____ their old king even though he was blind and senile.

    a. squandered

    b. extrapolated

    c. beleaguered

    d. exacerbated

    e. venerated

4. The hikers were _____ by the billions of mosquitoes that descended upon them as soon as they hit the trail.

    a. extolled

    b. vitiated

    c. palliated

    d. vexed

    e. promulgated

5. Seeing the pictures of our old home made us feel _____ and nostalgic.

    a. adept

    b. fastidious

    c. wistful

    d. infamous

    e. impartial

Final Exam Drill #38: Relationships

For each question below, decide whether the pair of words are roughly similar (S) in meaning, roughly opposite (O) in meaning, or unrelated (U) to each other.

1.	ardent	indifferent
2.	adherent	forsaker
3.	poignant	redolent
4.	inundate	reconcile
5.	abject	exalted
6.	proselytize	implement
7.	latent	manifest
8.	burgeon	accost
9.	immutable	static
10.	perfidy	piety

Final Exam Drill #39: Odd Man Out

Each question below consists of four words. Three of them are related in meaning. Find the word that does not fit.

1. quixotic	scintillating	chimerical	visionary
2. antipathy	malfeasance	digression	malevolence
3. absolute	unqualified	categorical	wistful
4. static	cerebral	inert	immutable
5. destitute	insolvent	affable	indigent
6. altruist	benevolent	philanthropic	ideological
7. vexed	unequivocal	unalloyed	unmitigated
8. comprehensive	stringent	rigorous	exacting
9. abstract	abstruse	intangible	impervious
10. discernment	tirade	discrimination	sagacity

Final Exam Drill #40: Relationships

For each question below, decide whether the pair of words are roughly similar (S) in meaning, roughly opposite (O) in meaning, or unrelated (U) to each other.

1. plethora	dearth
2. autonomy	subjugation
3. aggregate	augment
4. vocation	avocation
5. extraneous	intrinsic
6. implicit	inferred
7. invective	eulogy
8. acerbic	caustic
9. insinuation	hyperbole
10. adulterated	unalloyed

Final Exam Drill #41: Completions

For each question below, choose the word that best completes the meaning of the sentence.

1. An _____ current of dissatisfaction among the soldiers indicated to the ambassador that revolution was becoming a possibility.
   a. incipient
   b. inert
   c. impervious
   d. impeccable
   e. inept

2. The _____ baker had burnt an entire batch of chocolate chip cookies.
   a. bucolic
   b. ursine
   c. cosmopolitan
   d. infinitesimal
   e. incompetent

3. Irene's _____ cure for her husband's snoring was a paper bag tied snugly around his head.
   a. agnostic
   b. congenital
   c. extrinsic
   d. ingenious
   e. diffident

4. Myron looked harmless, but there was nothing _____ about his plan to enslave the human race.
   a. terse
   b. innocuous
   c. mendacious
   d. nominal
   e. preeminent

5. Attempting to bask in reflected glory, the candidate _____ the names of eleven past presidents in his speech to the convention of schoolteachers.
   a. absolved
   b. implied
   c. litigated
   d. invoked
   e. allocated

Final Exam Drill #42: Relationships

For each question below, decide whether the pair of words are roughly similar (S) in meaning, roughly opposite (O) in meaning, or unrelated (U) to each other.

1.	ambience	milieu
2.	literal	figurative
3.	hypothetical	empirical
4.	subjugate	enfranchise
5.	taciturn	integral
6.	congenital	innate
7.	enfetter	expedite
8.	peripheral	tangential
9.	usurp	abdicate
10.	consummate	abortive

Final Exam Drill #43: Odd Man Out

Each question below consists of four words. Three of them are related in meaning. Find the word that does not fit.

1.	cacophony	antagonism	rancor	antipathy
2.	discord	benefactor	contention	incongruity
3.	apathy	indifference	manifesto	languor
4.	amenable	tractable	docile	reciprocal
5.	clandestine	surreptitious	provisional	furtive
6.	intrepid	blithe	squalid	equanimity
7.	callow	apocryphal	dubious	spurious
8.	putative	overt	explicit	patent
9.	desultory	derisory	cursory	perfunctory
10.	conciliate	proscribe	appease	placate

Word Smart

Final Exam Drill #44: Antonyms

For each question below, match the word on the left with the word most nearly its **OPPOSITE** on the right.

1.	deferential	a.	irreverent
2.	remonstrate	b.	assiduous
3.	tacit	c.	amorous
4.	clement	d.	explicit
5.	indolent	e.	acquiesce
6.	ambivalent	f.	intemperate
7.	aloof	g.	aversion
8.	lucid	h.	antagonist
9.	partisan	i.	enigmatic
10.	affinity	j.	resolute

Final Exam Drill #45: Relationships

For each question below, decide whether the pair of words are roughly similar (S) in meaning, roughly opposite (O) in meaning, or unrelated (U) to each other.

1.	artifice	machination
2.	obtuse	myopic
3.	respite	premise
4.	exalt	laud
5.	assimilate	appreciate
6.	edify	obfuscate
7.	pensive	ruminating
8.	narcissist	egocentric
9.	precipitate	stigmatize
10.	polemical	contentious

Final Exam Drill #46: Completions

For each question below, choose the word that best completes the meaning of the sentence.

1. The three-year-old was _____ in her refusal to taste the broccoli.
   a. recondite
   b. didactic
   c. fortuitous
   d. resolute
   e. genteel

2. We _____ the fine print in the document but were unable to find the clause the lawyer had mentioned.
   a. scrutinized
   b. reconciled
   c. exculpated
   d. cajoled
   e. accrued

3. A state in which one can see, hear, feel, smell, and taste little or nothing is known as _____ deprivation.
   a. aggregate
   b. subversive
   c. sensory
   d. sensual
   e. sensuous

4. The children tried to be _____ about the fact that their parents couldn't afford to give them Christmas presents, but you could tell that they were really quite depressed inside.
   a. tangential
   b. abysmal
   c. stoic
   d. disingenuous
   e. eclectic

5. We felt repeatedly _____ by the impersonal and inflexible bureaucracy in our attempt to win an exemption to the rule.

a. vindicated
b. deluged
c. stymied
d. reiterated
e. gesticulated

Final Exam Drill #47: Relationships

For each question below, decide whether the pair of words are roughly similar (S) in meaning, roughly opposite (O) in meaning, or unrelated (U) to each other.

1. cliché   platitude
2. malevolent   macroeconomic
3. juxtaposed   contiguous
4. defame   laud
5. idyllic   bucolic
6. inexorable   irrevocable
7. despondent   sanguine
8. lethargy   zeal
9. dogma   tenet
10. ebullient   stoic

Final Exam Drill #48: Completions

For each question below, choose the word that best completes the meaning of the sentence.

1. The gasoline spill had so thoroughly _____ the town's main well that it was possible to run an automobile on tap water.

a. exulted
b. exalted
c. engendered
d. adulterated
e. preempted

2. Mr. Jones _____ the teenagers after they had driven the stolen car into his living room and put a dent in his new color TV.

a. admonished
b. usurped
c. enervated
d. alleged
e. professed

3. Elsa's legs were so severely injured in the roller-skating accident that she didn't become fully _____ again until more than a year later.

a. decadent
b. exemplified
c. querulous
d. portentous
e. ambulatory

4. The kitchen in the new house had an electronic vegetable peeler, an automatic dish scraper, a computerized meat slicer, and dozens of other futuristic _____.

a. proponents
b. genres
c. amenities
d. mendicants
e. protagonists

5. When Joe began collecting stamps, he had hoped that the value of his collection would _____ rapidly; instead, the collection has slowly become worthless.

a. qualify
b. appreciate
c. polarize
d. belabor
e. rebuke

CHAPTER 4

SAT Key Terms

Need-to-Know Words for the SAT

Although the Evidence-Based Reading and Writing section of the SAT emphasizes critical reading and writing skills, many questions nevertheless test your vocabulary knowledge, such as vocabulary-in-context questions. Other questions are related to vocabulary in a more peripheral way; the reading passages, grammar sections (especially those involving diction), and even the essay will be more easily dealt with if you have an erudite vocabulary. If you learn every word on the main word list in this book, you'll have a big advantage on the SAT. The bigger your vocabulary, the better you'll do. But not every word on the main list is the sort of word that is tested on the SAT. If you're getting ready to take the SAT or a similar standardized test, you should focus your attention on the words in the following list.

We've included short definitions to make it easier for you to learn the words. These definitions aren't always exactly like the ones you'll find in the dictionary or the main word list of this book; the y're the definitions of the words *as they are tested* on the SAT.

Keep in mind that these are not the *only* words you need to know for the SAT. They're just the words that have been tested most frequently in the past—the words that the test writers tend to come back to over and over again

Some SATs are absolutely loaded words on this list; others don't contain as many. One of the most important things these key terms will teach you is the *level* of the vocabulary on the test. Once you get a feel for this level, you'll be able to spot other possible so-called SAT words in your reading.

After you review these key terms, you should also turn to the GRE list starting on page 298. Of course, all of the words in this book are ones that will help you on standardized tests.

ABSTRACT Theoretical; lacking substance (the opposite of *concrete*)

ACUTE Sensitive; sharp; discerning

ADVOCATE *v* To promote; *n* one who promotes a cause

AESTHETIC Having to do with artistic beauty; artistic (not to be confused with *ascetic*)

ALLEVIATE To relieve, especially pain

AMASS To accumulate

AMBIVALENT Simultaneously feeling opposing feelings; uncertain

ANALOGY A comparison

ANARCHY Absence of government or control; lawlessness; disorder

ANECDOTE A short account of an interesting incident

ANIMATED Alive; moving

ANOMALY Something that is abnormal or irregular

APATHY Lack of emotion or interest

APPEASE To soothe; to pacify by giving in to

APPREHENSIVE Fearful about the future

ARROGANT Feeling superior to others; snooty

ARTICULATE Speaking clearly and well

ASCERTAIN To determine with certainty

AUTHENTIC Real

BELITTLE To make to seem little

BELLIGERENT Combative; quarrelsome; waging war

BENEVOLENT Kind; good-hearted; generous

BENIGN Gentle; not harmful; kind; mild

BIAS Prejudice; tendency; tilt

BREVITY The quality or state of being brief in duration

CANDOR Completely honest, straightforward

COMPLACENT Satisfied with the current situation and unconcerned with changing it

COMPLIANT Yielding; submissive

CONCISE Brief and to the point; succinct

CONDONE To overlook; to permit to happen

CONGENIAL Agreeably suitable; pleasant

CONSPICUOUS Easy to notice; obvious (antonym: *inconspicuous*)

CONTEMPT Reproachful disdain

DEBILITATE To weaken

DEFERENCE Submission or courteous respect

DENOUNCE To condemn openly

DEPLETE To use up; to reduce; to lessen

DESPONDENT Depressed

DETER To prevent; to stop; to keep from doing something

DIGRESS To go off the subject

DILIGENT Hardworking

DISCERNMENT Insight; ability to see things clearly

DISCRIMINATE To differentiate; to make a clear distinction; to see the difference

DISDAIN To regard with contempt

DISPARAGE To speak of negatively; to belittle

DISPASSIONATE Without passion; objective; neutral

DISSENT Disagreement

DISTINGUISH To tell apart; to cause to stand out

DIVERSE Varied

DIVERT To change the direction of; to alter the course of; to amuse

DUBIOUS Doubtful; of unlikely authenticity

ECCENTRIC Not conventional; a little kooky; irregular

ELABORATE Detailed; careful; thorough

ELOQUENT Well-spoken

EMPIRICAL Derived from observation or experiment

ENCROACH To make gradual inroads; to trespass

ENHANCE To make better; to augment

EVOKE To summon or draw forth

EXPLICIT Fully and clearly expressed

EXTRANEOUS Irrelevant; extra; unnecessary; unimportant

FANATIC One who is extremely devoted to a cause or idea

FICKLE Capricious; whimsical; unpredictable

FRIVOLOUS Not serious; not solemn; with levity

FUTILE Hopeless; without effect

GULLIBLE Overly trusting; willing to believe anything

HEED To listen to

HYPOTHETICAL Uncertain; unproven

IMPARTIAL Unbiased; neutral

IMPERATIVE Completely necessary

IMPLICIT Implied

INADVERTENT Lax; careless; without intention

INCESSANT Unceasing; never-ending

INCOHERENT Jumbled; chaotic; impossible to understand

INDIFFERENT Having no interest or concern

INDIGNATION Anger aroused by something perceived as unjust

INDULGENT Lenient; yielding to desire

INEVITABLE Unavoidable; bound to happen

INNATE Existing since birth; inborn; inherent

INNOVATION The act of introducing something new

INSTIGATE To provoke; to stir up

IRONIC Satiric; unexpected

JEOPARDY Danger

LAMENT To mourn

LETHARGY Sluggishness; laziness; drowsiness; indifference

MALICIOUS Deliberately harmful

MALLEABLE Capable of being shaped

MEDIATION A settlement between conflicting parties

MERGER A joining or marriage

NEGLIGENCE Carelessness

NEUTRAL Unbiased; not taking sides; objective

NOSTALGIA A bittersweet longing for things of the past

NOVEL *adj* Fresh; original; new

OBSCURE *adj* Not readily noticed; vague

OBJECTIVE *adj* Uninfluenced by emotions; *n* a goal

OMINOUS Menacing; threatening

PERIPHERAL Unimportant

PERVADE To be present throughout

PRAGMATIC Practical; down-to-earth; based on experience rather than theory

PREDECESSOR Someone or something that came before another

PROFOUND Deep; insightful (antonym: *superficial*)

PROFUSE Flowing; extravagant

PROVOCATIVE Giving rise to action or feeling

PRUDENT Careful; wise

RECIPROCATE To mutually take or give; to respond in kind

REDUNDANT Repetitive; unnecessary; excessively wordy

REFUTE To disprove; to prove to be false

REJUVENATE To make young and strong again

RELEVANT Important; pertinent

REMORSE Sadness; regret

REPRESS To hold down

REPUDIATE To reject; to deny

RESIGNATION Unresisting acceptance; submission

RETRACT To take back; to withdraw; to pull back

RIGOROUS Strict; harsh; severe

SCANTY Inadequate; minimal

SCRUTINIZE To examine closely

SKEPTICAL Doubting (antonym: *gullible*)

SOLEMN Serious; grave

SQUANDER To waste

STAGNATION Motionlessness; inactivity

STRINGENT Strict; restrictive

SUBSTANTIATE To support with proof or evidence; verify

SUBTLE Not obvious; able to make fine distinctions; ingenious; crafty

SUPERFICIAL Near the surface; shallow; unimportant

TANGIBLE Touchable; palpable

TEMPERATE Moderate; restrained

TENACIOUS Tough; hard to defeat

TENTATIVE Experimental; temporary; uncertain

UNDERMINE To weaken

UNDERSCORE To put emphasis on

UNIFORM Consistent; unchanging; the same for everyone

UNPRECEDENTED Happening for the first time; novel; never seen before

VOLATILE Quick to evaporate; highly unstable; explosive

VOLUNTARY willing; unforced

WILLFUL Deliberate; obstinate; insistent on having one's way

CHAPTER 5

GRE Key Terms

Need-to-Know Words for the GRE

The GRE (Graduate Record Examination) is essentially the SAT for graduate school. How well you do on the verbal section of the GRE is largely determined by your vocabulary. If you know a lot of words, you'll do better than most other test takers; if you don't, you'd better start learning some. Today.

The word list in this chapter includes the terms most likely to appear on the GRE. These are not the only words that can appear on the GRE, but they are the most likely. This list is a start. If you know all of these words, get cracking on the other *Word Smart* definitions.

ABSTRUSE Hard to understand or grasp

ACUTE Sharp; shrewd

ADORN To lend beauty to

ADROIT Skillful; dexterous; clever; shrewd; socially at ease

ADVERSE Unfavorable; antagonistic

AESTHETIC Having to do with artistic beauty; artistic

AFFECTATION Unnatural or artificial behavior, usually intended to impress

AMBIGUOUS Unclear in meaning; confusing; capable of being interpreted in different ways

AMBIVALENT Undecided; having opposed feelings simultaneously

AMELIORATE To make better or more tolerable

ANOINT To choose by or as if by divine intervention

ARCANE Mysterious; known only to a select few

ARCHAIC Extremely old; ancient; outdated

ARTLESS Honest or sincere; natural; uncultured and ignorant

ASCENDANCY Supremacy; domination

ASPIRATION A strong desire for high achievement

ASSIDUOUS Hardworking; busy; diligent

ASTONISHMENT Great surprise or amazement

AUGMENT To make bigger; to add to; to increase

AUSTERE Unadorned; stern; forbidding; without excess

AVARICE Greed; excessive love of riches

AVERSION A fixed, intense dislike

BANAL Unoriginal; ordinary

BASE *adj* Having or showing a lack of decency

BELIE To give a false impression of; to contradict

BENIGN Gentle; not harmful; kind; mild

BOON A timely blessing or benefit

BUCOLIC Charmingly rural; rustic; country-like

CANDOR Truthfulness; sincere honesty

CANNY Careful and shrewd

CANONIZE To treat as sacred; glorify

CLANGOR A loud racket; a din

COALESCE To come together as one; to fuse; to unite

COLLUSION Conspiracy; secret cooperation

COMMENSURATE Equal; proportionate

COMPREHENSIVE Covering or including everything

CONCOCT To devise, using skill and intelligence

CONCOMITANT Occurring or existing concurrently

CONFOUND To cause to become confused or perplexed

CONJURE To summon or bring into being as if by magic

CONSTRUE To interpret

CONTINUITY An uninterrupted succession or flow; a coherent whole

CONVENTIONAL Common; customary; unexceptional

COSMOPOLITAN At home in many places or situations; internationally sophisticated

COVET To wish for enviously

COW *v* To frighten or subdue with threats or a show of force

CREDENCE Acceptance as true or valid

CUNNING Marked by or given to artful subtlety and deceptiveness

CURSORY Hasty; superficial

DAUNT *v* To make fearful; to intimidate

DEBACLE Violent breakdown; sudden overthrow; overwhelming defeat

DEFIANT Boldly resisting

DEFLECT To turn aside or cause to turn aside

DELIMIT To establish the limits or boundaries of

DERIVATIVE Copied or adapted from others

DISPARATE Different; incompatible; unequal

DISPASSIONATE Not influenced by strong feelings or emotions

DISSEMBLE To disguise or conceal behind a false appearance

DISSEMINATE To spread the seeds of something; to scatter; to make widely known

DOCTRINAIRE Inflexibly committed to a doctrine or theory without regard to its practicality

DOGMATIC Arrogantly assertive of unproven ideas; stubbornly claiming that something (often a system of beliefs) is beyond dispute

DUBIOUS Full of doubt; uncertain

DUPLICITY The act of being two-faced; double-dealing; deception

DYNAMISM Continuous change, activity, or progress

EBULLIENT Boiling; bubbling with excitement; exuberant

ECCENTRIC Not conventional; a little kooky; irregular

ECLECTIC Choosing the best from many sources; drawn from many sources

EFFICACY Effectiveness

EFFLORESCENCE A gradual process of unfolding or developing; the point or time of greatest vigor

EGALITARIANISM The belief in the social and economic equality of all people

EGOISM The doctrine that human behavior is motivated by self-interest

EMINENT Well-known and respected; standing out from all others in quality or accomplishment; outstanding

ENIGMA A mystery

EPITOME A brief summary that captures the meaning of the whole; the perfect example of something; a paradigm

EQUIVOCAL Ambiguous; intentionally confusing; capable of being interpreted in more than one way

ERRONEOUS Containing or derived from error; mistaken

ERSTWHILE In the past; at a former time; formerly

ERUDITE Scholarly; deeply learned

ETHOS The disposition, character, or fundamental values peculiar to a specific person, people, culture, or movement

EXACERBATE To make worse

EXIGENT Demanding prompt action; urgent

EXPLICIT Clearly and directly expressed

EXPLOIT *v* To employ to the greatest possible advantage; to make use of selfishly or unethically

EXTANT Still in existence; not destroyed

EXTEMPORANEOUS Carried out or performed with little or no preparation

EXTRANEOUS Unnecessary; irrelevant; extra

EXTRAPOLATE To project or deduce from something known; to infer

FACETIOUS Humorous; not serious; clumsily humorous

FECKLESS Careless and irresponsible

FEEBLE Lacking bodily strength; weak

FEIGN To give a false appearance of

FORTUITOUS Accidental; occurring by chance

GARRULOUS Talkative; chatty

GLUM Moody and melancholy

HARBINGER A forerunner; a signal of

HERALD *v* To proclaim, especially with enthusiasm

HETERODOX Not in agreement with accepted beliefs

HIDEBOUND Stubbornly prejudiced, narrow-minded, or inflexible

HOMOGENEOUS Uniform; made entirely of one thing

HORTATORY Marked by exhortation or strong urging

HUMANISM A system of thought that focuses on humans and their values, capacities, and worth

HYPOTHESIS Something taken to be true for the purpose of argument or investigation; an assumption

ICONOCLAST One who attacks popular beliefs or institutions

ILLUMINATE To make understandable; to clarify

IMMINENT Just about to happen

IMPECUNIOUS Having little or no money

IMPEDIMENT A hindrance or obstruction

IMPENETRABLE Impossible to penetrate or enter; impossible to understand

IMPERATIVE Necessary or urgent

IMPERCEPTIBLE Impossible or difficult to perceive by the mind or senses

IMPETUS An impelling force; an impulse

IMPLICIT Implied rather than expressly stated

INALIENABLE Unable to be transferred to others

INCENDIARY Tending to arouse strong emotion or conflict

INCENSE *v* To make very angry

INCLUSIVE Taking in a great deal or everything within its scope

INDEFATIGABLE Having or showing a capacity for persistent effort

INDICT To accuse of wrongdoing; to criticize severely

INDIFFERENT Not caring one way or the other; apathetic; mediocre

INDOLENT Lazy

INDUSTRIOUS Energetic in work or study

INHIBIT To hold back; to restrain

INNOCUOUS Harmless

INNOVATION The act of introducing something new

INSCRUTABLE Difficult to understand or interpret

INSIPID Dull; bland

INSULAR Like an island; isolated

INTEGRATE To combine two or more things into a whole

INVALIDATE To nullify

IRKSOME Causing annoyance or weariness

IRONIC Meaning the opposite of what you seem to say; using words to mean something other than what they seem to mean

KINDRED Having a similar or related origin, nature, or character

LACONIC Using few words, especially to the point of being rude

LAUD To praise; to applaud; to extol; to celebrate

LUCID Clear; easy to understand

LUCRATIVE Producing wealth; profitable

LUMINARY A person who inspires others or achieves eminence in a field

MAGNIFY To make more intense or extreme

MAKESHIFT Suitable as a temporary substitute

MALIGN To make evil, harmful statements about, especially untrue statements

MARGINALIZE To relegate or confine to a lower or outer limit or edge

MEAGER Deficient in quantity, fullness, or extent

MENDACIOUS Lying; dishonest

MITIGATE To moderate the effect of something

MORBID Unwholesome thoughts or feelings, especially of death or disease

MORTIFY To humiliate

MUNDANE Ordinary; pretty boring; not heavenly and eternal

MUNIFICENT Very generous; lavish

NAIVETÉ Lacking worldly experience and understanding

NARCISSISM Excessive love of one's body or oneself

NOTORIOUS Known widely and usually unfavorably

NOVEL *adj* New; original

OBJECTIVE *adj* Uninfluenced by emotions or personal prejudices

OBSCURE Unknown; hard to understand; dark

OFFSET To counterbalance, counteract, or compensate for

OMNIPRESENT Present everywhere simultaneously

OPAQUE Impossible to see through; impossible to understand

OPULENT Luxurious

ORTHODOX Conventional; adhering to established principles or doctrines, especially in religion; by the book

OUTSTRIP To move past or ahead of

OVERSHADOW To make insignificant by comparison

PAINSTAKING Extremely careful; taking pains

PANACEA Something that cures everything

PARADOX A true statement or phenomenon that nonetheless seems to contradict itself; an untrue statement or phenomenon that nonetheless seems logical

PARTIAL Favoring one person or side over another or others

PARTISAN One who supports a particular person, cause, or idea

PATENT *adj* Obvious

PEDDLE To travel about selling; to seek to disseminate; to give out

PENCHANT Strong taste or liking

PERFUNCTORY Unenthusiastic; careless

PERIPHERY The outside edge of something

PERTURB To disturb greatly

PERUSE To read carefully

PERVADE To spread throughout

PHYSIOLOGICAL Characteristic of the normal functioning of a living organism

PIVOTAL Crucial

PLURALISM A condition in which numerous distinct ethnic, religious, or cultural groups are present and tolerated within a society

POLARIZE To break up into opposing factions or groupings

PRECARIOUS Dangerously lacking in security or stability

PRECOCIOUS Characterized by development, aptitude, or interests considered advanced for a given age

PREDILECTION A natural preference for something

PRESCIENCE Knowledge of actions or events before they occur

PRETENTIOUS Behaving as if one is important or deserving of merit when such is not the case

PREVARICATE To speak or write dishonestly

PROLIFERATE To spread or grow rapidly

PROLIX Tending to speak or write at excessive length

PROMULGATE To proclaim; to publicly or formally declare something

PROPITIOUS Marked by favorable signs or conditions

PROVIDENT Preparing or providing for the future; frugal

PROVOCATIVE Tending to provoke or stimulate

PROXY One appointed or authorized to act for another

PRUDENT Careful; having foresight

PUNCTILIOUS Strictly attentive to minute details of form in action or conduct

QUOTIDIAN Everyday; commonplace

REBUT To contradict; to argue in opposition to; to prove to be false

RECAPITULATE To make a summary

RECONCILE To settle; to resolve

RECONDITE Hard to understand; over one's head

REFERENDUM The submission of a proposed public measure or statute to a direct popular vote

REFUGE Protection or shelter

RELENTLESS Continuous; unstoppable

RELISH Hearty enjoyment or appreciation

REPUDIATE To reject; to renounce; to disown; to have nothing to do with

RESOLUTE Determined; firm; unwavering

RESONANT Strong and deep in tone; resounding; having a lasting presence or effect

REVERE To respect highly; to honor

RIDICULE To make fun of

RUTHLESS Having no compassion or pity

SANGUINE Cheerful; optimistic; hopeful

SCANTY Small; insufficient

SCINTILLATE To sparkle, either literally or figuratively

SECULAR Having nothing to do with religion or spiritual concerns

SERENDIPITY Accidental good fortune; discovering good things without looking for them

SHREWD Clever awareness or resourcefulness

SINISTER Evil, wicked; foreshadowing evil, trouble, or wickedness

SOLICITOUS Eager and attentive, often to the point of hovering; anxiously caring or attentive

SOLIDARITY Unity of purpose, interest, or sympathy

SPECULATIVE Based on guesswork

SPORADIC Stopping and starting; scattered; occurring in bursts every once in a while

SPURIOUS Doubtful; bogus; false

SUBJECTIVE Based on a given person's experience, understanding, and feelings

SUPERFICIAL On the surface only; shallow; not thorough

SUPPLANT To take the place of or substitute for

SURROGATE Substitute

SYNTHESIS The combining of parts to form a whole

TACIT Implied; not spoken

TACITURN Not talkative

TEMPERANCE Moderation and self-restraint

TEMPORAL Lasting only for a time; not eternal; passing

TENABLE Defensible, as in one's position in an argument; capable of being argued successfully; valid

TENSILE Capable of being stretched or extended

TEPID Lacking in emotional warmth or enthusiasm

TRANSGRESS To violate (a law); to sin

TRIFLING Of little worth or importance

TRIVIAL Of little significance or value

TUMULTUOUS Very loud; noisy; disorderly

UBIQUITOUS Being everywhere at the same time

UNDERMINE To weaken

UNDERSCORE To put emphasis on; to stress

UNIFORM *adj* Consistent; unchanging; the same for everyone

VAIN Having or showing excessive pride in one's appearance or accomplishments

VANQUISH To defeat or conquer in battle

VERACIOUS Truthful

VEX To annoy; to pester; to confuse

VINDICATE To clear from all blame or suspicion; to justify

VINTAGE Old or outmoded

CHAPTER 6

Word Roots You Should Know

You Don't Have to Memorize These Roots—You Already Know Them!

Here is a list of the most helpful roots to know. As mentioned earlier, learning roots helps you memorize words. We've focused on roots that will help you learn the *Word Smart* words, but this list will help you memorize hundreds of other words, too.

When you look up the definition of a word on this list, try to relate that definition to the root. Some students go through this list one root at a time. They look up all the words under one root and learn the definitions together. As always, whatever works for you is best.

To show you how each root relates to words you already know, each list includes an easy word or two. For example, the root *spec-* comes from a Latin word meaning to look or see, as in the easy words *spectator* and *spectacles.* Recognizing that will help you memorize the definition of the less common words *specter and circumspect,* which are on the same list. And you thought you didn't know Latin!

You will notice that the same root can be spelled in different ways. We have included the most common spelling variations in the heading. Remember that roots tell us the common heritage of words thousands of years old. Over the centuries spelling variations are bound to occur.

A note to philologists (etymologically, "word lovers"): In keeping with our pragmatic philosophy, we have sometimes taken liberties in compiling this list.

a (without)
amoral
atheist
atypical
anonymous
apathy
amorphous
atrophy
apartheid
anomaly
agnostic

***ab/abs* (off, away from, apart, down)**
abduct
abhor
abolish
abstract
abnormal
abdicate
abstinent
absolution
abstruse
abrogate
abscond
abjure
abstemious
ablution
abominate
aberrant

***ac/acr* (sharp, bitter)**
acid
acute
acerbic
exacerbate
acrid
acrimonious
acumen

***act/ag* (to do, to drive, to force, to lead)**
act
agent
agile
agitate

exacting
litigate
prodigal
prodigious
pedagogue
demagogue
synagogue

***ad/al* (to, toward, near)**
adapt
adjacent
addict
admire
address
adhere
administer
adore
advice
adjoin
adultery
advocate
allure
alloy

***al/ali/alter* (other, another)**
alternative
alias
alibi
alien
alter ego
alienation
altruist
altercation
allegory

***am* (love)**
amateur
amatory
amorous
enamored
amity
paramour
inamorata
amiable
amicable

amb (to go, to walk)
ambitious
amble
preamble
ambulance
ambulatory
perambulator
circumambulate

amb/amph (around)
amphitheater
ambit
ambience
ambient

amb/amph (both, more than one)
ambiguous
amphibian
ambivalent
ambidextrous

anim (life, mind, soul, spirit)
unanimous
animosity
equanimity
magnanimous
pusillanimous

annu/enni (year)
annual
anniversary
biannual
biennial
centennial
annuity
perennial
annals
millennium

ante (before)
ante
anterior
antecedent
antedate
antebellum
antediluvian

anthro/andr (man, human)
anthropology
android
misanthrope
philanthropy
anthropomorphic
philander
androgynous
anthropocentric

anti (against)
antidote
antiseptic
antipathy
antipodal

apo (away)
apology
apostle
apocalypse
apogee
apocryphal
apotheosis
apostasy
apoplexy

apt/ept (skill, fitness, ability)
adapt
aptitude
apt
inept
adept

arch/archi (chief, principal)
architect
archenemy
archetype
archipelago

archy (ruler)
monarchy
matriarchy
patriarchy
anarchy
hierarchy
oligarchy

art (skill, craft)
art
artificial
artifice
artisan
artifact
artful
artless

auc/aug/aux (to increase)
auction
auxiliary
augment
august

auto (self)
automatic
autopsy
autocrat
autonomy

be (to be, to have a certain quality)
belittle
belated
bemoan
befriend
bewilder
begrudge
bequeath
bespeak
belie
beguile
beset
bemuse
bereft

bel/bell (war)
rebel
belligerent
bellicose
antebellum

ben/bon (good)
benefit
beneficiary
beneficent

benefactor
benign
benevolent
benediction
bonus
bon vivant
bona fide

bi (twice, doubly)
binoculars
biannual
biennial
bigamy
bilateral
bilingual
bipartisan

bri/brev (brief, short)
brief
abbreviate
abridge
brevity

cad/cid (to fall, to happen by chance)
accident
coincidence
decadent
cascade
recidivism
cadence

cand (to burn)
candle
incandescent
candor

cant/cent/chant (to sing)
chant
enchant
accent
recant
incantation
incentive

cap/cip/capit/cipit (head, headlong)

capital
cape
captain
disciple
principle
principal
precipice
precipitate
precipitous
capitulate
capitalism
precipitation
caption
recapitulate

cap/cip/cept (to take, to get)

capture
anticipate
intercept
susceptible
emancipate
recipient
incipient
percipient
precept

card/cord/cour (heart)

cardiac
courage
encourage
concord
discord
accord
concordance
cordial

carn (flesh)

carnivorous
carnival
carnal
carnage
reincarnation
incarnation

cast/chast (cut)

caste
castigate
chastise
chaste

caust (to burn)

caustic
holocaust

ced/ceed/cess (to go, to yield, to stop)

exceed
precede
recess
concede
cede
access
predecessor
precedent
antecedent
recede
abscess
cessation
incessant

centr (center)

central
concentrate
eccentric
concentric
centrifuge
egocentric

cern/cert/cret/crim/crit (to separate, to judge, to distinguish, to decide)

concern
critic
secret
crime
discrete
ascertain
certitude
hypocrite
discriminate

criterion
discern
recrimination

chron (time)
synchronize
chronicle
chronology
chronic
chronological
anachronism
chronometer

circu (around, on all sides)
circumference
circumstances
circuit
circumspect
circumvent
circumnavigate
circumambulate
circumlocution
circumscribe
circuitous

cis (to cut)
scissors
precise
exorcise
excise
incision
incisive
concise

cit (to set in motion)
excite
incite
solicit
solicitous

cla/clo/clu (shut, close)
closet
enclose
conclude
claustrophobia
disclose

exclusive
recluse
preclude
seclude
cloister
foreclose
closure

claim/clam (to shout, to cry out)
exclaim
proclaim
acclaim
clamor
disclaim
reclaim
declaim

cli (to lean toward)
decline
recline
climax
proclivity
disinclination

co/col/com/con (with, together)
connect
confide
concede
coerce
cohesive
cohort
confederate
collaborate
compatible
coherent
comply
conjugal
connubial
congenial
convivial
coalesce
coalition
contrite
conciliate
conclave
commensurate

crat/cracy (to govern)
bureaucracy
democracy
aristocracy
theocracy
plutocracy
autocracy

cre/cresc/cret (to grow)
creation
increase
crescendo
increment
accretion
accrue

cred (to believe, to trust)
incredible
credibility
credentials
credit
creed
credo
credence
credulity
incredulous

cryp (hidden)
crypt
cryptic
apocryphal
cryptography

cub/cumb (to lie down)
cubicle
succumb
incubate
incumbent
recumbent

culp (blame)
culprit
culpable
exculpate
inculpate
mea culpa

cur/cour (running, a course)
occur
recur
current
curriculum
courier
cursive
excursion
concur
concurrent
incur
incursion
discourse
discursive
precursor
recourse
cursory

de (away, off, down, completely, reversal)
descend
detract
decipher
deface
defile
defraud
deplete
denounce
decry
defer
defame
delineate
deferential

dem (people)
democracy
epidemic
endemic
demagogue
demographics
pandemic

di/dia (apart, through)
dialogue
diagnose
diameter

dilate
digress
dilatory
diaphanous
dichotomy
dialectic

dic/dict/dit (to say, to tell, to use words)
dictionary
dictate
predict
contradict
verdict
abdicate
edict
dictum
malediction
benediction
indict
indite
diction
interdict
obiter dictum

dign (worth)
dignity
dignitary
dignify
deign
indignant
condign
disdain
infra dig

dis/dif (away from, apart, reversal, not)
disperse
disseminate
dissipate
dissuade
diffuse

doc/dac (to teach)
doctor
doctrine

indoctrinate
doctrinaire
docile
didactic

dog/dox (opinion)
orthodox
paradox
dogma
dogmatic

dol (suffer, pain)
condolence
indolence
doleful
dolorous

don/dot/dow (to give)
donate
donor
pardon
condone
antidote
anecdote
endow
dowry

dub (doubt)
dubious
dubiety
indubitable

duc/duct (to lead)
conduct
abduct
conducive
seduce
induct
induce
ductile

dur (hard)
endure
durable
duress
dour
obdurate

dys (faulty)
dysfunction
dystopia
dyspepsia
dyslexia

epi (upon)
epidemic
epilogue
epidermis
epistle
epitome
epigram
epithet
epitaph

equ (equal, even)
equation
adequate
equivalent
equilibrium
equable
equidistant
equity
iniquity
equanimity
equivocate
equivocal

err (to wander)
err
error
erratic
erroneous
errant
aberrant

esce (becoming)
adolescent
obsolescent
iridescent
luminescent
coalesce
quiescent
acquiescent

effervescent
incandescent
evanescent
convalescent
reminiscent

eu (good, well)
euphoria
euphemism
eulogy
eugenics
euthanasia
euphony

e/ef/ex (out, out of, from, former, completely)
evade
exclude
extricate
exonerate
extort
exhort
expire
exalt
exult
effervesce
extenuate
efface
effusion
egregious

extra (outside of, beyond)
extraordinary
extrasensory
extraneous
extrapolate

fab/fam (speak)
fable
fabulous
affable
ineffable
fame
famous
defame
infamous

fac/fic/fig/fait/feit/fy
(to do, to make)
factory
facsimile
benefactor
facile
faction
fiction
factitious
efficient
deficient
proficient
munificent
prolific
soporific
figure
figment
configuration
effigy
magnify
rarefy
ratify
ramification
counterfeit
feign
fait accompli
ex post facto

fer (to bring, to carry, to bear)
offer
transfer
confer
referendum
infer
fertile
proffer
defer
proliferate
vociferous

ferv (to boil, to bubble, to burn)
fervor
fervid
effervescent

fid (faith, trust)
confide
confident
confidant
affidavit
diffident
fidelity
infidelity
perfidy
fiduciary
infidel
semper fidelis
bona fide

fin (end)
final
finale
confine
define
definitive
infinite
affinity
infinitesimal

flag/flam (to burn)
flame
flamboyant
flammable
inflammatory
flagrant
conflagration
in flagrante delicto

flect/flex (to bend)
deflect
flexible
inflect
reflect
genuflect

flict (to strike)
afflict
inflict
conflict
profligate

flu, flux (to flow)
fluid
influence
fluent
affluent
fluctuation
influx
effluence
confluence
superfluous
mellifluous

fore (before)
foresight
foreshadow
forestall
forgo
forbear

fort (chance)
fortune
fortunate
fortuitous

fra/frac/frag/fring (to break)
fracture
fraction
fragment
fragile
refraction
fractious
infraction
refractory
infringe

fruit/frug (fruit, produce)
fruitful
fruition
frugal

fund/found (bottom)
foundation
fundamental
founder
profound

fus (to pour)
confuse
transfusion
profuse
effusive
diffuse
suffuse
infusion

gen (birth, creation, race, kind)
generous
generate
genetics
photogenic
degenerate
homogeneous
genealogy
gender
genre
genesis
carcinogenic
genial
congenial
ingenuous
ingenue
indigenous
congenital
progeny
engender
miscegenation
sui generis

gn/gno (know)
ignore
ignoramus
recognize
incognito
diagnose
prognosis
agnostic
cognitive
cognoscente
cognizant

grand (big)
grand
grandeur
grandiose
aggrandize
grandiloquent

grat (pleasing)
grateful
ingrate
ingratiate
gratuity
gratuitous

grav/griev (heavy, serious)
grave
grief
aggrieve
gravity
grievous

greg (herd)
congregation
segregation
aggregation
gregarious
egregious

gress/grad (to step)
progress
graduate
gradual
aggressive
regress
degrade
retrograde
transgress
digress
egress

her/hes (to stick)
coherent
cohesive
adhesive
adherent
inherent

(h)etero (different)
heterosexual
heterogeneous
heterodox

(h)om (same)
homogeneous
homonym
homosexual
anomaly
homeostasis

hyper (over, excessive)
hyperactive
hyperbole

hypo (under, beneath, less than)
hypodermic
hypochondriac
hypothesis
hypocritical

_id_ (one's own)
idiot
idiom
idiosyncrasy

_im/in_ (not, without)
inactive
indifferent
innocuous
insipid
indolence
impartial
inept
indigent

_im/in/em/en_ (in, into)
in
embrace
enclose
ingratiate
intrinsic
influx
incarnate
implicit
indigenous

infra (beneath)
infrastructure
infrared
infrasonic

inter (between, among)
interstate
interim
interloper
interlude
intermittent
interplay
intersperse
intervene

intra (within)
intramural
intrastate
intravenous

ject (to throw, to throw down)
inject
eject
project
trajectory
conjecture
dejected
abject

join/junct (to meet, to join)
junction
joint
adjoin
subjugate
juxtapose
injunction
rejoinder
conjugal
junta

jur (to swear)
jury
perjury
abjure
adjure

lect/leg (to select, to choose)
collect
elect
select
electorate
predilection
eclectic
elegant

lev (lift, light, rise)
elevator
relieve
lever
alleviate
levitate
relevant
levee
levity

loc/log/loqu (word, speech)
dialogue
eloquent
elocution
locution
interlocutor
prologue
epilogue
soliloquy
eulogy
colloquial
grandiloquent
philology
neologism
tautology
loquacious

luc/lum/lus (light)
illustrate
illuminate
luminous
luminescent
illustrious
lackluster
translucent
lucid
elucidate

lud/lus (to play)
illusion
ludicrous
delude
elude
elusive
allude
collusion
prelude
interlude

lut/lug/luv (to wash)
lavatory
dilute
pollute
deluge
antediluvian

mag/maj/max (big)
magnify
magnitude
major
maximum
majestic
magnanimous
magnate
maxim
magniloquent

mal/male (bad, ill, evil, wrong)
malfunction
malodorous
malicious
malcontent
malign
malignant
malaise
dismal
malapropism
maladroit
malevolent
malinger
malfeasance
malefactor
malediction

man (hand)
manual
manufacture
emancipate
manifest
mandate
mandatory

mater/matr (woman, mother)
matrimony
maternal
maternity
matriculate
matriarch

min (small)
minute
minutiae
diminution
miniature
diminish

min (to project, to hang over)
eminent
imminent
prominent
preeminent

mis/mit (to send)
transmit
manumit
emissary
missive
intermittent
remit
remission
demise

misc (mixed)
miscellaneous
miscegenation
promiscuous

mon/monit (to warn)
monument
monitor
summons

admonish
remonstrate

morph (shape)
amorphous
metamorphosis
polymorphous
anthropomorphic

mort (death)
immortal
morgue
morbid
moribund
mortify

mut (change)
commute
mutation
mutant
immutable
transmutation
permutation

nam/nom/noun/nown/nym (rule, order)
astronomy
economy
autonomy
antimony
gastronomy
taxonomy

nat/nas/nai (to be born)
natural
native
naive
cognate
nascent
innate
renaissance

nec/nic/noc/nox (harm, death)
innocent
noxious
obnoxious

pernicious
internecine
innocuous
necromancy

nom/nym/noun/nown (name)
synonym
anonymous
nominate
pseudonym
misnomer
nomenclature
acronym
homonym
nominal
ignominy
denomination
noun
renown
nom de plume
nom de guerre

nov/neo/nou (new)
novice
novel
novelty
renovate
innovate
neologism
neophyte
nouvelle cuisine
nouveau riche

nounc/nunc (to announce)
announce
pronounce
denounce
renounce

ob/oc/of/op (toward, to, against, completely, over)
obese
object
obstruct
obstinate
obscure

obtrude
oblique
oblivious
obnoxious
obstreperous
obtuse
opprobrium
obsequious
obfuscate

omni (all)
omnipresent
omniscient
omnipotent

pac/peac (peace)
peace
appease
pacify
pacifist
pacifier
pact

pan (all, everywhere)
panorama
panacea
panegyric
pantheon
panoply
pandemic

par (equal)
par
parity
apartheid
disparity
disparate
disparage

para (next to, beside)
parallel
paraphrase
parasite
paradox
parody
paragon

parable
paradigm
paramilitary
paranoid
paranormal
parapsychology
paralegal

pas/pat/path (feeling, suffering, disease)
apathy
sympathy
empathy
antipathy
passionate
compassion
compatible
dispassionate
impassive
pathos
pathology
sociopath
psychopath

pater/patr (father, support)
patron
patronize
paternal
paternalism
expatriate
patrimony
patriarch
patrician

pau/po/pov/pu (few, little, poor)
poor
poverty
paucity
pauper
impoverish
puerile
pusillanimous

ped (child, education)
pedagogue
pediatrician
encyclopedia

ped/pod (foot)
pedal
pedestal
pedestrian
podiatrist
expedite
expedient
impede
impediment
podium
antipodes

pen/pun (to pay, to compensate)
penal
penalty
punitive
repent
penance
penitent
penitentiary
repine
impunity

pend/pens (to hang, to weigh, to pay)
depend
dispense
expend
stipend
spend
expenditure
suspense
compensate
propensity
pensive
indispensable
impending
pendulum
appendix
append

appendage
ponderous
pendant

per (completely, wrong)
persistent
perforate
perplex
perspire
peruse
pervade
perjury
perturb
perfunctory
perspicacious
permeate
pernicious
perennial
peremptory
pertinacious

peri (around)
perimeter
periscope
peripheral
peripatetic

pet/pit (to go, to seek, to strive)
appetite
compete
petition
perpetual
impetuous
petulant
propitious

phil (love)
philosophy
philanthropy
philatelist
philology
bibliophile

phone (sound)
telephone
symphony
megaphone

euphony
cacophony

plac (to please)
placid
placebo
placate
implacable
complacent
complaisant

ple (to fill)
complete
deplete
complement
supplement
implement
plethora
replete

plex/plic/ply (to fold, to twist, to tangle, to bend)
complex
complexion
complicate
duplex
replica
ply
comply
implicit
implicate
explicit
duplicity
complicity
supplicate
accomplice
explicate

pon/pos/pound (to put, to place)
component
compound
deposit
dispose
expose
exposition
expound
juxtapose

depose
proponent
repository
transpose
superimpose

port (to carry)
import
portable
porter
portfolio
deport
deportment
export
portmanteau
portly
purport
disport
importune

post (after)
posthumous
posterior
posterity
ex post facto

pre (before)
precarious
precocious
prelude
premeditate
premonition
presage
presentiment
presume
presuppose
precedent
precept
precipitous
preclude
predilection
preeminent
preempt
prepossess
prerequisite
prerogative

prehend/prise (to take, to get, to seize)
surprise
comprehend
enterprise
impregnable
reprehensible
apprehension
comprise
apprise
apprehend
comprehensive
reprisal

pro (much, for, a lot)
prolific
profuse
propitious
prodigious
profligate
prodigal
protracted
proclivity
proliferate
propensity
prodigy
proselytize
propound
provident
prolix

prob (to prove, to test)
probe
probation
approbation
probity
opprobrium
reprobate

pug (to fight)
pugilism
pug
pugnacious
impugn
repugnant

punc/pung/poign/point (to point, to prick)
point
puncture
punctual
punctuate
pungent
poignant
compunction
expunge
punctilious

que/quis (to seek)
acquire
acquisition
exquisite
acquisitive
request
conquest
inquire
inquisitive
inquest
query
querulous
perquisite

qui (quiet)
quiet
disquiet
tranquil
acquiesce
quiescent

rid/ris (to laugh)
ridicule
derision
risible

rog (to ask)
interrogate
arrogant
prerogative
abrogate
surrogate
derogatory
arrogate

sal/sil/sault/sult (to leap, to jump)
insult
assault
somersault
salient
resilient
insolent
desultory
exult

sanct/sacr/secr (sacred)
sacred
sacrifice
sanctuary
sanctify
sanction
execrable
sacrament
sacrilege

sci (to know)
science
conscious
conscience
unconscionable
omniscient
prescient
conscientious
nescient

scribe/scrip (to write)
scribble
describe
script
postscript
prescribe
proscribe
ascribe
inscribe
conscription
scripture
transcript
circumscribe
manuscript
scribe

se (apart)
select
separate
seduce
seclude
segregate
secede
sequester
sedition

sec/sequ (to follow)
second
prosecute
sequel
sequence
consequence
inconsequential
obsequious
non sequitur

sed/sess/sid (to sit, to be still, to plan, to plot)
preside
resident
sediment
session
dissident
obsession
residual
sedate
subside
subsidy
subsidiary
sedentary
dissident
insidious
assiduous
sedulous

sens/sent (to feel, to be aware)
sense
sensual
sensory
sentiment
resent

consent
dissent
assent
consensus
sentinel
insensate
sentient
presentiment

sol (to loosen, to free)
dissolve
soluble
solve
resolve
resolution
irresolute
solvent
dissolution
dissolute
absolution

spec/spic/spit (to look, to see)
perspective
aspect
spectator
specter
spectacles
speculation
suspicious
auspicious
spectrum
specimen
introspection
retrospective
perspective
perspicacious
circumspect
conspicuous
respite
specious

sta/sti (to stand, to be in a place)
static
stationary
destitute

obstinate
obstacle
stalwart
stagnant
steadfast
constitute
constant
stasis
status
status quo
homeostasis
apostasy

sua (smooth)
suave
assuage
persuade
dissuade

sub/sup (below)
submissive
subsidiary
subjugate
subliminal
subdue
sublime
subtle
subversive
subterfuge
subordinate
suppress
supposition

super/sur (above)
surpass
supercilious
superstition
superfluous
superlative
supersede
superficial
surmount
surveillance
survey

tac/tic (to be silent)
reticent
tacit
taciturn

tain/ten/tent/tin (to hold)
contain
detain
pertain
pertinacious
tenacious
abstention
sustain
tenure
pertinent
tenant
tenable
tenet
sustenance

**tend/tens/tent/tenu
(to stretch, to thin)**
tension
extend
tendency
tendon
tent
tentative
contend
contentious
tendentious
contention
contender
tenuous
distend
attenuate
extenuating

theo (god)
atheist
apotheosis
theocracy
theology

tom (to cut)
tome
microtome

epitome
dichotomy

tort (to twist)
tort
extort
torture
tortuous

tract (to drag, to pull, to draw)
tractor
attract
contract
detract
tract
tractable
intractable
protract
abstract

trans (across)
transfer
transaction
transparent
transport
transition
transitory
transient
transgress
transcendent
intransigent
translucent

us/ut (to use)
abuse
usage
utensil
usurp
utility
utilitarian

**ven/vent (to come, to move
toward)**
adventure
convene
convenient
event

venturesome
avenue
intervene
advent
contravene
circumvent

ver (truth)
verdict
verify
veracious
verisimilitude
aver
verity

vers/vert (to turn)
controversy
revert
subvert
invert
divert
diverse
aversion
extrovert
introvert
inadvertent
versatile
traverse
covert
overt
avert
advert

vi (life)
vivid
vicarious
convivial
viable
vivacity
joie de vivre
bon vivant

vid/vis (to see)
evident
television
video
vision
provision
adviser
provident
survey
vista
visionary
visage

voc/vok (to call)
vocabulary
vocal
provocative
advocate
equivocate
equivocal
vocation
avocation
convoke
vociferous
irrevocable
evocative
revoke
convoke
invoke

vol (to wish)
voluntary
volunteer
volition
malevolent
benevolent

CHAPTER 7

Common Usage Errors

Some of the most embarrassing language errors involve words so common and so apparently simple that almost no one would think of looking them up. The following list contains a number of the most frequently misused words and expressions in the language.

ALL RIGHT Not "alright."

AMONG/BETWEEN *Among* is used with three or more people or things; *between* is used with two.
- The tin-can telephone line ran *between* the two houses.
- *Among* the twelve members of the committee were only three women.
- Mr. Nuñez distributed the candy *among* the four of us.

Between you and I is incorrect; *between you and me* is correct.

ANXIOUS This word properly means "filled with anxiety," not "eager." Don't say you're *anxious* for school to end unless the ending of school makes you feel fearful.

AS FAR AS...IS CONCERNED Not a stylish expression, but if you use it, don't leave out the is *concerned*. It is not correct to say, "As far as money, I'd like to be rich." Instead, you should say, "As far as money *is concerned*, I'd like to be rich."

AS/LIKE You can run like a fox, but you can't run like a fox runs.

Like is used only with nouns, pronouns, and grammatical constructions that act like nouns.
- Joe runs *like* a fox.
- Joe runs *as* a fox runs.
- Joe runs the way a fox runs.

BIWEEKLY, BIMONTHLY. *Biweekly* means either twice a week or once every two weeks, depending on who is using it. Likewise with *bimonthly*. If you need to be precise, avoid these words by saying "twice a week" or "every other week" instead. *Fortnightly* means once every two weeks.

CAN/MAY *Can* denotes ability; *may* denotes permission. If you *can* do something, you are *able* to do it. If you *may* do something, you are *permitted* to do it.

CAPITAL/CAPITOL Washington, D.C., is the *capital* of the United States. The building where Congress meets is the *Capitol*.

COMMON/MUTUAL *Common* means "shared"; *mutual* means "reciprocal." If Tim and Tom have a *common* dislike, they both dislike the same thing (anchovies). If Tim and Tom have a *mutual* dislike, they dislike each other.

COMMONPLACE In careful usage, this word is an adjective meaning "ordinary" or "uninteresting." It can also be used as a noun meaning a "trite or obvious observation" or a "cliché." It should not be used sloppily as a substitute for the word "common."

- To say that French food is the best in the world is a *commonplace*.
- It is *commonplace* but neither interesting nor perceptive to say that French food is the best in the world.

COMPARE TO/COMPARE WITH *To compare* an apple *to* an orange is to say that an apple is like an orange. *To compare* an apple *with* an orange is to discuss the similarities and differences between the two fruits.

- Daisuke *compared* his girlfriend's voice *to* the sound of a cat howling in the night; that is, he said his girlfriend sounded like a cat howling in the night.
- I *compared* my grades *with* Beth's and discovered that she had done better in every subject except math.

DIFFERENT FROM *Different from* is correct; "different than" is not.

- My dog is *different from* your dog.

EACH OTHER/ONE ANOTHER Each other is used with two; one another is used with three or more.

- A husband and wife should love each other.
- The fifteen members of the group had to learn to get along with one another.

EQUALLY AS Nothing is ever "equally as" anything as anything else.

- Your car and Dave's car might be equally fast.

You should never say that the two cars are equally as fast. Nor should you say that your car is equally as fast as Dave's. You should simply say that it is as fast.

(THE) FACT THAT/THAT You almost never need to use "the fact that"; *that* alone will suffice.

Instead of saying, "I was appalled by *the fact that* he was going to the movies," say, "I was appalled *that* he was going to the movies."

FARTHER/FURTHER *Farther* refers to actual, literal distance—the kind measured in inches and miles. *Further* refers to figurative distance. Use *farther* if the distance can be measured; use *further* if it cannot.

- Paris is *farther* from New York than London is.
- Paris is *further* from my thoughts than London is.
- We hiked seven miles but then were incapable of hiking *farther*.
- I made a nice outline for my thesis but never went any *further*.

FEWER, LESS *Fewer* is used with things that can be counted, *less* with things that cannot. That is, *fewer* refers to number; *less* refers to quantity.

- I have *fewer* sugar lumps than Henry does.
- I have *less* sugar.

Despite what you hear on television, it is *not* correct to say that one soft drink contains "less calories" than another. It contains *fewer* calories (calories can be counted); it is *less* fattening.

FORMER, LATTER *Former* means the first of two people or things; *latter* means the second of two. If you are referring to three or more things, you shouldn't use *former* and *latter*.

It is incorrect to say, "The restaurant had hamburgers, hot dogs, and pizzas; we ordered the *former*." Instead, say, "We ordered the first," or, "We ordered hamburgers."

IF/WHETHER Almost everyone uses *if* in situations that call for *whether*. *If* should be used when something may or may not happen and is usually followed by *then*. *Whether* should be used when more than one alternative is being discussed. For example: "We need to decide *whether* we should go to the show or stay home." The use of *if* in this situation is widely accepted, but the use of *if* in some situations might cause confusion. Consider this sentence: "Let me know *if* you're coming tonight." Someone might interpret this to mean "*If* you're coming tonight, then let me know. *If* you're not coming tonight, then you don't have to reply." To make it clear that you expect a response, use *whether*: "Let me know *whether* you're coming tonight." This should be interpreted as "No matter what you decide, please let me know your plans."

IRREGARDLESS This is not a word. Say *regardless* or *irrespective*.

LAY/LIE The only way to "*lay* down on the beach" is to take small feathers and place them in the sand.
To *lay* is to place or set.

- Will the widow *lay* flowers by the grave? She already *laid* them, or she has already *laid* them. Who *lies* in the grave? Her former husband *lies* there. He *lay* there yesterday, too. In fact, he has *lain* there for several days.

PLURALS AND SINGULARS
The following words take plural verbs:

> both
> criteria
> media
> phenomena

The following words take singular verbs:

> criterion
> each
> either
> every, everybody, everyone, everything
> medium
> neither
> none, no one, nobody, nothing
> phenomenon

PRESENTLY *Presently* means "soon," not "now" or "currently."
- The mailman should be here *presently*; in fact, he should be here in about five minutes.
- The mailman is here now.

STATIONARY/STATIONERY *Stationary* means not moving; *stationery* is notepaper.

THAT/WHICH Most people confuse these two words. Many people who know the difference have trouble remembering it. Here's a simple rule that will almost always work: *that* can never have a comma in front of it; *which* always will.

- There is the car *that* ran over my foot.
- Ed's car, *which* ran over my foot, is over there.
- I like sandwiches *that* are dripping with mustard.
- My sandwich, *which* was dripping with mustard, was the kind I like.

Which is used in place of *that* if it follows another *that*: "We were fond of *that* feeling of contentment *which* follows victory."

CHAPTER 8

Abbreviations

Abbreviations may not technically be considered vocabulary, but being able to recognize certain acronyms and other abbreviations will definitely help you understand what you read. Here are some of the most common abbreviations you may encounter in your reading, whether everyday or academic.

AP	Advanced Placement
ASAP	As soon as possible
Assn.	Association
Assoc.	Associates
asst.	Assistant
ATM	Automated teller machine
attn.	To the attention of
aux.	Auxiliary
AWOL	Absent without leave
BA	Bachelor of Arts
BMOC	Big man on campus
BS	Bachelor of Science
BW	Black and white
C	Celsius, centigrade
c/o	In care of
cc	Cubic centimeter; carbon copy
CD	Certificate of Deposit; compact disc
cf.	[Latin—*confer*] See also
CMYK	Cyan-magenta-yellow-black
CO	Commanding officer
Co.	Company
COD	Cash on delivery
Corp.	Corporation
CPA	Certified public accountant
CPU	Central processing unit
CRT	Cathode ray tube
DA	District Attorney
db	Decibels
DDM	Doctor of Dental Medicine
DDS	Doctor of Dental Science
dept.	Department

DUI	Driving under the influence
DVD	Digital video disk; digital versatile disk
DWI	Driving while intoxicated
ED	Executive director
e.g.	[Latin—*exempli gratia*] For example
EKG	Electrocardiogram
EP	Extended-play record
ESP	Extrasensory perception
et al.	[Latin—*et alii*] And others
et seq.	[Latin—*et sequens*] And following
ETA	Estimated time of arrival
etc.	[Latin—*et cetera*] And so on
ETD	Estimated time of departure
ETS	Educational Testing Service
F	Fahrenheit
ff.	And following pages
FYI	For your information
GI	Government issue
govt.	Government
GRE	Graduate Record Examinations
IB	International Baccalaureate
ibid	[Latin—*ibidem*] In the same place
i.e.	[Latin—*id est*] That is
Inc.	Incorporated
IQ	Intelligence quotient
ISO	in search of
ISP	Internet service provider
IV	Intravenous
JD	[Latin—*jurisdoctor*] Doctor of Law
K	[Latin—*kilo*] Thousand
km	Kilometer
LLP	Limited liability partnership
LP	Long-playing record
LPG	Liquefied petroleum gas
MA	Master of Arts
MC	Master of Ceremonies
MD	Doctor of Medicine
MIA	Missing in action

mm	Millimeter
MP	Member of Parliament or military police
Ms	Manuscript
MS	Master of Science
Mss	Manuscripts
MVP	Most valuable player
op. cit.	[Latin—*opere citato*] In the work previously cited
OS	Operating system
p.	Page
PA	Public address
PC	Personal computer
PhD	Doctor of Philosophy
PIN	Personal identification number
POW	Prisoner of war
pp.	Pages
P.S.	[Latin—*postscriptum*] Postscript
QED	[Latin—*quod erat demonstrandum*] Which was to be demonstrated
R & D	Research and development
Rep.	Representative
RGB	Red-green-blue
ROTC	Reserve Officers' Training Corps
RSVP	[French—*Répondez s'il vous plaît*] Please reply
SRO	Standing room only
SWAK	Sealed with a kiss
TKO	Technical knockout
TLC	Tender loving care
UFO	Unidentified flying object
VIP	Very important person
viz.	[Latin—*videlicet*] Namely
w/	With
w/o	Without
WWW	World wide web

CHAPTER 9

The Arts

You don't need to be a master of music, literature, film, or another artistic discipline to keep up in a conversation or course about the arts. Here are some major key art terms to keep in your back pocket.

ALLITERATION   A poetic device involving the use of two or more words with the same initial consonant sounds. Big Bird is an *alliterative* name.

BAUHAUS   A German school of art and architecture founded in 1919. *Bauhaus* style is characterized by harsh geometric form and great austerity of detail.

BIOPIC   A biographical film. *Gandhi* and *Malcolm X* are well-known biopics. Some, such as *The Hours* (about Virginia Woolf) and *Capote* (about Truman Capote and Harper Lee), interweave real and fictitious plots or use a single incident to shed light on a person's entire life.

BLANK VERSE   Unrhymed verse, especially in **iambic pentameter**.

CHAMBER MUSIC   Music written for and performed by small ensembles of players. The string quartet (two violins, viola, and cello) is the most influential form of *chamber music* ensemble.

CHIAROSCURO   An artistic technique in which form is conveyed by light and dark only, not by color.

CONCERTO   A musical composition for an orchestra and one or more soloists.

CUBISM   An early 20th century artistic movement involving, among other things, the fragmented portrayal of three-dimensional objects. *Cubism* was given its highest expression by Pablo Picasso.

DOCUMENTARY   A nonfiction film intended to record or capture (and often comment on) some part of reality. *Hoop Dreams, March of the Penguins,* and *Fahrenheit 9/11* are examples of well-known documentaries.

FREE VERSE   Unrhymed and unmetered (or irregularly rhymed and metered) verse.

FRESCO   An artistic technique in which paint is applied to wet plaster, causing the painted image to become bound into the decorated surface.

HAIKU A three-line, non-rhyming poem in which the first and third lines contain five syllables, and the second contains seven. Traditional Japanese haiku (plural and singular forms are identical) often evoke the seasons.

IAMBIC PENTAMETER A poetic metrical form in which each line of verse consists of ten syllables, of which only the even-numbered syllables are stressed.

IMPRESSIONISM A late 19th century French movement in painting that attempted, among other things, to convey the effect of light more vividly than had previously been done. Claude Monet was among the most influential of the *Impressionists*.

JAZZ An influential American music style rooted in African and African-American traditions with input from diverse sources. Jazz has many spin-offs and subgenres. Famous jazz musicians have included Duke Ellington and Charlie Parker.

LIBERAL ARTS A general course of study focusing on literature, art, history, philosophy, and related subjects rather than on specifically vocational instruction.

METAPHOR A figure of speech involving the use of words associated with one thing in connection with another in order to point up some revealing similarity between the two. To refer to someone's nose as his or her beak is to use *metaphor* to say something unflattering about the person's nose.

MOSAIC An art form in which designs are produced by inlaying small tiles or pieces of stone, glass, or other materials.

NARRATIVE FILM A fiction film told primarily in chronological order. Most popular films fall into this category.

NOIR A film and literature style portraying crime and sleaze in an atmosphere of mystery, bleakness, cynicism, and/or glamour. *Noir* (pronounced "nwar") often contains a political subtext of corruption or paranoia. Well-known examples include *The Big Sleep* and *Chinatown*.

OPERA A drama set to music, in which the dialogue is sung rather than spoken.

OVERTURE An introductory musical piece for an opera or other work of musical drama.

POSTCOLONIALISM   A literary and philosophical movement concerned with life and identity in formerly colonized cultures. Well-known postcolonial writers include Franz Fanon, Jamaica Kincaid, and Salman Rushdie.

RENAISSANCE   The blossoming of art, literature, science, and culture in general that transformed Europe between the fourteenth and seventeenth centuries.

ROMAN À CLEF   A novel in which the characters and events are disguised versions of real people and events.

ROMANTICISM   An anticlassical literary and artistic movement that began in Europe in the late 18th century. William Wordsworth and John Keats were perhaps the preeminent *Romantic* poets.

SIMILE   A figure of speech in which one thing is likened to something else. A *simile* will always contain the word *like* or *as*. To call someone's nose a beak is to use a *metaphor;* to say that someone's nose is *like* a beak is to use a *simile.*

SONATA   An instrumental musical composition consisting of several movements.

SONNET   A verse form consisting of fourteen lines of **iambic pentameter** rhymed in a strict scheme.

STILL LIFE   An artistic depiction of arranged objects.

STREAM OF CONSCIOUSNESS   A literary technique in which an author attempts to reproduce in prose the unstructured rush of real human thought.

SURREALISM   A primarily French artistic and literary movement of the early 20th century that attempted to incorporate imagery from dreams and the unconscious into works of art.

SYMPHONY   A major work for orchestra, usually consisting of several movements.

CHAPTER 10

Finance

Reading the financial pages of the newspaper can be confusing if you don't know the lingo. Here are some of the terms that crop up most often.

ANNUAL PERCENTAGE RATE (APR) A loan's *annual percentage rate* is the loan's *true* interest rate when all the costs of borrowing are taken into account. Before lending you $10,000 at a nominal interest rate of 12 percent, a bank may charge you a fee of several hundred dollars. The effective interest rate on the loan—its *APR*—would include the cost of paying this fee and would thus be somewhat higher than 12 percent.

ASSET An *asset* is something you own. A *liability* is something you owe.

BANKRUPTCY A procedure by which a deeply indebted person or company sacrifices most or all remaining *assets* in exchange for being relieved of the obligation to repay any remaining debts.

BEAR MARKET A falling stock market.

BONDS When you buy a *bond* you are, in effect, lending money to the city, company, or other entity that issued it. In return, the issuer pays you interest.

There are many different kinds of *bonds.* U.S. government *bonds* are *bonds* issued by the federal government. When you buy a *government bond,* you're helping to finance the federal deficit. *Municipal bonds* are *bonds* issued by cities, counties, and states. They are often issued to finance specific projects, such as the construction of a highway or an athletic stadium. *Corporate bonds* are *bonds* issued by companies. *Junk bonds* are high-interest, high-risk *bonds* issued by relatively uncredit-worthy borrowers.

BOOK VALUE A company's *book value* is what the company would be worth if its *assets* (including office buildings and furniture) were all sold and its *liabilities* were all paid off.

BULL MARKET A rising stock market.

CALL An *option* to buy stock at a certain price within a certain period of time. A *put* is an option to sell stock at a certain price within a certain period of time. *Puts* and *calls* are not for amateurs.

CAPITAL GAIN The profit on the sale of stocks, bonds, real estate, and other so-called capital *assets.* If you buy a stock for $5 a share and sell it a few weeks later for $1,000 a share, you have a capital gain of $995 a share. A *capital loss* is the same thing in reverse.

COMMODITIES Pork bellies, beef fat, wheat, corn, gold, silver, and other animal, vegetable, and mineral products are a few examples of *commodities*. Contracts for these items are traded in highly risky markets that are no place for someone who can't afford to lose a lot of money.

COMMON STOCKS A share of *common stock* represents a (usually tiny) piece of the company that issues it. If you own a share of stock in a company, you own a fraction of the company itself and are entitled to a corresponding fraction of the company's profits, usually paid in the form of quarterly *dividends*.

COMPOUND INTEREST *Compound interest* is interest paid on interest that's already been paid. If you put $100 in a savings account and don't withdraw the interest payments, the effective interest rate on your initial investment rises as each new interest payment increases the value of your account. The compounding of interest causes an account earning 10 percent interest to double in value in about seven years instead of the ten you might expect.

CORPORATE BONDS See *bonds*.

DISCOUNT BROKERAGE A stockbrokerage that charges lower commissions than traditional stockbrokerages but provides fewer services.

DIVIDEND When a company earns profits, it typically reinvests some in itself and distributes the rest to its shareholders, who are the company's owners. These profit distributions are typically paid quarterly and are called *dividends*.

DOW JONES INDUSTRIAL AVERAGE An index based on the stock prices of thirty big industrial companies. The *Dow Jones* isn't a representative sample of either the stock market or the economy in general, but it has traditionally been used as a barometer of both.

EQUITY *Equity* is the difference between *assets* and *liabilities*. If your house (an *asset*) is worth $100,000 and you owe $45,000 on it (a *liability*), your *equity* in your house is $55,000.

A *home equity loan* is a loan backed by your *equity* in your home. *Home equity loans* used to be called *second mortgages.* If you stop paying off your *home equity loan,* you risk losing your house.

FEDERAL DEPOSIT INSURANCE CORPORATION The *FDIC* is the government agency that insures bank deposits.

HOME EQUITY LOAN See *equity*.

MARGIN Buying stock on *margin* is buying stock in part with money borrowed from the stockbroker. Buying on *margin* is risky. If the price of a stock you bought on *margin* falls below a certain point, the broker will require you to put up more money. If you don't have the money, you may be forced to sell the stock immediately at a loss in order to cover your position.

MORTGAGE When you obtain a *mortgage* to buy a house, what you are really doing is persuading a bank to buy a house for you and let you live in it in exchange for your promise to pay back the bank, with interest, over a period of years. If you stop paying back the bank, the bank may take back the house. In other words, the bank lends you enough money to buy the house with the understanding that the bank gets the house if you don't pay back the loan. A traditional *mortgage* runs for thirty years at a fixed interest rate with fixed monthly payments, but there are many variations.

MUTUAL FUND A *mutual fund* is an investment pool in which a large number of investors put their money together in the hope of making more money than they would have if they had invested on their own. *Mutual funds* are run by professional managers who may or may not be better than the average person at picking good investments. Some *mutual funds* invest only in stocks; some invest only in *bonds;* some invest only in metals; some invest only in Japanese stocks; some invest in a little of everything; some invest in whatever looks good at the moment.

ODD LOT Less than 100 shares of a company's stock. Groups of shares in multiples of 100 are known as *round lots.* Brokerages typically charge slightly higher commissions on transactions involving *odd lots.*

OPTION The opportunity to do something else (such as buy a certain number of shares at a certain price) at some time in the future.

OVER-THE-COUNTER STOCK An *OTC* stock is one that isn't traded on the New York Stock Exchange or the NASDAQ; one of several smaller stock exchanges. A stock exchange is a big marketplace where buyers and sellers (or, usually, their representatives) gather to do business within a framework of mutually agreed-upon rules and limitations. But not all stocks are bought and sold through stock exchanges. These stocks (typically those of smaller, less-established companies) are said to be bought and sold "over the counter." To buy or sell such a stock, you have to do business directly with someone who deals in it, or "makes a market" in it. Most stockbrokers of any size have *over-the-counter* departments that handle such transactions.

PRICE/EARNINGS RATIO A stock's *P/E* is the ratio of its price and the value of the company's earnings in the past year divided by the number of shares outstanding. If a stock sells for $20 a share and had earnings of $2 a share, its *P/E* is 10, and its share price is said to be "ten times earnings." In theory, if everything else is equal, a stock with a high *P/E* is a worse buy than a stock with a low *P/E,* but there are many exceptions.

PRIME RATE The interest rate that banks charge their biggest and best loan customers. Everybody else pays more. Many loan rates are keyed to the prime, which is why a change in the *prime rate* affects more than just the biggest and best loan customers.

PROXY Ownership of a share of stock entitles the shareholder to vote at the company's annual meeting. Shareholders who can't attend the meeting can still vote by sending in a *proxy*—essentially, an absentee ballot.

SECURITIES AND EXCHANGE COMMISSION The *SEC* is the government agency that oversees the trading of stocks, bonds, and other securities.

SELLING SHORT To sell a stock short is to sell it before you own it. Sounds impossible? It's not. *Selling short* is a way to make money on a stock when its price is going down. What you do, technically, is sell stock borrowed from your broker, then buy the same number of shares later, when the price has fallen. What happens if the price doesn't fall? You lose money.

STOCK SPLIT When a stock "splits two for one," shareholders are issued an additional share for every share they own at the time of the split. The effect is to halve the price per share, because each share is now worth half of what it was worth when there were only half as many. Companies generally split their stocks in order to knock the share price down to a level at which, the company hopes, it will be more attractive to investors.

Stock splits are sometimes referred to as *stock dividends.* But a stock dividend isn't really a dividend at all, because it doesn't have any value.

TAX SHELTER Any investment that permits the investor to protect income from taxation. Tax reform has eliminated most of these. *Tax shelters* that sound too good to be true tend to be not only too good to be true but also illegal. There are still a lot of humbler *tax shelters,* though. Buying a house is one: interest on mortgage payments is deductible, and the resulting tax savings amounts to a federal housing subsidy for people wealthy enough to buy their own homes.

WARRANT An option to buy a certain amount of stock at a certain price within a certain period of time.

YIELD The annual income generated by an investment expressed as a percentage of its cost. If a stock has a *yield* of 4 percent, it pays dividends equal to 4 percent of purchase price of a share of its stock.

CHAPTER 11

Foreign Words and Phrases

People in France buy their prescriptions at "le drug-store" and look forward to "le weekend"—useful words borrowed from English. Similarly we supplement English with many words and phrases borrowed directly from other languages. Here are some of the most useful recent imports.

À PROPOS (ah pruh POH) *adj* [French—"to the purpose"] to the point; pertinent

A comment is *à propos* (or *apropos*) if it is exactly appropriate for the situation.

AD HOC (ad HAHK) *adj* [Latin—"for this"] for a particular purpose; only for the matter at hand

An *ad hoc* committee is a committee established for a particular purpose or to deal with a particular problem.

AFICIONADO (uh fish yuh NAH doh, ah fee syow NAH doh) *n* [Spanish—"affectionate one"] fan

An *aficionado* of football is a football fan. An *aficionado* of theater is a theater fan.

AL FRESCO (al FRES koh) *adj* [Italian—"in the fresh"] outside; in the fresh air

An *al fresco* meal is a picnic.

APPARATCHIK (app uh RAT shik) *n* [Russian—"apparat (Communist party machine) member"] loyal functionary; bureaucrat

- Recent articles have described Mr. Petroleum as "an energy company *apparatchik*" and Mayor Atlanta as "a Democratic Party *apparatchik* turned popular leader."

AU COURANT (oh koo RAWN) *adj* [French—"in the current"] up to date; informed

To be *au courant* is to know all the latest information.

BONA FIDE (BO na FIDE) *adj* [Latin—"in/with good faith"] authentic; sincere; genuine

The noun form is *bona fides* (singular), meaning proof of credentials or of sincerity.

- A *bona fide* linguistic expert, Alli speaks forty languages, including six Aboriginal tongues.

CARTE BLANCHE (kahrt blanch, kahrt blawnch) *n* [French—"blank card"] the power to do whatever one wants

To give someone *carte blanche* is to give that person the license to do anything.

DE FACTO (dee FAK toh) *adj* [Latin—"from the fact"] actual

Your *de facto* boss is the person who tells you what to do. Your *de jure* (dee JYUR) boss is the person who is technically in charge of you. *De jure* ("from the law") means according to rule of law.

DE RIGUEUR (duh ri GUR, duh ree GUER) *adj* [French—"indispensable"] obligatory; required by fashion or custom

Long hair for men was *de rigueur* in the late 1960s. Evening wear is *de rigueur* at a formal party.

DÉJÀ VU (DAY zhah vu) *n* [French—"already seen"] an illusory feeling of having seen or done something before

To have *déjà vu* is to believe that one has already done or seen what one is in fact doing or seeing for the first time.

ENNUI (AHN wee) *n* [French—"annoyance"] boredom; weary dissatisfaction
- Masha thinks *ennui* is sophisticated, but her jaded remarks bore me to tears.

FAIT ACCOMPLI (fet uh kohm PLEE, fayt ah kahm PLEE) *n* [French—"accomplished fact"] something that is already done and that cannot be undone
- Our committee spent a long time debating whether to have the building painted, but the project was a *fait accompli*. The chairman had already hired someone to do it.

FAUX PAS (foh PAH) *n* [French—"false step"] an embarrassing social mistake
- Henry committed a *faux pas* when he told the hostess that her party had been boring.

IDÉE FIXE (ee day FEEKS) *n* [French—"fixed idea"] a fixed idea; an obsession

An *idée fixe* is an idea that obsesses you or that you can't get out of your mind.

IPSO FACTO (IP soh FAC toh) *adv* [Latin—"by the fact itself"] by or because of that very fact
- Under the discriminatory employment policy, people with children are *ipso facto* ineligible for promotion.

JOIE DE VIVRE (zhwah duh VEE vruh) *n* [French—"joy of living"] deep and usually contagious enjoyment of life
- Antonia's *joie de vivre* made her office a pleasant place to work for everyone connected with it.

JUNTA (HOON tuh, JUN tuh) *n* [Spanish—"joined"] a small group that rules a country after its government is overthrown
- After the rebels had driven out the president, the Latin American country was ruled by a *junta* of army officers.

LAISSEZ-FAIRE (les ay FAIR, lay zay FAIR) *n* [French—"let do"] a doctrine of noninterference by government in the economy; noninterference in general

To believe in *laissez-faire* is to believe the government should exert no control over business. It's also possible to adopt a *laissez-faire* attitude about other matters.

MEA CULPA (may ah KOOL pah, may uh KUL puh) *n* [Latin—"my fault"] my fault
- *Mea culpa, mea culpa.* I was the one who put the dog in the cat's bed.

NOLO CONTENDERE (noh loh kahn TEN duh ree) *n* [Latin—"I do not wish to contend"] no contest

A plea in a court case that is the equivalent of a guilty plea, but it doesn't include an actual admission of guilt.

NON SEQUITUR (nahn SEK wi tur) *n* [Latin—"it does not follow"] a statement that does not follow logically from what has gone before
- Bill's saying, "Forty-three degrees," when Lola asked, "May I have the butter?" was a *non sequitur.*

PERSONA NON GRATA (per SOH nuh nahn GRAH tuh) *adj* [Latin—"unacceptable person"] specifically unwelcome

In diplomacy, *persona non grata* often refers to an emissary blacklisted (for suspected espionage or crime, or for political reasons) by a host country.
- Fernando's altercation with the principal made him *persona non grata* in the Parent-Teacher Association.

QUID PRO QUO (kwid proh KWOH) *n* [Latin—"something for something"] something given or done in return for something else
- The politician said she would do what we had asked her to do, but there was a *quid pro quo:* she said we had to bribe her first.

RAISON D'ÊTRE (ray zohn DET, ray zohn DET ruh) *n* [French—"reason to be"] reason for being
- Money was the greedy rich man's *raison d'être.*

RENDEZVOUS (RAHN day voo, RAHN duh voo) *n* [French—"present yourselves"] a meeting; a meeting place
- The young couple met behind the bleachers for a discreet *rendezvous.*

SAVOIR-FAIRE (sav wahr FER) *n* [French—"to know how to do"] tact; the ability to act confidently and appropriately in different situations
- While Jo tended to be tactless, her sister Meg was full of *savoir-faire* and had the ability to charm whomever she met.

SINE QUA NON (sin ay kwoh NOHN, sye nee kway NAHN) *n* [Latin—"without which not"] something essential
- Understanding is the *sine qua non* of a successful marriage.

STATUS QUO (stayt us KWOH, stat us KWOH) *n* [Latin—"state in which"] the current state of affairs

The *status quo* is the way things are now.

SUI GENERIS (soo ee JEN ur is) *adj* [Latin—"of one's own kind"] unique; in a class of one's own

To be *sui generis* is to be unlike anyone else.

TÊTE-À-TÊTE (tayt uh TAYT, tet ah TET) *n* [French—"head to head"] a private conversation between two people
- The two attorneys resolved their differences in a brief *tête-à-tête* before the trial began.

VIS-À-VIS (vee zuh VEE) *prep* [French—"face to face"] in relation to; compared with
- The students' relationship *vis-à-vis* the administration was one of confrontation.

ZEITGEIST (TSYTE gyste) *n* [German—"time spirit"] the spirit of the times
- Nudnik was always out of step with the *zeitgeist;* he had short hair in 1970 and long hair in 1980.

CHAPTER 12

Science

Here's a list of scientific terms that turn up in newspapers and magazines with great frequency. You won't learn much science by learning this list, but you'll learn some words that may help you keep your bearings.

ABSOLUTE ZERO   The temperature at which atoms become so cold they stop moving: −459.67°F or −273.15°C. This is theoretically the lowest possible temperature.

ANTIBODY   The key part of the immune system. An *antibody* is a protein produced by the body in response to invasion of the body by a virus, bacterium, or other threatening substance. The *antibody* attacks the invader and then remains in the bloodstream, providing continuing immunity.

ANTIMATTER   In effect, the mirror image of ordinary matter. Each of the **elementary particles** has a corresponding anti-particle, with an opposite electrical charge. When matter and *antimatter* collide, both are annihilated, and energy is released.

ARTIFICIAL INTELLIGENCE   The general name for attempts to reproduce human mental processes with computers.

BEHAVIORISM   A branch of psychology whose principal tenet is that all behavior consists of reflexive responses to external stimuli.

BIG BANG   A massive explosion that theoretically began the universe between 10 billion and 20 billion years ago.

CHROMOSOME   A structure in the nucleus of a cell that contains **DNA** and carries genetic information.

CLONING   A technology used to produce an organism that is genetically identical to another organism.

COSMOLOGY   The study of the origins, structure, and future of the universe.

DARK ENERGY   A hypothetical force that some cosmologists believe counteracts gravity and accounts for the accelerating expansion of the universe; Einstein was first to posit the existence of dark energy, though he later referred to the idea as his "biggest blunder."

DARK MATTER   Invisible hypothetical matter thought by some scientists to constitute as much as 90 percent of the mass in the universe.

DNA An abbreviation for deoxyribonucleic acid, the substance that is the principal component of **genes;** hence, *DNA* is the primary carrier of genetic information.

ELECTROMAGNETIC RADIATION Visible light, radio signals, microwaves, ultraviolet light, and X rays are all examples of *electromagnetic radiation*, which is energy radiated in waves from certain electrically charged **elementary particles**.

ELECTRON MICROSCOPE A device that uses streams of electrons to provide greatly magnified images of objects far too small to be seen by the human eye or even by ordinary optical microscopes.

ELEMENTARY PARTICLES The tiny particles that make up atoms and are thus the building blocks of all matter. Protons, neutrons, and electrons were once believed to be the only *elementary particles*, but it is now known that these particles are themselves made up of smaller particles and that the list of *elementary particles* is quite long. Among the newer additions to the list are quarks, muons, pions, gluons, positrons, and neutrinos.

ENDORPHINS Sometimes referred to as the body's own narcotics, *endorphins* are substances produced by the pituitary gland that can reduce pain, alter moods, and have other effects.

ENZYME Any of a large number of substances in organisms that speed up or make possible various biological processes.

GENE A chemical pattern on a **chromosome**. *Genes* make up units of information that govern the inheritance of all biological structures and functions.

GENETIC ENGINEERING A science devoted to altering **genes** in order to produce organisms with more desirable characteristics, such as resistance to disease.

GENOME The complete set of a creature's **genes**.

GREENHOUSE EFFECT The phenomenon whereby the earth's atmosphere (especially when altered by the addition of various pollutants) traps some of the heat of the sun and warms the surface of the earth.

HOLOGRAM A three-dimensional image produced by a photographic process called **holography**, which involves **lasers**.

HYDROCARBON Any of a large number of organic compounds composed of hydrogen and carbon. Butane, methane, and propane are three of the lighter *hydrocarbons*. Gasoline, kerosene, and asphalt are all mixtures of (mostly relatively heavy) *hydrocarbons*.

IN VITRO FERTILIZATION The fertilization of an egg outside the mother's body.

ISOTOPE An atom with the same number of protons as a second atom but a different number of neutrons is said to be an *isotope* of that second atom.

LASER A device that produces an extraordinarily intense beam of light. The word *laser* is an acronym for Light Amplification by Simulated Emission of Radiation.

LIGHT-YEAR The distance that light travels in a year, or approximately 5,878,000,000,000 miles.

NATURAL SELECTION The theory that species originate and become differentiated as certain characteristics of organisms prove more valuable than others at enabling those organisms to reproduce. These valuable characteristics are in effect "selected" by nature for preservation in succeeding generations, while other characteristics disappear. *Natural selection* was a key element in Charles Darwin's monumental theory of evolution.

NEBULA An enormous cloud of dust and gas in outer space.

NUCLEAR ENERGY The vast energy locked in the infinitesimal nucleus of an atom. This energy can be released through *fission* (the splitting of certain atomic nuclei) and *fusion* (the combining of certain atomic nuclei). It is also released naturally in a few elements through a process of decomposition called *radioactivity*. Fission, fusion, and radioactivity are all processes involving the conversion of small amounts of matter into enormous amounts of energy. The release of this energy is the basis of nuclear weapons (such as atomic bombs and hydrogen bombs) and nuclear reactors used in the production of electricity.

NUCLEAR WINTER A hypothetical chilling of the earth resulting from the contamination of the atmosphere by radioactive materials, dust, and other substances in the aftermath of a nuclear war.

OSMOSIS The equalization of fluid concentrations on both sides of a permeable membrane.

OZONE LAYER Ozone is a compound of oxygen. The *ozone layer* is a part of the atmosphere that, among other things, filters out radiation that is harmful to human beings. In recent decades the *ozone layer* has been found to be decomposing at an alarming rate, owing in large part to the release of certain pollutants into the atmosphere.

PASTEURIZATION A sterilization process in which foods are heated in order to kill harmful organisms in them. The process is named for Louis Pasteur, the 19th-century French scientist who developed it.

PERIODIC TABLE A chart depicting the known elements arranged according to certain characteristics—a must-have in chemistry classrooms and textbooks.

PHEROMONE Substances secreted by animals that influence the behavior of other animals, primarily through the sense of smell.

PHOTON The smallest unit of **electromagnetic radiation**.

PHOTOSYNTHESIS The process whereby green plants transform energy from the sun into food.

PLATE TECTONICS A revolutionary geological theory holding that the earth's crust consists of enormous moving plates that are constantly shifting position and, among other things, altering the shape and arrangement of the continents.

PULSAR Any of a number of less than thoroughly understood objects in outer space that emit regular pulses of radio waves.

QUASAR Any of a number of starlike objects believed to occupy the very farthest fringes of the universe.

RADIO TELESCOPE A large antenna capable of receiving the radio waves naturally emitted by stars and other objects in outer space. A *radio telescope* is a telescope capable of "seeing" forms of **electromagnetic radiation** not visible to the human eye or to an ordinary optical telescope.

RELATIVITY Albert Einstein's monumental theory, which holds, among a great many other things, that space and time are not separate entities but elements of a single continuum called *space time*.

RNA An abbreviation for ribonucleic acid, a substance similar to **DNA** that is a crucial element in the synthesis of proteins.

SEISMOLOGY The study of earthquakes and other tremors (including man-made ones) in the earth's crust.

SPEED OF LIGHT The speed at which light travels through a vacuum, or 186,282 miles per second.

SUPERCONDUCTIVITY The ability of certain substances to conduct electricity with no resistance. *Superconductivity* has usually been produced by cooling certain substances to temperatures approaching **absolute zero**. More recently, scientists have discovered materials that become *superconductive* at vastly warmer temperatures.

THERMODYNAMICS A branch of science concerned with heat and the conversion of heat into other forms of energy.

VACCINE A substance that, when introduced into an organism, causes the organism to produce **antibodies** against, and hence immunity to, a particular disease.

CHAPTER 13

The Answers

Quick Quiz #1

1. **j** abash—embarrass
2. **f** abate—subside
3. **a** abdicate—step down from power
4. **i** aberration—deviation
5. **g** abhor—detest
6. **b** abject—hopeless
7. **k** abnegate—renounce
8. **c** abortive—unsuccessful
9. **h** abridge—shorten
10. **e** absolute—total
11. **d** absolve—forgive

Quick Quiz #2

1. **b** abstinent—voluntarily avoiding
2. **h** abstract—theoretical
3. **a** abstruse—hard to understand
4. **c** abysmal—wretched
5. **i** accolade—award
6. **j** accost—approach someone aggressively
7. **k** acerbic—sour
8. **e** acquiesce—comply
9. **f** acrid—harsh
10. **d** acrimonious—bitter
11. **g** acumen—mental sharpness

Quick Quiz #3

1. **a** acute—sharp
2. **h** adulation—wild admiration
3. **g** adamant—unyielding
4. **e** address—speak to
5. **b** adherent—follower
6. **d** admonish—scold gently
7. **f** adroit—skillful
8. **f** dexterous—skillful
9. **c** gauche—socially awkward

Quick Quiz #4

1. **f** adulterate—contaminate
2. **h** adverse—unfavorable
3. **a** averse—opposed to
4. **e** aesthetic—artistic
5. **b** affable—friendly
6. **d** affectation—unnatural behavior
7. **g** affinity—sympathy
8. **c** affluent—rich
9. **i** agenda—program

Quick Quiz #5

1. **g** aggregate—sum total
2. **a** congregate—get together
3. **e** segregate—keep apart
4. **b** integrate—unite
5. **c** agnostic—someone unconvinced about the existence of a god
6. **k** agrarian—relating to land
7. **j** alacrity—cheerful eagerness
8. **i** allege—assert
9. **d** alleviate—relieve
10. **h** allocate—distribute
11. **f** alloy—combination of metals

Quick Quiz #6

1. **e** allusion—indirect reference
2. **b** aloof—standoffish
3. **d** altruism—generosity
4. **a** ambience—atmosphere
5. **c** ambiguous—confusing
6. **f** ambivalent—undecided

Quick Quiz #7

1. **f** ameliorate—make better
2. **c** amenable—obedient
3. **a** amenity—pleasantness
4. **j** amiable—friendly
5. **h** amicable—politely friendly
6. **i** amnesty—official pardon
7. **d** amoral—without moral feeling
8. **e** amorous—feeling loving
9. **g** amorphous—shapeless
10. **k** anachronism—incongruity
11. **b** analogy—comparison

Quick Quiz #8

1. **i** anarchy—lawlessness
2. **h** monarchy—government by king or queen
3. **g** anecdote—amusing account
4. **f** anguish—agonizing pain
5. **a** animosity—resentment
6. **d** anomaly—irregularity
7. **e** antecedent—what went before
8. **c** antipathy—firm dislike
9. **j** antithesis—direct opposite
10. **b** apartheid—racial oppression

Quick Quiz #9

1. **d** apathy—lack of interest
2. **i** aphorism—witty saying
3. **f** apocalypse—prophetic revelation
4. **a** apocryphal—of dubious authenticity
5. **h** apotheosis—the perfect example
6. **e** appease—soothe
7. **c** appreciate—increase in value
8. **g** depreciate—decrease in value
9. **j** apprehensive—worried
10. **b** misapprehension—misunderstanding

Quick Quiz #10

1. **f** approbation—approval
2. **c** appropriate—take without permission
3. **a** misappropriate—misuse public money
4. **h** expropriate—take property officially
5. **j** aptitude—natural ability
6. **i** arbiter—judge
7. **d** arbitrate—weigh opposing views
8. **g** arbitrary—random
9. **e** arcane—mysterious
10. **b** archaic—extremely old

Quick Quiz #11

1. **i** archetype—original model
2. **a** ardent—passionate
3. **e** arduous—difficult
4. **b** aristocratic—of noble birth
5. **h** artful—crafty
6. **f** artifice—trickery
7. **c** ascendancy—supremacy
8. **g** ascetic—hermitlike
9. **d** assiduous—hardworking

Quick Quiz #12

1. **g** assimilate—absorb
2. **e** assuage—soothe
3. **a** astute—shrewd
4. **i** attrition—gradual wearing away
5. **b** audacity—boldness
6. **d** augment—make bigger
7. **c** auspicious—favorable
8. **h** austere—unadorned
9. **f** autocratic—extremely bossy

Quick Quiz #13

1. **d** autonomous—acting independently
2. **a** avarice—greed
3. **e** avow—claim
4. **b** avuncular—like an uncle
5. **f** awry—off course
6. **c** axiom—self-evident truth

Quick Quiz #14

1. **b** banal—unoriginal
2. **e** bane—poison
3. **d** bastion—stronghold
4. **h** beget—give birth to
5. **c** belabor—go over repeatedly
6. **g** beleaguer—surround
7. **f** belie—give a false impression
8. **a** belittle—make to seem little

Quick Quiz #15

1. **g** belligerent—combative
2. **e** bemused—confused
3. **b** benefactor—donor
4. **i** beneficiary—one who receives benefits
5. **f** benevolent—generous
6. **c** benign—not harmful
7. **d** malignant—deadly
8. **h** malign—injure with lies
9. **a** malevolent—intending harm
10. **j** malefactor—evildoer

Quick Quiz #16

1. **b** bequest—something left in a will
2. **e** bequeath—leaving in a will
3. **a** bereaved—left desolate
4. **c** beset—harass
5. **f** blasphemy—irreverence
6. **d** blatant—offensively noisy

Quick Quiz #17

1. **n** blight—plant disease
2. **c** blithe—carefree
3. **g** bourgeois—middle class
4. **e** bovine—cowlike
5. **m** canine—doglike
6. **d** feline—catlike
7. **h** equine—horselike
8. **l** piscine—fishlike
9. **j** porcine—piglike
10. **b** ursine—bearlike
11. **i** brevity—briefness
12. **o** broach—open a subject
13. **f** bucolic—charmingly rural
14. **k** bureaucracy—inflexible administration
15. **a** burgeon—flourish
16. **p** burlesque—ludicrous imitation

Quick Quiz #18

1. **b** cacophony—harsh mixture of sounds
2. **l** cadence—rhythm
3. **j** cajole—persuade deceptively
4. **f** callow—immature
5. **a** candor—truthfulness
6. **g** capitalism—free enterprise
7. **c** capitulate—surrender
8. **i** recapitulate—summarize
9. **e** capricious—unpredictable
10. **d** caricature—distorted portrait
11. **k** castigate—criticize severely
12. **h** catalyst—something that makes things happen

Quick Quiz #19

1. **a** categorical—unconditional
2. **b** catharsis—relieving purification
3. **i** catholic—universal
4. **g** caustic—corrosive
5. **c** celibacy—abstinence from sex
6. **h** censure—condemn severely
7. **d** cerebral—brainy
8. **e** chagrin—humiliation
9. **f** charisma—magical attractiveness

Quick Quiz #20

1. **h** charlatan—fraud
2. **i** chasm—gaping hole
3. **d** chastise—punish
4. **j** chicanery—trickery
5. **g** chimera—illusion
6. **c** choleric—hot-tempered
7. **b** chronic—constant
8. **a** chronological—in order of occurrence
9. **f** chronology—a list in time order
10. **e** chronicle—an account of past times

Quick Quiz #21

1. **e** circuitous—roundabout
2. **h** circumlocution—indirect expression
3. **b** circumscribe—draw a line around
4. **a** circumspect—cautious
5. **f** circumvent—frustrate
6. **d** civil—polite
7. **i** clique—exclusive group
8. **c** clemency—mercy
9. **j** inclement—bad, as in weather
10. **g** cliché—overused saying

Quick Quiz #22

1. **b** coalesce—unite
2. **g** coalition—group with a purpose
3. **d** coerce—force someone to do something
4. **h** cogent—powerfully convincing
5. **l** cognitive—dealing with how we know our environment
6. **a** cognizant—perceptive
7. **f** coherent—making sense
8. **c** colloquial—conversational
9. **k** collusion—conspiracy
10. **e** commensurate—proportionate
11. **j** compelling—forceful
12. **i** compendium—summary

Quick Quiz #23

1. **h** complacent—self-satisfied
2. **b** complement—complete
3. **g** complicity—participation in wrongdoing
4. **a** comprehensive—covering everything
5. **c** comprise—consist of
6. **d** compose—make up
7. **d** constitute—make up
8. **f** conciliatory —making peace
9. **e** concise—brief and to the point

Quick Quiz #24

1. **c** concord—harmony
2. **i** discord—disharmony
3. **h** concurrent—happening at the same time
4. **f** condescend—stoop or patronize
5. **g** condone—overlook
6. **e** conducive—promoting
7. **d** confluence—flowing together
8. **a** congenial—agreeably suitable
9. **b** congenital—innate

Quick Quiz #25
1. **i** congregate—get together
2. **h** conjecture—guess
3. **e** conjure—summon as if by magic
4. **g** connoisseur—artistic expert
5. **c** consecrate—make sacred
6. **f** desecrate—treat irreverently
7. **d** consensus—unanimity
8. **b** consonant—harmonious
9. **a** dissonant—incompatible

Quick Quiz #26
1. **b** construe—interpret
2. **c** consummate—perfect
3. **h** contentious—argumentative
4. **g** contiguous—adjoining
5. **e** contingent—dependent
6. **a** contrite—admitting guilt
7. **d** contrived—labored
8. **j** conventional—common
9. **i** convivial—festive
10. **f** copious—abundant

Quick Quiz #27
1. **g** corollary—natural consequence
2. **d** corroborate—confirm
3. **a** cosmopolitan—worldly and sophisticated
4. **b** countenance—face
5. **f** coup—brilliant victory
6. **e** covenant—solemn agreement
7. **h** covert—secret
8. **c** covet—wish for enviously

Quick Quiz #28
1. **e** credulous—eager to believe
2. **b** credible—believable
3. **g** incredible—unbelievable
4. **f** incredulous—unbelieving
5. **c** credence—believability
6. **d** creditable—worthy of praise
7. **i** criterion—standard
8. **j** cryptic—mysterious
9. **a** culinary—related to cooking
10. **h** culminate—climax

Quick Quiz #29
1. **e** culpable—guilty
2. **a** exculpate—free from guilt
3. **d** cursory—hasty
4. **b** curtail—shorten
5. **c** cynic—one who distrusts humanity

Quick Quiz #30
1. **e** daunt—make fearful
2. **b** dearth—lack
3. **i** debacle—violent breakdown
4. **j** debauchery—wild living
5. **h** debilitate—weaken
6. **f** decadent—decaying or decayed
7. **c** decimate—kill a large part of
8. **g** decorous—proper
9. **a** deduce—conclude from evidence
10. **d** defame—libel or slander

Quick Quiz #31

1. **d** deference—respect
2. **e** definitive—conclusive
3. **a** degenerate—deteriorate
4. **g** deleterious—harmful
5. **c** delineate—describe accurately
6. **i** delude—deceive
7. **j** deluge—flood
8. **l** demagogue—rabble-rousing leader
9. **h** denizen—inhabitant
10. **k** depravity—extreme wickedness
11. **f** deprecate—express disapproval of
12. **b** deride—ridicule

Quick Quiz #32

1. **h** derogatory— disapproving
2. **g** desiccate—dry out
3. **b** despondent—extremely depressed
4. **i** despot—absolute ruler
5. **e** destitute—extremely poor
6. **a** desultory—without purpose
7. **m** dextrous—skillful
8. **k** dialectical—relating to discussions
9. **l** dictum—authoritative saying
10. **j** didactic—intended to teach
11. **f** diffident—timid
12. **d** digress—stray from the main subject
13. **c** dilettante—amateur

Quick Quiz #33

1. **a** discern—have insight
2. **f** discreet—prudent
3. **g** discrete—unconnected
4. **c** indiscrete—not separated
5. **h** discriminate—differentiate
6. **e** disdain—arrogant scorn
7. **d** disinterested—not taking sides
8. **b** disparage—belittle

Quick Quiz #34

1. **i** disparate—incompatible
2. **j** disseminate—spread seeds
3. **b** dissipate—thin out
4. **k** dissolution—disintegration
5. **g** distend—swell
6. **h** distinguish—tell apart
7. **e** docile—easily taught
8. **a** doctrinaire—committed to a theory
9. **f** dogmatic—arrogantly assertive
10. **d** dogma—firmly held system of ideas
11. **c** domestic—of the household

Quick Quiz #35

1. **c** dormant—inactive
2. **a** dubiety—uncertainty
3. **b** duplicity—double-dealing

Quick Quiz #36

1. **f** ebullient—bubbling with excitement
2. **d** eccentric—not conventional
3. **e** eclectic—drawn from many sources
4. **i** edify—enlighten
5. **g** efface—erase
6. **a** effusion—pouring forth
7. **j** egalitarian—believing in social equality
8. **h** egocentric—selfish
9. **b** egotist—self-obsessed person
10. **c** egregious—extremely bad

Quick Quiz #37

1. **b** elicit—bring out
2. **g** elliptical—obscure
3. **c** elusive—hard to pin down
4. **e** emigrate—move from a country
5. **f** immigration—moving into a country
6. **a** eminent—well-known
7. **d** empirical—relying on experience

Quick Quiz #38

1. **g** emulate—strive to equal
2. **j** encroach—trespass
3. **e** endemic—native
4. **d** enervate—reduce the strength
5. **f** enfranchise—grant voting rights
6. **c** disfranchise—remove voting rights
7. **a** engender—cause to exist
8. **b** enigma—mystery
9. **i** enormity—extreme evil
10. **h** ephemeral—lasting a very short time

Quick Quiz #39

1. **i** epigram—brief, witty saying
2. **e** epigraph—apt quotation
3. **g** epitaph—inscription on a gravestone
4. **j** epithet—characterizing term
5. **a** epitome—brief summary
6. **c** equanimity—composure
7. **b** equitable—fair
8. **d** equivocal—intentionally confusing
9. **f** equivocate—say confusing things
10. **h** erudite—scholarly

Quick Quiz #40

1. **a** esoteric—peculiar
2. **i** espouse—advocate
3. **h** ethereal—heavenly
4. **e** euphemism—inoffensive substitute term
5. **j** evanescent—fleeting
6. **b** exacerbate—make worse
7. **c** exacting—extremely demanding
8. **d** exalt—raise high
9. **g** exasperate—annoy thoroughly
10. **k** exemplify—illustrate by example
11. **l** exhaustive—thorough
12. **f** exhort—urge strongly

Quick Quiz #41

1. **m** exigency—emergency
2. **d** existential—having to do with existence
3. **a** exonerate—free from blame
4. **l** expatriate—throw out of native land
5. **i** expedient—immediately advantageous
6. **f** expedite—speed up
7. **b** explicit—clearly expressed
8. **c** implicit—indirectly expressed
9. **o** extol—praise highly
10. **j** extraneous—unnecessary
11. **g** extrapolate—infer
12. **h** extricate—free from difficulty
13. **e** extrovert—outgoing person
14. **k** introvert—inwardly directed person
15. **n** exult—rejoice

Quick Quiz #42

1. **i** fabrication—lie
2. **e** facetious—humorous
3. **g** facile—superficially skillful
4. **h** faction—group with a cause
5. **c** farcical—absurd
6. **j** fastidious—meticulous
7. **d** fatalist—one who believes in fate
8. **k** fatuous—foolish
9. **f** fauna—animals
10. **a** flora—plants
11. **b** fecund—fertile

Quick Quiz #43

1. **j** felicity—happiness
2. **l** fervor—zeal
3. **c** fetter—restrain
4. **a** fidelity—loyalty
5. **g** figurative—based on figures of speech
6. **d** literal—meaning exactly what is says
7. **i** finesse—skillful maneuvering
8. **k** flagrant—glaringly bad
9. **f** flaunt—show off
10. **h** flout—to disregard contemptuously
11. **e** foible—minor character flaw
12. **b** foment—stir up

Quick Quiz #44

1. **e** forbear—refrain from
2. **b** forebear—ancestor
3. **d** forgo—do without
4. **i** forsake—abandon
5. **h** fortuitous—accidental
6. **f** founder—sink
7. **c** flounder—move in confusion
8. **j** frenetic—frantic
9. **a** frugal—economical
10. **g** furtive—secretive

Quick Quiz #45

1. **g** futile—hopeless
2. **a** garrulous—chatty
3. **m** gauche—awkward
4. **l** genre—type of art
5. **h** genteel—refined
6. **f** gesticulate—make gestures
7. **b** glut—surplus
8. **j** grandiloquent—pompous
9. **k** grandiose—absurdly exaggerated
10. **d** gratuitous—unjustified
11. **e** gravity—seriousness
12. **i** gregarious—sociable
13. **c** guile—cunning

Quick Quiz #46

1. **f** hackneyed—overused; trite
2. **j** hapless—unlucky
3. **d** harbinger—forerunner
4. **p** hedonism—lifelong pursuit of pleasure
5. **a** hegemony—leadership
6. **q** heresy—strongly contrary belief
7. **c** hermetic—airtight
8. **h** heyday—golden age
9. **m** hiatus—break
10. **e** hierarchy—pecking order
11. **l** histrionic—overly dramatic
12. **n** homily—sermon
13. **b** homogeneous—uniform
14. **i** heterogeneous—varied
15. **o** husbandry—thrifty management of resources
16. **g** hyperbole—exaggeration
17. **k** hypothetical—uncertain; unproven

Quick Quiz #47

1. **e** iconoclast—attacker of popular beliefs
2. **h** ideology—system of social ideas
3. **a** idiosyncrasy—peculiarity
4. **b** idyllic—naturally peaceful
5. **j** ignominy—deep disgrace
6. **l** illicit—illegal
7. **f** imminent—just about to happen
8. **k** immutable—unchangeable
9. **g** impartial—fair
10. **d** impeccable—flawless
11. **c** imperial—like an emperor
12. **i** imperious—bossy

Quick Quiz #48

1. **d** impervious—impenetrable
2. **g** impetuous—impulsive
3. **b** implement—carry out
4. **c** impotent—powerless
5. **f** impugn—attack the truth of
6. **e** inane—silly
7. **a** inaugurate—begin officially

Quick Quiz #49

1. **j** incandescent—brilliant
2. **d** incantation—chant
3. **b** incense—make very angry
4. **i** incessant—unceasing
5. **c** incipient—beginning
6. **h** incisive—cutting right to the heart
7. **e** incongruous—not harmonious
8. **f** incorrigible—incapable of being reformed
9. **a** increment—increase
10. **g** indifferent—not caring; mediocre

Quick Quiz #50

1. **a** indigenous—native
2. **f** indigent—poor
3. **h** indignant—angry
4. **c** indolent—lazy
5. **j** indulgent—lenient
6. **k** ineffable—inexpressible
7. **i** inept—clumsy
8. **b** inert—inactive
9. **g** inexorable—relentless
10. **e** infamous—shamefully wicked
11. **d** infatuated—foolish

Quick Quiz #51

1. **f** infer—conclude
2. **c** imply—hint at
3. **i** infinitesimal—infinitely small
4. **d** ingenuous—artless
5. **b** inherent—part of the nature of
6. **j** injunction—court order
7. **e** innate—inborn
8. **h** innocuous—harmless
9. **g** inordinate—excessive
10. **a** insatiable—hard or impossible to satisfy

Quick Quiz #52

1. **c** insidious—treacherous
2. **a** insinuate—hint
3. **h** insipid—dull
4. **j** insolent—arrogant
5. **e** instigate—provoke
6. **f** insular—like an island
7. **g** insurgent—rebel
8. **d** integral—essential
9. **k** integrate—combine
10. **b** intractable—uncontrollable
11. **i** intransigent—uncompromising

Quick Quiz #53

1. **e** intrinsic—inherent
2. **f** introspective—examining one's feelings
3. **d** inundate—flood
4. **b** invective—insulting speech
5. **j** inveterate—habitual
6. **i** irascible—irritable
7. **g** ironic—meaning other than what's said
8. **a** irrevocable—irreversible
9. **h** itinerant—moving from place to place
10. **c** itinerary—planned trip route

Quick Quiz #54

1. **m** judicious—exercising sound judgment
2. **e** juxtapose—place side by side
3. **h** kinetic—active
4. **d** labyrinth—maze
5. **c** laconic—using few words
6. **k** lament—mourn
7. **j** lampoon—satirize
8. **i** languish—become weak
9. **f** latent—present but not visible
10. **l** laud—praise
11. **g** legacy—bequest
12. **a** lethargy—sluggishness
13. **b** levity—lightness

Quick Quiz #55

1. **e** libel—written injurious falsehood
2. **f** slander—spoken injurious falsehood
3. **b** litigate—try in court
4. **g** loquacious—talking a lot
5. **d** lucid—easy to understand
6. **c** lugubrious—exaggeratedly mournful
7. **a** luminous—giving off light

Quick Quiz #56

1. **e** machination—scheming evil activity
2. **a** magnanimous—forgiving
3. **n** magnate—rich businessperson
4. **c** malaise—depression
5. **p** malevolent—wishing to do evil
6. **k** malfeasance—illegal act
7. **o** malignant—harmful
8. **g** malinger—pretend to be sick
9. **b** malleable—easy to shape
10. **d** mandate—command to do something
11. **h** manifest—visible
12. **f** manifesto—public declaration
13. **j** marshal—arrange in order
14. **m** martial—warlike
15. **i** martyr—one who dies for a cause
16. **l** matriculate—enroll

Quick Quiz #57
1. **i** maudlin—overly sentimental
2. **f** maverick—nonconformist
3. **b** maxim—fundamental principle
4. **d** mediate—help settle differences
5. **e** mellifluous—sweetly flowing
6. **c** mendacious—lying
7. **k** mendicant—beggar
8. **a** mentor—teacher
9. **j** mercenary—hired soldier
10. **g** mercurial—emotionally unpredictable
11. **h** metamorphosis—magical change in form

Quick Quiz #58
1. **m** microcosm—world in miniature
2. **j** milieu—environment
3. **h** minuscule—very tiny
4. **n** misanthropic—hating mankind
5. **b** mitigate—moderate the effect of
6. **f** mollify—soften
7. **c** monolithic—massive and unyielding
8. **l** moribund—dying
9. **i** morose—gloomy
10. **d** mortify—humiliate
11. **e** mundane—ordinary
12. **k** munificent—very generous
13. **g** myopia—nearsightedness
14. **a** myriad—a huge number

Quick Quiz #59
1. **a** narcissism—excessive love of self
2. **h** nebulous—vague
3. **e** nefarious—evil
4. **l** neologism—new word
5. **j** nepotism—favoritism
6. **k** nihilism—belief in the absence of all values and morals
7. **b** nominal—in name only
8. **i** nostalgia—longing for the past
9. **g** notorious—famous for something bad
10. **d** novel—original
11. **c** noxious—harmful
12. **f** nuance—subtle difference

Quick Quiz #60
1. **c** obdurate—stubborn
2. **k** obfuscate—confuse
3. **g** oblique—indirect
4. **a** oblivion—forgetfulness
5. **b** obscure—hard to understand
6. **l** obsequious—fawning
7. **d** obtuse—insensitive
8. **n** officious—annoyingly helpful
9. **e** onerous—burdensome
10. **j** opaque—impossible to see through
11. **f** opulent—luxurious
12. **m** orthodox—conventional
13. **h** ostensible—misleadingly apparent
14. **i** ostentatious—showing off

Quick Quiz #61

1. **g** pacify—calm someone down
2. **j** painstaking—extremely careful
3. **l** palliate—alleviate
4. **a** palpable—obvious
5. **i** paltry—insignificant
6. **h** panacea—cure for everything
7. **b** paradigm—model
8. **e** paradox—contradictory truth
9. **d** parochial—narrow in point of view
10. **k** parody—satirical imitation
11. **f** parsimonious—stingy
12. **c** partisan—supporter of a cause

Quick Quiz #62

1. **i** patent—obvious
2. **l** paternal—fatherly
3. **f** pathology—science of diseases
4. **a** patriarch—male head of a family
5. **j** patrician—aristocrat
6. **g** patronize—treat as an inferior
7. **k** paucity—scarcity
8. **b** peccadillo—minor offense
9. **e** pedantic—boringly scholarly
10. **c** pedestrian—unimaginative
11. **h** pejorative—negative
12. **n** penchant—strong liking
13. **m** penitent—sorry
14. **d** pensive—thoughtful and sad

Quick Quiz #63

1. **k** peremptory—final
2. **f** perennial—continual
3. **j** perfidy—treachery
4. **b** perfunctory—unenthusiastic
5. **l** peripatetic—wandering
6. **a** periphery—outside edge of something
7. **d** perjury—lying under oath
8. **c** permeate—penetrate
9. **n** pernicious—deadly
10. **e** perquisite—job-related privilege
11. **h** prerequisite—necessity
12. **m** pertinent—relevant
13. **g** perturb—disturb greatly
14. **i** peruse—read carefully

Quick Quiz #64

1. **b** pervade—spread throughout
2. **i** petulant—rude
3. **k** philanthropy—love for mankind
4. **d** philistine—smugly ignorant person
5. **g** pious—reverent
6. **j** pivotal—crucial
7. **c** placate—pacify
8. **f** plaintive—expressing sadness
9. **h** platitude—trite remark
10. **l** plebeian—low class
11. **e** plethora—excess
12. **a** poignant—painfully emotional

Quick Quiz #65

1. **g** polarize—cause opposing positions
2. **d** polemic—powerful refutation
3. **a** ponderous—massive and clumsy
4. **j** portent—omen
5. **h** portentous—ominous
6. **k** postulate—axiom
7. **c** pragmatic—practical
8. **i** precedent—earlier example
9. **b** precept—rule to live by
10. **f** precipitate—cause to happen abruptly
11. **e** precipitous—steep

Quick Quiz #66

1. **k** preclude—prevent
2. **j** precursor—forerunner
3. **f** predilection—natural preference
4. **a** preeminent—outstanding
5. **c** preempt—seize by prior right
6. **i** premise—assumption
7. **g** prepossess—preoccupy
8. **h** prerogative—right or privilege
9. **b** prevail—triumph
10. **e** pristine—unspoiled
11. **d** prodigal—wastefully extravagant

Quick Quiz #67

1. **f** prodigious—extraordinary
2. **e** prodigy—extremely talented child
3. **b** profane—irreverent
4. **a** profess—declare
5. **i** proficient—thoroughly competent
6. **j** profligate—extravagantly wasteful
7. **h** profound—deep
8. **d** profuse—flowing
9. **k** proletariat—industrial working class
10. **g** proliferate—spread rapidly
11. **c** prolific—abundantly productive

Quick Quiz #68

1. **l** promulgate—proclaim
2. **a** propensity—natural inclination
3. **j** propitious—marked by favorable signs
4. **c** proponent—advocate
5. **g** proprietary—constituting property
6. **b** propriety—good manners
7. **i** prosaic—dull
8. **d** proscribe—prohibit
9. **k** proselytize—convert
10. **f** protagonist—leading character
11. **e** protract—prolong
12. **h** provident—frugal

Quick Quiz #69
1. **c** provincial—narrow in outlook
2. **f** provisional—conditional
3. **b** proximity—nearness
4. **e** prudent—careful
5. **d** purported—rumored
6. **a** putative—commonly accepted

Quick Quiz #70
1. **d** qualify—modify or restrict
2. **e** qualitative—having to do with quality
3. **a** quantitative—having to do with quantity
4. **c** querulous—complaining
5. **b** quixotic—foolishly romantic

Quick Quiz #71
1. **c** ramification—consequence
2. **f** rancor—bitter resentment
3. **j** rapacious—greedy
4. **b** rebuke—criticize sharply
5. **i** rebut—contradict
6. **g** recalcitrant—stubbornly defiant
7. **h** recant—publicly deny
8. **d** reciprocal—mutual
9. **e** reclusive—hermitlike
10. **a** recondite—hard to understand

Quick Quiz #72
1. **h** recrimination—bitter counteraccusation
2. **e** redolent—fragrant
3. **i** redundant—unnecessarily repetitive
4. **j** refute—prove to be false
5. **g** reiterate—say again
6. **f** relegate—banish
7. **a** relinquish—surrender
8. **d** remonstrate—argue against
9. **c** renaissance—rebirth
10. **b** renounce—disown

Quick Quiz #73
1. **g** reparation—paying back
2. **d** repercussion—consequence
3. **j** replenish—fill again
4. **f** replete—completely filled
5. **c** reprehensible—worthy of blame
6. **a** reprisal—act of revenge
7. **e** reproach—scold
8. **i** reprove—criticize mildly
9. **k** repudiate—reject
10. **h** requisite—necessary
11. **b** resolute—determined

Quick Quiz #74
1. **g** respite—period of rest
2. **e** reticent—restrained
3. **i** revere—honor
4. **d** rhetoric—formal writing or speaking
5. **h** rigorous—strict
6. **c** robust—vigorous
7. **j** rogue—scoundrel
8. **a** rudimentary—basic
9. **b** ruminate—contemplate
10. **f** rustic—rural

Quick Quiz #75
1. **c** saccharine—sweet
2. **a** sacrilege—blasphemy
3. **h** sacrosanct—sacred
4. **j** sagacious—discerning
5. **b** sage—wise
6. **i** salient—sticking out
7. **e** salutary—healthful
8. **d** sanctimonious—pretending to be devout
9. **g** sanguine—cheerful
10. **f** sardonic—mocking

Quick Quiz #76
1. **a** scintillate—sparkle
2. **f** scrupulous—strict
3. **h** scrutinize—examine very carefully
4. **b** secular—having nothing to do with religion
5. **c** sedition—treason
6. **k** segregate—separate
7. **d** sensory—having to do with the senses
8. **i** sensual—devoted to pleasure
9. **g** sensuous—delighting the senses
10. **j** sentient—conscious
11. **e** sequester—set apart

Quick Quiz #77
1. **a** serendipity—accidental good fortune
2. **e** servile—submissive
3. **j** singular—unique
4. **k** sinister—wicked
5. **i** slavish—extremely subservient
6. **g** sloth—laziness
7. **h** sobriety—state of being sober
8. **c** solicitous—eager and attentive
9. **d** solvent—not bankrupt
10. **f** insolvent—broke
11. **b** soporific—sleep inducing

Quick Quiz #78
1. **h** sordid—vile
2. **g** spawn—bring forth
3. **l** specious—deceptively plausible
4. **b** sporadic—stopping and starting
5. **m** spurious—false
6. **n** squander—waste
7. **d** stagnation—inactivity
8. **k** static—stationary
9. **i** staunch—firmly committed
10. **i** steadfast—firmly committed
11. **a** stigmatize—disgrace
12. **e** stipulate—require
13. **f** stoic—indifferent to pain, pleasure
14. **j** stratum—layer
15. **c** stricture—restriction

Quick Quiz #79

1. **k** strife—bitter conflict
2. **h** stringent—strict
3. **d** stymie—thwart
4. **e** subjugate—subdue
5. **b** sublime—awesome
6. **i** subordinate—lower in importance
7. **g** insubordinate—not respectful of authority
8. **j** substantive—having substance
9. **a** subtle—not obvious
10. **f** subversive—corrupting
11. **c** succinct—brief and to the point

Quick Quiz #80

1. **b** succumb—yield
2. **a** supercilious—haughty
3. **f** superficial—on the surface only
4. **e** superfluous—unnecessary
5. **h** surfeit—excess
6. **g** surreptitious—sneaky
7. **d** surrogate—substitute
8. **c** sycophant—flatterer
9. **i** synthesis—combining of parts

Quick Quiz #81

1. **i** tacit—implied
2. **b** taciturn—naturally untalkative
3. **e** tangential—not deeply relevant
4. **j** tangible—touchable
5. **d** tantamount—equivalent to
6. **f** tautological—redundant
7. **c** temerity—boldness
8. **g** temperate—mild
9. **h** tenable—defensible
10. **a** tenacious—persistent

Quick Quiz #82

1. **h** tenet—shared principle
2. **e** tentative—experimental
3. **k** tenuous—flimsy
4. **a** terse—without unnecessary words
5. **j** torpor—sluggishness
6. **m** theology—study of religion
7. **g** tirade—bitter speech
8. **n** touchstone—standard
9. **c** tout—brag publicly about
10. **b** transcend—go beyond
11. **o** transgress—violate
12. **f** transient—not lasting long
13. **f** transitory—not lasting long
14. **l** trepidation—fear
15. **d** intrepid—fearless
16. **i** turpitude—wickedness

Quick Quiz #83

1. **c** ubiquitous—everywhere at once
2. **f** unconscionable—unscrupulous
3. **a** unctuous—oily; slick
4. **i** uniform—consistent
5. **j** unremitting—unceasing
6. **h** unwitting—unintentional
7. **b** urbane—poised and sophisticated
8. **e** usurp—seize wrongfully
9. **d** utilitarian—pragmatic
10. **g** utopia—an ideal society

Quick Quiz #84

1. **b** vacillate—be indecisive
2. **f** vapid—dull
3. **o** vehement—intense
4. **l** venal—corrupt
5. **h** venerate—revere
6. **k** veracity—truthfulness
7. **m** verbose—wordy
8. **j** verisimilitude—similarity to reality
9. **n** vernacular—slang
10. **i** vestige—last trace
11. **a** vex—annoy
12. **d** viable—capable of living
13. **e** vicarious—experienced through another
14. **g** vicissitude—upheaval
15. **c** vilify—defame

Quick Quiz #85

1. **e** vindicate—clear from suspicion
2. **h** vindictive—seeking revenge
3. **b** virtuoso—masterful musician
4. **a** virulent—extremely poisonous
5. **c** visionary—dreamer
6. **j** vitiate—make impure
7. **d** vitriolic—caustic
8. **i** vocation—occupation
9. **k** vociferous—noisy
10. **g** volatile—quick to evaporate
11. **f** volition—will

Quick Quiz #86

1. **d** wanton—malicious
2. **c** willful—deliberate
3. **b** wistful—yearning
4. **a** zealous—fervent

Final Exam Drill #1

1. **d**
2. **e**
3. **b**
4. **e**
5. **c**

Final Exam Drill #2

1. **b**
2. **a**
3. **f**
4. **h**
5. **g**
6. **e**
7. **i**
8. **j**
9. **d**
10. **c**

Final Exam Drill #3
1. address
2. integral
3. delineate
4. relegate
5. didactic
6. labyrinthine
7. amoral
8. analogous
9. magnanimous
10. malleable

Final Exam Drill #4
1. O
2. S
3. U
4. S
5. O
6. O
7. S
8. S
9. U
10. S

Final Exam Drill #5
1. a
2. c
3. d
4. b
5. b

Final Exam Drill #6
1. O
2. U
3. O
4. S
5. O
6. O
7. O
8. S
9. S
10. S

Final Exam Drill #7
1. renaissance
2. requisite
3. apprehensive
4. sacrosanct
5. replenish
6. arbitrary
7. eclectic
8. elliptical
9. allocate
10. avuncular

Final Exam Drill #8
1. S
2. O
3. O
4. S
5. O
6. S
7. S
8. U
9. S
10. U

Final Exam Drill #9
1. e
2. d
3. e
4. c
5. e

Final Exam Drill #10
1. U
2. S
3. S
4. O
5. O
6. S
7. O
8. S
9. U
10. U

Final Exam Drill #11
1. O
2. O
3. S
4. O
5. U
6. O
7. O
8. O
9. U
10. O

Final Exam Drill #12
1. awry
2. ascendancy
3. cadence
4. oblivion
5. nominal
6. equitable
7. nostalgic
8. bereft
9. bourgeois
10. pejorative

Final Exam Drill #13
1. O
2. O
3. U
4. U
5. U
6. S
7. U
8. S
9. O
10. S

Final Exam Drill #14
1. a
2. c
3. b
4. e
5. c

Final Exam Drill #15
1. a
2. f
3. g
4. b
5. d
6. e
7. h
8. c
9. j
10. i

Final Exam Drill #16
1. U
2. S
3. S
4. U
5. S
6. O
7. S
8. U
9. O
10. O

Final Exam Drill #17
1. existential
2. flaunt
3. felicity
4. pivotal
5. salutary
6. ubiquitous
7. succinct
8. eminent
9. farcical
10. volition

Word Smart

Final Exam Drill #18

1. U
2. U
3. S
4. S
5. U
6. S
7. U
8. O
9. S
10. U

Final Exam Drill #19

1. b
2. d
3. a
4. a
5. b

Final Exam Drill #20

1. S
2. O
3. U
4. U
5. S
6. O
7. S
8. O
9. S
10. O

Final Exam Drill #21

1. officious
2. scrutinize
3. reprehensible
4. founder
5. palpable
6. qualify
7. culinary
8. corollary
9. proximity
10. vicarious

Final Exam Drill #22

1. S
2. O
3. S
4. S
5. O
6. S
7. O
8. S
9. S
10. O

Final Exam Drill #23

1. d
2. d
3. b
4. a
5. a

Final Exam Drill #24

1. S
2. U
3. O
4. U
5. U
6. U
7. S
8. S
9. O
10. S

Final Exam Drill #25

1. omnipotent
2. fortuitous
3. verisimilitude
4. pertinent
5. conducive
6. prolific
7. vicissitude
8. obsequious
9. euphemism
10. diffident

Final Exam Drill #26
1. U
2. O
3. O
4. O
5. S
6. O
7. O
8. O
9. S
10. O

Final Exam Drill #27
1. d
2. a
3. c
4. b
5. b

Final Exam Drill #28
1. U
2. U
3. O
4. S
5. O
6. S
7. O
8. S
9. S
10. S

Final Exam Drill #29
1. comprise
2. bemuse
3. provident
4. anecdotal
5. prodigy
6. cadence
7. soporific
8. staunch
9. vacillate
10. vestige

Final Exam Drill #30
1. U
2. O
3. U
4. S
5. U
6. O
7. U
8. S
9. S
10. U

Final Exam Drill #31
1. e
2. c
3. a
4. e
5. b

Final Exam Drill #32
1. O
2. S
3. O
4. O
5. U
6. S
7. O
8. O
9. S
10. O

Final Exam Drill #33
1. innocuous
2. assimilate
3. unctuous
4. exult
5. surrogate
6. tantamount
7. catharsis
8. complacency
9. recrimination
10. patronize

Final Exam Drill #34

1. O
2. S
3. O
4. O
5. S
6. S
7. O
8. S
9. O
10. U

Final Exam Drill #35

1. f
2. g
3. h
4. b
5. i
6. a
7. e
8. c
9. j
10. d

Final Exam Drill #36

1. U
2. O
3. O
4. S
5. S
6. O
7. U
8. S
9. S
10. U

Final Exam Drill #37

1. c
2. b
3. e
4. d
5. c

Final Exam Drill #38

1. O
2. O
3. U
4. U
5. O
6. U
7. O
8. U
9. S
10. O

Final Exam Drill #39

1. scintillating
2. digression
3. wistful
4. cerebral
5. affable
6. ideological
7. vexed
8. comprehensive
9. impervious
10. tirade

Final Exam Drill #40

1. O
2. O
3. S
4. O
5. O
6. S
7. O
8. S
9. O
10. O

Final Exam Drill #41
1. a
2. e
3. d
4. b
5. d

Final Exam Drill #42
1. S
2. O
3. O
4. O
5. U
6. S
7. O
8. S
9. O
10. O

Final Exam Drill #43
1. cacophony
2. benefactor
3. manifesto
4. reciprocal
5. provisional
6. squalid
7. callow
8. putative
9. derisory
10. proscribe

Final Exam Drill #44
1. a
2. e
3. d
4. f
5. b
6. j
7. c
8. i
9. h
10. g

Final Exam Drill #45
1. S
2. S
3. U
4. S
5. U
6. O
7. S
8. S
9. U
10. S

Final Exam Drill #46
1. d
2. a
3. c
4. c
5. c

Final Exam Drill #47
1. S
2. U
3. S
4. O
5. S
6. S
7. O
8. O
9. S
10. O

Final Exam Drill #48
1. d
2. a
3. e
4. c
5. b

Word Smart

NOTES